WORLD AFFAIRS
National and International Viewpoints

WORLD AFFAIRS
National and International Viewpoints

The titles in this collection were selected
from the Council on Foreign Relations' publication:
The Foreign Affairs 50-Year Bibliography

Advisory Editor
RONALD STEEL

THE PRINCIPLES
OF POWER

❖❖❖

THE GREAT POLITICAL CRISES
OF HISTORY

❖❖❖

By GUGLIELMO FERRERO

ARNO PRESS
A NEW YORK TIMES COMPANY
New York • 1972

Reprint Edition 1972 by Arno Press Inc.

Copyright © 1942 by Guglielmo Ferrero
Reprinted by permission of Nina Ferrero Raditsa

Reprinted from a copy in The Newark Public Library

World Affairs: National and International Viewpoints
ISBN for complete set: 0-405-04560-3
See last pages of this volume for titles.

Manufactured in the United States of America

Library of Congress Cataloging in Publication Data

Ferrero, Guglielmo, 1871-1942
  The principles of power.

    (World affairs: national and international view-
points)
  Translation of Potere.
    1. Europe--History--Philosophy. 2. Revolution.
I. Title. II. Series.
D16.9.F4413 1972   940   72-4274
ISBN 0-405-04569-7

THE PRINCIPLES OF POWER

THE PRINCIPLES
OF POWER

THE GREAT POLITICAL CRISES
OF HISTORY

By GUGLIELMO FERRERO

TRANSLATED BY
THEODORE R. JAECKEL

G. P. PUTNAM'S SONS

NEW YORK

Designed by Robert Josephy

Manufactured in the United States of America

To my dear Children,
Nina and Bogdan,
who so bravely helped me
in the last and most terrible tempest
of my stormy existence

PREFACE

The Principles of Power is the third volume of a trilogy.
The first two volumes—*The Gamble* and *The Reconstruction of Europe*—were originally published in Paris. *The Principles of Power* is appearing in New York because it could not be published in Europe on account of the greatly increased censorship.

Merely a tiny incident in a great tragedy. Yet it helps us to understand the situation into which Europe was thrown in 1940 by the fall of France, the last great legitimate power left on the continent after the flood of revolutions that started with Russia and ended with Spain. Europe is dying of a disease that threatens to infect the whole world. It might seem that it would want to read, study, and discuss books such as this, which delve into the history of the last few centuries for the causes of the disease and for possible remedies. But instead it condemns them, destroys them, scatters them to the four winds. Is the disease so far advanced that the patient no longer even wants to be cured? After seeing the work of the new inquisitions that have sprung up all over Europe, one is tempted to believe so.

In any event, the book is being published in the United States; and from the United States its effect will spread to Europe, too. But, even if the Old World remains closed to the book, and if it is read only in the New, the author will not feel that he has worked in vain. The disease of which Europe is dying is a canker that might infect the rest of the world if the other continents did not know how to protect themselves. It is as necessary for them as for Eu-

vii

rope to understand the origin, the nature, and the growth of this fearful pestilence that threatens to deform and mutilate the whole of mankind.

The thesis with which this book is concerned is a very simple one. It may be summed up as follows: The cause of the frightful disorder to which Europe has succumbed is not the disturbance of international relations among the various states of which it is composed. That disturbance is itself the result of something far more profound—the internal crises that completely upset nearly all the Old World states. The war now devastating the world is the result of the revolutions that, since 1917, have convulsed practically the whole of the European continent. Therein lies the chief significance of the questions that this book attempts to answer: What do all these revolutions mean? Where did they come from? Where are they heading?

The answer to these questions, which I have discovered after a great deal of thought and research, is a political one. From the Middle Ages to 1914, Europe was governed by the great dynasties. Monarchy was the only political system in almost the whole of Europe—except for a few states unaware of their privileged position, England, France, Belgium, Holland, and the Scandinavian countries—that ensured an organized government. Gradually weakened by the developments in Western civilization after the French Revolution, the monarchic system was completely overthrown at the end of the First World War. All the European peoples, except for the small minority of privileged states, suddenly found themselves without the governments by which they had been guided for centuries; they were obliged to try to govern themselves, and they proclaimed republics. Then, all over Europe the same tragedy took place that had ravaged France at the end of the eighteenth century, when for the first time, the monarchy having collapsed, the French people attempted to found a republic. In almost all of Europe after 1919, as in France after 1789, the difficulty of organizing a republic in a country saturated with monarchic traditions led to all sorts of chaos, which resulted in the creation of revolutionary governments.

It was these revolutionary governments that finally unleashed a general war, for the same reasons and in exactly the same manner as the French Revolution. We are witnessing the repetition of Napoleon's adventure on a worldwide scale—Napoleon's adventure translated into German. In this book I have endeavored particularly to demonstrate, by comparing the French Revolution with existing revolutions, why the revolutionary governments that had been multiplying in Europe for the past twenty years were fated to end up in a general war; and why peace can only be established and maintained in Europe with the help of legitimate governments. This was the great truth that the Congress of Vienna had understood and used as a foundation for its magnificent reconstruction, and that was the chief reason for the latter's success. It is a truth that was never recognized by the men who guided the League of Nations, and it is especially because of this that their work failed miserably in one of the most lamentable fiascos of history.

I believe that this truth, in itself extremely simple, will once more be able to save the world, as it saved Europe in 1814. That is why I give this book to the United States with the utmost confidence, happy in the thought that a country still exists in which one is able to think and to write with sincerity in the hope of securing the welfare of the world, and not merely in order to serve illegitimate powers. It is one of the strongest reasons for not giving way to despair in this dread hour in the history of mankind!

G. FERRERO.

Geneva,
December 31, 1941.

CONTENTS

I. "And One Day at Last the Light . . . ." 3

II. The Genii of the City 13

III. The Four Principles of Legitimacy 20

IV. Some Reflections on Fear, Progress, and Civilization 28

V. The Fear of Bonaparte 38

VI. The Genius of the Old Regime and the Genius of the Revolution 49

VII. A Crucial Turning Point in History 67

VIII. The First Day of the Revolutionary Apocalypse: July 14, 1789 82

IX. A Restless World 102

X. Legitimacy and Prelegitimacy 131

XI. Legitimate Monarchy 145

XII. Legitimate Democracy 167

XIII. Revolutionary Government 187

XIV. Quasi Legitimacy 213

XV. The Catastrophic Effects of Quasi Legitimacy (France, 1848—Italy, 1915) 230

XVI. Government (Past, Present, and Future) 277

Index 321

THE PRINCIPLES OF POWER

I

"AND ONE DAY AT LAST THE LIGHT . . . . "

Having been appointed *dictator perpetuus* in the first part of February, Julius Caesar, on March 15, went alone and unarmed to the session of the Senate. Sixty well-sharpened daggers were waiting for him, prepared to relieve the Republic, once and for all, of the perpetual dictatorship. With so trustful a dictator, this proved to be the work of a mere minute or two. And the perpetual dictatorship, after only a month's existence, disappeared forever.

Senatus mala bestia, as the classical saying goes. The Roman Senate was not a parliament, like many modern parliaments, in which the abstract sovereignty of the people is embodied in a crowd of lower and upper bourgeois, all of whom are trained to serve it. The Roman Senate was an assembly of sovereigns among whom the Republic, at stated intervals, redistributed portions of its sovereignty in domestic and imperial affairs. Caesar had forgotten that every sovereignty is a monster, capable of murder when it knows or believes itself to be threatened. Forty years ago, when I was writing about Caesar, this forgetfulness on his part did not surprise me. At the time I thought, like everyone else, that a dictator who has already crossed his Rubicon must be afraid of nothing or no one. Caesar had gone so carelessly to meet the murderous attack of the *mala bestia* because of an excess of courage—a fault typical of men who are fated to be leaders.

More than twenty years went by after my study of Caesar. Sick of the endless tumult and disorder caused by the World War, Italy had also begun, toward 1922, to clamor for a new Caesar, a dauntless leader or leaders who would cross the Rubicon and subdue the rebellious masses. In a few months the country was swarming with Caesars in embryo—little, medium, and great; municipal, provincial, and national—who, at the head of large and tiny followings, screamed to the four winds that they were afraid of nothing, that if they were given the power they would perform miracles. While they were waiting for their opportunity, all these apprentice dictators practiced to their hearts' content, with sublime obliviousness to the penal code; they indulged in all sorts of bastinados, incendiaries, extortions, assassinations, and general havoc, thanks to a compliant police force and a drugged justice. Finally the king determined on the *coup d'état:* the Rubicon was crossed, and the fiery shock troops of the new revolution took the government by storm as though it were a trench.

Cosa fatta, capo ha, was the popular comment. The die was cast: henceforth a war-tempered generation of steel was going to put new life into our sad history, softened by half a century of legislative and democratic cowardice. Had not all these great and small leaders shown themselves to be utterly fearless while they were violating most of the Ten Commandments, including the one which forbids men to kill? That was the general opinion. And so I was more than a little surprised to learn that, hardly had they got into power, these village, town, and city Caesars—those with whom the public came in contact—far from courageously exposing themselves to real conspiracies, were everywhere taking ridiculous precautions against all kinds of conspiracies which existed only in their imaginations: in private letters entrusted to the mails and in private telephone conversations; in the privacy of families and in the back rooms of taverns; in assemblies and meetings of all kinds where men might gather to exchange opinions; in the secrecy of the confessional and in between the lines of newspapers. If not everyone, at any rate the majority of the people had welcomed the new government with sympathy and hope—the hope of a great change which would take place in Italy's history. Why, then, was this sympathy met from the very beginning with a distrust which was rapidly to become a public scourge? Never before had Italy seen so suspicious a government. Weren't all these dictators satisfied with being in power and having the enthusiastic support of a majority which was generally indifferent? What more did they want? That every one of the forty million Italians should be convinced that they were perfect, innocent, and above suspicion?

At first it was thought that this would pass. "It is the apprenticeship of power," people said. Instead, the evil grew as time went on. In his march on Rome, the new dictator had not been met by a sovereign assembly bearing even the remotest resemblance to the Senate which had assassinated Caesar. The parliament—Chamber and Senate —was a group of bourgeois, trained to serve, even when they bore titles, and they had bowed to the king's *coup d'état*. In 1923, when it was presented to the parliament, the new electoral law, designed to legalize the *coup d'état*, had nothing more serious to fear than a few academic and completely inoffensive opposition speeches. Nevertheless, the dictatorship was so frightened that it threatened to burn the houses of deputies and senators who spoke and voted against the law. It was passed by a great majority, and assured the government of an unshakable majority of two thirds under any and all circumstances and for all time. What more could it want? In spite of the charity which gave it a third of the seats, the opposition in the new Chamber was nothing but a constitutional fiction, designed to maintain a semblance of representative government. Yet hardly had one of the leaders of this phantom opposition made a speech when the next day he disappeared. Hired assassins had carried him off in broad daylight and stabbed him. This time the country did try to revolt. To save itself, the dictatorship was obliged to load it with heavy chains.

At first I was completely stupefied. It was obvious that the new masters were afraid. But afraid of what, since they were the masters? On one point I was in doubt: to what extent did the head of the government share the fear of his subordinates? Was he also subject to it, unable to conquer it? He seemed so sure of himself when he spoke! But one day I was able to ascertain, by a rather singular accident, that his fear was as great as that of his subordinates. Informed by the prefect of Florence that he had something urgent to communicate to me, I went to the Palazzo Riccardi. Although he usually wore a brilliant smile, this time the prefect received me with the grim visage of an inquisitor at his work. He drew a paper out of a drawer and read a lengthy invective and denunciation personally addressed to me by the head of the state. It concluded with this textual sentence: "Say to Signor Ferrero that the French Revolution treated its enemies in quite a different fashion." What crime had I committed for the all-powerful dictator to mention the scaffold as a possible climax to my unfortunate career? A private letter in which, having been refused a passport, I was slightly ridiculing the advantages which the World War for liberty, democracy, and law had brought to Italy, had come to the attention of a New York reporter, who had used it for a few rather caustic lines appearing in a daily paper. The Italian Consulate had cabled the text of the article to Rome, and the dictator had seen fit to show his displeasure by threatening me with dire consequences. The world, together with Italy, was everywhere falling to pieces; full powers had been given to a dictator in the hope of averting the disaster; and, while every day he had to overcome fearful obstacles in order to accomplish his herculean task, this dictator found time to be frightened by a few lines hidden in a paper published on another continent seven or eight thousand miles away! It was incredible. A British prime minister or a French premier would never have even heard about so insignificant an article!

Another few years elapsed. I had accepted a position to teach modern history at the University of Geneva. At one point in my course I was obliged to penetrate the obscurity surrounding the story of the 18 Brumaire and Bonaparte. There, again, what courage Bonaparte must have exhibited while he was going over the text of the Constitution of the Year VIII behind the locked doors of the Luxembourg, surrounded by committees formed that same evening! He had not even hesitated before a concept of government which would shackle the people in the same breath that it proclaimed the latter sovereign. A sovereign in chains! Never in history had there been such a fantastic plan. Bonaparte, who in 1797, at the command of the Directory, had tried a colonial experiment of this revolutionary absurdity in Italy, had not thought twice before introducing it into France and embodying it in a fantastic Constitution which had neither precedent, model, nor doctrinal justification in all history. At the top was a Senate composed of eighty members, risen from the ranks of the Revolution, who were elected by co-optation and were enthroned above the clouds in a manner resembling the conception of God held by certain classical painters. Below this were two parliaments elected not by the people but by the Senate: the Législature, which, in spite of its title, was forbidden to speak, in other words a mute parliament with a vocabulary consisting of two monosyllables —yes and no—with which it either approved or rejected legislation; and a Tribunate, which did nothing but talk, and criticized bills before the Legislature without having a vote on them. Utterly remote from the Senate and far below it, solidly planted on the ground instead of seated in the clouds but completely independent, was the omnipotent executive power, flanked by a Council of State, whose function was to prepare the bills and defend them from the attacks of the Tribunate. Bonaparte had not used any half measures when he established the powers of the First Consul, that is, his own future powers. He had taken them all for himself, with no division and no checks: the supreme administration of peace and war, the initiation of legislation, and the appointment of all administrative, military, diplomatic, and judicial personnel, except for the Court of Cassation and the justices of peace. The Senate and the First Consul, with their dependencies—the Legislature, the Tribunate, and the State Council—were the real rulers in this fantastic Constitution, and at their feet lay the pretended sovereign—the people. Limited as they were to drawing up three lists of notables in a sort of pyramid, from which the Senate and the First Consul would choose, as they saw fit, the representatives of the popular will in the legislative assemblies and the municipal or departmental councils, the people were given the status of a slave and hidden away at the bottom of the Constitution as in a dungeon. With the Senate composed entirely of friends and interested parties, with the legislative power dependent on the Senate, and with the executive and administrative power completely in his hands, Bonaparte was the real ruler of the State, the absolute power. No king of France had ever possessed such authority.

He had been courageous enough while he had remained closeted in the gilded chambers of the Luxembourg, drafting the constitutional document and having it voted upon. But when he emerged, the new constitution in hand, ready to be applied—what happened then? "If I should give the press a free hand, I would not remain in power three months," he said the day after the 18 Brumaire. And a few weeks later: "Freedom of press? No, that they will *surely* not get. I might just as well climb into my carriage and go and live on a farm a hundred leagues from Paris."[1] Less than a month after he had seized the power, the matter was attended to: a decree—they had not dared to pass a law—was proclaimed, the first article of which read:

The Secretary of Police shall not permit the printing, publication, or distribution of any but the following papers for the entire duration of the war: the *Moniteur Universel*, the *Journal des débats et décrets*, the *Journal de Paris*, the *Bien Informé*, the *Publiciste*, the *Amis des Lois*, the *Chef du Cabinet*, the *Citoyen Français*, the *Gazette de France*, the *Journal des Hommes Libres*, the *Journal du Soir*, the *Journal des Défenseurs de la Patrie*, the *Décade philosophique*, and those papers dealing exclusively with the sciences, the arts, literature, commerce, announcements, and notices.

The bitter hurricane of words that had been raging over France ever since 1789, was reduced to a more discreet chorus of tame, supervised murmurs that soothed rather than annoyed the all-powerful master. And yet they were only insignificant sheets, most of them badly edited by obscure and mediocre men without prestige!

The Tribunate was hardly any better. This was no sovereign assembly capable of doing away with a too ambitious member, but a chorus of subordinates who asked nothing better than to sing the praises of the real power. Having been chosen by the small group that had engineered the *coup d'état*, the tribunes trembled before the leaders of the group, now at the head of the State. And yet . . . The consular government had begun to function on December 22; ten days had barely passed when, on January 2, the First Consul laid before the Legislature a "bill concerning the respective functions and communica-

[1] E. d'Hauterive, "Napoléon et la presse," *Revue des deux mondes*, January 1, 1940, p. iii.

tions of the authorities charged by the Constitution to concur in the formation of the law." Behind this imposing title a law was hidden that gave the government the right to fix the day on which the Tribunate might send its speakers to the Legislature in order to express its views on the bills presented by the government. In short, the bill proposed to limit the time during which the Tribunate could study government bills, and gave the government power to conduct the discussions as it pleased. And so the tribunes were disarmed, not of daggers, which they did not carry under their togas as did the Roman senators on the Ides of March, but of the speeches they carried to the Palais Royal in their portfolios. The would-be new Caesar was more afraid of words than the old Caesar, the real one, had been afraid of daggers.

It seemed obvious that the enormous powers created by the Constitution of the Year VIII did not give the government any sense of security against a pack of snarling pamphleteers or the more or less well-cadenced phrases of the Tribunate orators. The most ingenious explanations of these strange measures that apologist historians could offer failed to convince me in the face of one very simple fact: a government born of the Revolution, of the Revolution that had promised France the right of opposition, would not, from the very first, have muzzled the press and the parliament if, after the success of the *coup d'état*, Bonaparte had felt himself to be the master, as his admirers have pretended. Moreover, having the rather acute perception of a historian, I could not help but see that every action taken by the consular power—during the provisional Consulate and at the beginning of the real Consulate—betrayed a constant indecision and anxiety that had nothing in common with the irresistible energy attributed to great dictatorships. For instance, the measures taken in favor of the *émigrés*, the nobles, and that part of the clergy which had not accepted the Constitution, evinced a desire on the part of the consular power to do something for the victims of the Directory; but it also feared to antagonize the revolutionaries by doing too much; it continually stopped at half measures that alarmed the persecutors and exasperated the victims instead of appeasing them. It was this exasperation of the victims against the first acts of clemency in their favor that seem especially to have frightened the First Consul and determined him to silence the clamor. The papers suppressed by the edict of January 17 were nearly all royalist and Catholic.

What is the explanation of this fear, this uncertainty and anxiety on the part of so strong a government, which contradicts all nineteenth-century ideas about dictators and dictatorships? The more I examined in detail the events during the first months of the Consulate, the greater became the analogy with what had at first surprised me in the dictatorship of my own country. Did not the immediate suppression of the press by decree of the Consulate stem from the same papyrophobia that caused the Italian dictator to lose some sleep over a few lines printed in a New York paper? From the same terror of mysterious voices coming from everywhere—no one knew where? Was not the muzzling of the newly created parliament the precedent, a century and a quarter before, for what happened in Rome in 1924? In Paris, as in Rome, the parliament was reduced to a harmless fiction by the removal of every means it might have to embarrass the government. And yet, in Paris as in Rome, at the first words that this fiction had uttered, with the sole aim of fulfilling its function, everyone had gone wild. Benjamin Constant, who on January 4 had made the first and only opposition speech—in connection with the bill limiting the discussions of the Tribunate—had had more luck than Matteotti. But all the official circles had protested that his speech was an intolerable scandal, and the next day the police had ordered Mme. de Stael to get some fresh air in the country. The analogy between the two cases was striking: it was the same inexplicable anxiety about a danger against which every imaginable and possible precaution had already been taken. And the more I compared what I had seen in Italy after 1922 with the pale and lifeless accounts of the historians that I was reading, the better I understood. The events of the past became alive once more to me in the light of my personal experiences, even when the historian had only half understood them or had not understood them at all.

And one day at last the light dawned upon me. Supposing the analogy were not an accident but a revelation? What if power acquired through a *coup d'état* had the diabolical property of frightening the one who had possessed himself of it before it frightened the others?

II

THE GENII OF THE CITY

***

"Your wine is excellent, Don Francesco, I will testify to that. . . . But as for knowing whether Horace would recognize it . . ."

Don Francesco was a wealthy landowner in southern Italy whose vineyards in the Campania produced a superlative white wine. But he had got it into his head that his wine was the Falernian of Horace. He had collected all the Latin works about the famous wine; and, with the help of these, he endeavored to establish the glorious genealogy of his cellar. Having heard that I was passing in the neighborhood of his lands on my way to Sicily, he sallied forth to meet me, brought me into his domain, and called upon me to acknowledge that he was giving me the true Falernian. As a historian of Rome, it seems that I was especially competent to decide. It was in vain that I sought to convince him of the impossibility of comparing a wine that is drunk today with a wine whose merits were sung by a poet twenty centuries ago. Later I learned that he was the terror of the local archeologists; every expert on antiquity was forced to prove his knowledge by instantly recognizing the proffered wine as the Falernian dear to Horace.

Don Francesco was merely a delightful individual with a minor and inoffensive eccentricity. But I often think of him during the innumerable political discussions in which I participate. Are we not trying to solve the same insoluble problem as that of Don Francesco when we compare the government under which we live with a government of the past? We know our own government, like the wine that is served at our table, through actual experience. We either like it or hate it according to the good or the harm it does us, or which we believe it does. We judge it from the inside. On the other hand, we judge the governments of the past from the outside, like objects on display in a window. "What lovely shoes!" In the brilliant lighting of the shoe-store window and on the gleaming glass shelves that support it, we admire the shapes, the colors, and the polish of a magnificent array of footgear. That does not mean we would be satisfied if we put on any pair of the shoes that delighted us so in the window. We admire or we detest past governments because we have learned at school or through tradition that they were good or bad; but how are we to know whether and to what extent, if we had lived under those regimes, we would have appreciated the same virtues and criticized the same faults that history has attributed to them, wrongly or justly? The two experiences—the real and literary—have nothing in common.

And, moreover, governments that are dead can be judged according to results. *"Dammelo morto,"* as they say in Italy when a living man is judged. Every political system that endures, works for the future, even though it may not want to or does not realize it. Although keeping pace with each passing day, at the end it discovers that it has overleaped centuries. But only posterity accompanies it down the centuries; each generation can only see the small daily march. The monarchy unified France; the papacy crystallized Italy into a parcel of tiny industrial and artistic centers. But the subjects of Louis XIV and the Italians of the sixteenth or seventeenth centuries were not aware of it. It is possible that the historians of the year 2500 will find that the Third Republic or the Kingdom of Italy have accomplished an important part in a providential plan about which we know nothing. A tax that raises the price of wine or of chicken will always have more importance for the contemporary generation than the mission of a regime, discovered by historians a century later. Such is the natural infirmity of human judgment.

In order to compare two regimes, it would be necessary to invent a time machine that would make the past real to us and enable us to live under Louis XV or in the grand-duchy of Tuscany with the same plenitude of experience as in our own epoch. And even so miraculous a machine would not eliminate all obstacles. Probably the duc de la Rochefoucauld or the archbishop of Florence, transported by time machine to the eighteenth or seventeenth centuries, would not have the same viewpoint as the corner grocer. A new problem would then be raised: which one would be right? Among the three points of view—that of the duke, that of the bishop, and that of the grocer—which standard of comparison should we take?

No, we can only compare different political regimes that have existed, that do exist, and that will exist by means of false reasonings based on arbitrary and fictitious premises. Only passion can transform these false reasonings into political and philosophical illusions. It is impossible to compare a direct experience with an intellectual perception. The same can be said of two contemporary political regimes, except in the case of enormous differences that strike the eye immediately because they depend on the degree of civilization of the peoples in question. No one will deny that the French Republic and the Swiss Republic are superior to the Liberian Republic. But in the case of regimes governing peoples equally civilized—for example, before 1914, the Third Republic and the German Empire—a comparison becomes impossible. France and Germany were faced with the same difficulty in appraising each other's regime: each knew his own from the inside, the other from the outside. The perplexity of a stranger trying to judge both countries from the outside would have been no less great. He would easily have been able to decide that in Germany there was more order and better organization and that in France there was more freedom and more equality. In order to judge between them, he would have had to decide which was the sovereign good. Order? Organization? Freedom? Equality?

Human intelligence, in this sphere, can only determine, at the moment when a state undergoes a change, the accentuation of certain faults or of certain virtues. The people who lived under a liberal regime before 1914 and who fully benefited from its liberties, felt and judged the totalitarian state to be decadent. But, supposing that the totalitarian state became a permanent and universally accepted regime, in twenty or thirty years it would be impossible to discover whether the generations who had accepted it would live more or less happily than those who had enjoyed a large measure of freedom. The problem is insoluble. But then why, since the beginning of time, have men made so many efforts, written so many books, invented so many doctrines, run so many dangers, spilled so much blood, in order to overthrow existing regimes and replace them with different regimes that they affirmed to be superior? History is full of revolutions and wars caused by revolutions. Since it is impossible to know if the new regime is better than the old, is all this enormous effort wasted? Continually to change the world, without knowing whether the changes are good or bad—is that not the delirium of a maniac?

No, though man is fundamentally rather senseless, he is not that mad. The struggle for power has played so large a

part in history for a reason more profound than a desire
to ameliorate the State: because of certain forces that act
inside human societies and prevent them from crystallizing into definitive forms. But it is extremely difficult to
describe these forces. They are born, develop, grow old,
and die, like human beings; and they can perish in their
cradle from a childhood disease, die of old age at the end
of a long career, or be violently destroyed in the prime of
life. Like all living things, they make up a family, composed of a certain number of different individuals who at
times quarrel and make war on each other. But they are
not, like living creatures, visible and tangible; they bear
a close resemblance to those beings, intermediary between
gods and men, which the Romans called *Genii,* and which
they imagined to be always present among men, either
benevolently or maliciously, but invisible and bodyless.
Because they are invisible, men are too often apt to be
unaware of their presence and even of their existence.
And yet these invisible Genii rule our entire existence.
When they are sick, men suffer; when they are at war,
men fight and the blood flows; when they interfere with
each other and quarrel, men lose themselves; when they
perish, either by violence or of old age, the great panic
sweeps over humanity, men become terrified and fall into
slavery and madness; when they are at peace, strong and
in good health, mankind is assured of that small measure
of peace, justice, order, and happiness which it can enjoy.
And they are not divided into good and bad Genii: they
are all by turns good and bad, they all both help and torment man.

What, then, are these invisible masters of our destiny?
I, too, had reached the age of forty-seven without having
suspected their existence. No one had ever told me about
them, either in my family, at school, or in the outside
world. I had read a great many books, and I had learned
many things from them, but not one of those books had
ever taught me what would have been the most important

of all: that these Genii, sometimes good, sometimes bad, surrounded me, helped and tormented me. It was they— in a benevolent mood—that had given me the idea from which was conceived *The Greatness and Decline of Rome,* which so astonished the world. It was they, become evil, that had caused me to live in anxiety and unhappiness for twenty years, unable to adapt myself to the Italy of my youth, feeling that everywhere thought and desire—ethics, philosophy, religion, literature, social life—were neither what they should have been nor what they pretended to be, but without knowing why, without being able to discover and define the cause of the evil. They surrounded me, they counseled me, they worried me, and I was unaware of their existence; under the influence of these invisible forces my life had become a hopeless enigma and an incurable torment. In order to resolve the enigma and appease the torment, to understand further and to suffer less, from 1909 to 1913 I had retired into seclusion, cut off from the world, from my family, and from my past, so as to devote myself to the tremendous labor out of which came *Between the Old World and the New.* After a concentrated study of the major problems of life, at the end of four years I had arrived as far as the door of the mystery. But I had failed to see that before me lay a door through which, in order to complete my journey, I had to force a passage. And so I had stopped, breathless and still unhappy.

It took five more years, a universal catastrophe, and a few pages from an old forgotten book, before I became aware of the existence of the mysterious Genii that were helping and persecuting me without my knowledge. During the first part of November, 1918, a peculiar stomach trouble forced me to take to my bed, though without any fever, for several weeks. The World War was just coming to an end, and the thrones of Europe were falling one on top of the other with a deafening clatter. To while away the hours, I started reading some ancient and forgotten tomes, which were somewhat in the spirit of the time. One day, while reading Talleyrand's *Mémoires*, I came across seven pages in the second volume (pp. 155-162) that revealed to me the existence of principles of legitimacy. The revelation was momentous. From then on I began to see clear in the history of mankind and in my own destiny. Before we can give a reason for this sudden illumination, we must first define a principle of legitimacy.

III

THE FOUR PRINCIPLES
OF LEGITIMACY

Everyone knows that Switzerland is a confederation consisting of twenty-two cantons. Formerly sovereign states, the cantons are no longer completely so, having abandoned the right to coin money and to raise armies. With the exception of a very few cantons, where pure democracy still exists, the legislative, executive, and judiciary powers of the cantons are elected by universal male suffrage. The federal government is in charge of the money, the post office, the railroads, the army, the customs, and the conduct of foreign affairs. It consists of two large legislative bodies—The National Council and States Council—and a large executive body—the Federal Council. The National Council and the States Council are elected by universal male suffrage, the Federal Council by the two legislative councils in joint session. The federal councilors are elected for three years. Finally, there is the referendum.

The Constitution, based on the principle of popular sovereignty, recognizes the rule of the majority. The sovereign people delegate their powers to representatives, charged either with making laws or applying them. These are chosen in free elections, by majority rule. In the same way the assemblies and the councils deliberate according to the majority. The majority has the right to govern, the minority has the right to criticize the government, to form an opposition against it, to speak and to write freely to convince the majority that it is wrong, and to become in its turn the majority. That is one example of a principle of legitimacy or, to be more exact, of two principles of legitimacy combined—the elective principle and the democratic principle. History has recorded the number of struggles, starting from the idea that the people are sovereign, the Swiss constitutions went through to attain that sovereignty, guaranteeing, by means of the elective principle and a certain number of rules providing for freedom of elections, that the majority should have the power and the minority the right of opposition. Today, after a long series of disputes, every Swiss will agree that the two principles of legitimacy on which the Swiss constitutions are based and the rules which determine their application, are both reasonable and just. The result is that he is convinced that all governments elected in accordance with constitutional law have the right to govern and that all the people, minority and majority, have the duty to obey.

The elective and democratic principles are not the only principles of legitimacy that have been recognized and followed by Western civilization. Two other principles were widely accepted in Europe before 1914—the aristo-monarchic principle and the hereditary principle. In the monarchies one family, from father to son, possessed the hereditary right to administer the sovereign power—legislative and executive—either in person or through bodies appointed by it or conjointly with bodies independently created. In the aristocratic republics, numerous until the end of the eighteenth century, the sovereignty belonged by hereditary right to a group of families that exercised it either directly through assemblies, in which the family heads had the right to a life membership, or through a supreme magistrate appointed by them. In the most glorious of these republics—Venice—the head of the government was called the doge. The aristo-monarchic principle always presupposes the superiority, more or less definite and confirmed, of one family or one group of families. Justified by this superiority, whether real or assumed, the heredity of the power becomes in its turn a final confirmation of superiority. It is because of this that heredity has been accepted as a just and reasonable rule for the transmission of power.

These four principles of legitimacy—the elective and the hereditary, the aristo-monarchic and the democratic—have for centuries been intermixed, either in conflict or in collaboration. The aristo-monarchic principle has always been inseparable from the hereditary principle. The democratic principle is irreconcilable with the latter and has only reluctantly tolerated a few remnants of it; the elective principle, fundamental for democracies, has also been utilized by monarchies, by aristocracies, and by certain authoritarian institutions like the Catholic Church. A great many monarchies have accepted the election of diets, estates, parliaments, or municipal councils. The doge of Venice and the head of the Holy Roman Empire were elected, as the pope is today, by electoral colleges especially constituted and governed by majority rule.

In short, principles of legitimacy are justifications of power, that is, of the right to rule. Of all human inequalities none is as important in its effects or has greater need of logical justification than that established by power. Except for certain rare enough individuals, one man is as good as another; why then do some men have the right to command and others the duty to obey? The answer to this lies in the principles of legitimacy. If you should ask a Swiss why the state council of such and such a canton has the right to govern, he will reply that it has been elected by a majority of the people. The same reply would

have been given, before 1939, by a Frenchman, an Eng-
lishman, a Belgian, a Dutchman, or a Scandinavian, if
you had put to each the same question about his country's
parliament. If, at the close of the year 1763, a Venetian
had been asked why the Serenissimo Doge, Alvisio Mocenigo, was acknowledged to be the head of the republic,
and obeyed as such by everybody, the Venetian would have
answered that he had been elected on April 19 of that
year by the Consiglio Maggiore, to which belonged, by
hereditary right, all male members of the four hundred
and fifty families inscribed in the Golden Book of Venice.
Similarly, fifty years ago, if a Prussian, Austrian, or Russian had been asked why such and such a minister governed the entire country in his own field of public administration, the reply would have been: "The King or
Emperor appointed him." And all these explanations
would have seemed absolutely pertinent and incontrovertible to everyone.

What are these principles, and what value should be
placed on them? They are characterized by a complete
lack of transcendence; by being just and rational up to a
certain point, that is, under certain conditions, and becoming absurd when these conditions are lacking; and by
never being able to force themselves immediately and irresistibly on man's consciousness. To the question, "Why
do these have the right to command and those the duty
to obey," there is but one reasonable reply, a reply, moreover, that is very simple and in daily use in family life. No
one will deny that a child of three or four must obey his
parents or that his father and mother have the right to
exercise control over him. Why? Because the parents know
what is good and what is bad better than does the child.
The right to govern can only be justified by superiority.
The only ruler by divine right is the wisest and the most
just. A majority proves nothing: neither the ability of a man
or a party, nor the truth of a doctrine, nor the wisdom
of a decision, nor the justice of a verdict. One man by him-

self may be right against the entire universe; that has been so, is so, and will be so until the end of time. The people sovereign? That enormous and shapeless aggregate of human beings, the majority of whom have themselves only a glimmering intelligence? Sovereignty implies superiority. The sovereignty of the people is the flock guiding the shepherd, it is the pyramid turned upside down. Furthermore, heredity is scarcely any better. Genealogy is no surer guarantee than a majority. The virtues and faults of a father may or may not be transmitted to the son, and no one can foretell which will happen. It is a mystery or, if you prefer, a gamble. But, though it is evident that the majority can be wrong, it is also evident that when the conduct of an important affair is given to a group or body of capable individuals their combined abilities will be of mutual benefit. A majority will have a better chance to reach a wise decision than a single individual, except in the case of extraordinary intelligence. The principle of the majority, therefore, is rational up to a point, that is, if its application is accompanied by the necessary precautions; and democracy is rationally justifiable under these conditions. Obviously it lies outside the bounds of reason to attribute the miraculous gift of the right choice to universal suffrage; and obviously, if a mass of millions of men and women, accustomed to obey, are suddenly told, "You are the sovereigns, now govern," God alone knows what will happen. Democracy, too, like all governments, must be organized, prepared, and trained. But the public school, the work of parties and of the press, the great currents of opinion, a belief in certain principles, can transform the people into a clear-sighted sovereign. Universal suffrage can also lead to rational choice, at least to a certain extent.

The same is true of the hereditary principle and of the aristo-monarchic principle. We are agreed that genealogy guarantees nothing. And yet it is obvious that the family may become an excellent school of preparation for government when the succession of the great state offices is intelligently established. In an aristocracy, every generation will always have a certain number of gifted younger men; by concentrating on their education, it is possible to prepare an elite of judges, warriors, legislators, diplomats, and administrators. An aristocracy that is capable, energetic, disinterested, and devoted, would be of inestimable advantage to any regime, even to a democracy, if their coexistence were possible. The deterioration of the old European nobility led to the gradual weakening, after 1848, of the monarchies as well as the parliaments.

Every principle of legitimacy, therefore, at least in part, is a rational implement that men may use to create an efficacious government if they want to. That is why chance is inadmissible as a means of bestowing power. Even the most unusual principle of legitimacy implies a minimum of rationality. In Tibet, for example, the sovereign is supposed to be Buddha in person, who after each death is reincarnated in a new-born child. As soon as the sovereign has died, the priests are charged with the immediate discovery of Buddha's new incarnation somewhere in the infant population; when they have found him, they take him away and begin to prepare him for his sovereignty. Would it be possible to imagine a more absurd principle of legitimacy? An infant chosen at random, declared sovereign and god, a perpetual game of hide-and-go-seek between Buddha in person and the Tibetan people! And yet even this baroque principle has an element of wisdom, of foresight, of intelligence, in the choice of the child and in its education. It is not quite pure chance, not quite Dame Fortune blindfolded.

But, if all principles of legitimacy are, at bottom, partially rational, they can all become absurd as soon as they are put into practice. In democracies the majority is right even when it is wrong, stands officially for truth, justice, and wisdom even when the errors and iniquities of which it can be guilty are glaringly evident. In the aristo-mon-

archic regimes, which assumed the infallibility of the government and denied the right of opposition, if the hereditary or elected ruler was not equal to his task, then logic
was forced to give way: incapacity was called genius, wisdom, divine inspiration, anything but what it was. In
short, the rational element in principles of legitimacy is
purely accidental, something added, not consubstantial. It
may be present in practice, but it may also be totally lacking or insufficient.

But at this point the Enemy intervenes and registers
his protest. This Enemy, against which all thoughts have
turned, is the revolutionary spirit of the nineteenth century, expressed for the last hundred and fifty years in
countless ways—books and speeches, philosophical doctrines and political programs, panegyric and obloquy. It
cries:

"And so your principles of legitimacy reveal what they
really are: absurdities that seem reasonable, arbitrary and
instable conventions that pass for unalterable truths because men are stupid. They are accustomed to stop short
in their rationalizations and judgments at a point beyond
which the absurdity becomes only too evident. Thus, in
the democracies everyone concedes the right of the majority without asking himself whether this right really
exists; while in the monarchies and aristocracies everyone
accepts the hereditary superiority of the nobility and the
dynasty without asking himself whether it is not an arbitrary assumption. And you want to make these principles
the invisible Genii of the City that regulate all human existence? That you have taken as the basis for your knowledge of the world and of yourself? You must be joking.
Your pretended Genii of the City are fragile conventions,
forever hovering between reason and absurdity, that men
take seriously when they become lazy and dream of order
as their ideal of life—order conceived as a great soft bed on
which they can lie all day and night. It is fortunate that
I am here; I have at my beck and call enough philosophers

and poets, journalists and professors, salons and taverns, judges and executioners, policemen and jailers, bombs and cannon, to prevent your pretended Genii from stuffing the City with their stupid prejudices and putting it to sleep."

The revolutionary spirit of the nineteenth century is right when it states that principles of legitimacy are limited, conventional, instable, extremely vulnerable to reason: we have admitted that ourselves. Nor is it wrong when it affirms that they seem just and true only because men stop at a certain point when they are discussing them —the point beyond which their weakness would be revealed. But it is wrong and shows ignorance of that same world which it periodically devastates, when it confuses these principles with all the other fragile conventions of a civilized society. These principles are to be distinguished from the other conventions because they are gifted with a magical power; fragile as they may be by themselves, hardly do men allow themselves to be persuaded by the revolutionary spirit to revolt against them than they are seized with fear, the awful fear that results from the violation of a law.

It is because of this magical power that the principles of legitimacy are the invisible Genii of the City, whose principal task is to combat and imprison that same revolutionary spirit which a while ago was calling out in protest. The fear of dictators is only one example of this magical power of the principles of legitimacy. The dictator becomes afraid of his power because he has acquired it by violating a principle of legitimacy. But where does this magical power of the invisible Genii spring from? To discover its source, we must plumb the most profound depths of human nature. For the awful fear of dictators springs from these depths; and it bears with it the essence of life.

IV

SOME REFLECTIONS ON FEAR, PROGRESS, AND CIVILIZATION

―――――――――❖❖❖❖―――――――――

"Progress" and "civilization" are words each of us uses a dozen times a day without the slightest hesitation. And yet we would be at a complete loss if asked to give a concise and exact definition of them.

Fundamentally, to our age progress means science and industry, discoveries and inventions. But this definition, if exact, is limited to viewing progress as the effort man has directed toward the invention of the tools that help him to live—from the discovery of metals, the cultivation of plants, and the domestication of animals to the latest developments of the radio, including the exploration of the planet. But inventions and discoveries are accomplished by the restlessness of certain periods of history; after a while the restlessness dies down and long periods follow when there are no great discoveries or inventions. For the last century and a half, the West has been in the throes of this restlessness, which has taken the form of scientific and technological inventions, just as the fifteenth and sixteenth centuries saw a feverish era of geographical explorations. Between these two periods, inventions and discoveries were made, but they were only a minor preoccupation of the times. If one goes back into the beginnings of known history in the Mediterranean world from the fifteenth century, one will find that only the discoveries of Greek science fit into this conception of progress, an accomplishment, moreover, that was limited both in time and in space. During this whole period of our history, which embraces approximately twenty centuries, technical and scientific achievements were very few and hardly discernible in the vast gulf of time that submerges them. And yet, during those centuries, tremendous advances were made: to cite only one example, the great monotheistic religions spread through the world. If progress is identified with science and industry, then all the work that went into the creation of Judaism, Christianity, and Mohammedanism was either harmful or useless, since it was not progress— an inadmissible conclusion.

Yet that is what we do admit in our confusion when we do not agree to identify progress with civilization, while being incapable of distinguishing between them. A civilized state is best for us because from it we obtain benefits unknown to barbarism—but what benefits? A greater refinement of taste, a greater mildness of manners, a stronger sense of justice or humanity? We are not in agreement, each of us has his preferences. We all agree, however, that those benefits, whatever they may be, do not depend either on science or on industry, in fact that these may weaken them, diminish them, may even destroy them.

In short, ideas of progress and civilization, which play so large a part in our life, are completely at variance. Is there any way to clear up this confusion to some extent? Obviously, in these two ideas of civilization and progress there is a common element—the idea of betterment, of an advantage, previously unknown, that has been acquired, of a former evil that has been suppressed or lightened. Is there a primordial evil, which we may easily recognize, and to which we may trace all those changes that we classify under the names of "civilization" and "progress"?

This primordial evil seems to be fear. Fear is the soul of the living universe. The universe cannot enter into the sphere of life without becoming afraid. Animals are creatures living in a perpetual state of alarm; they flee through life, multiplying their defenses in every direction; they are afraid and they create fear. What is the domestication of animals but a victory over fear before it becomes incurable? One can only tame extremely young animals, captured before their fear reflexes have become ungovernable. The highest living creature is man, who is also the most fearful and the most feared creature. He fears and is feared more than any other because he is the only creature with the idea, the obsession, and the terror of the great dark gulf of death into which the torrent of life has been pouring ever since the beginning of time; and because he is the only one that has the ability to invent and manufacture instruments to destroy life. Knowing that he may die at any moment and that one day or another he will have to die, he sees the danger of death everywhere. Unbalanced by this fear, his imagination darkens the face of the universe with imaginary dangers that he adds to the real ones, with fantastic beings or monstrous forces against which he is powerless. As far as we can tell, the dangers that animals fear are always, if not real, at any rate possible. The bird that is foraging in the middle of a deserted street and flies off as I approach, flees before a nonexistent but possible danger. I have no intention of harming it, but then again I might have. Since the bird has no way of knowing what I will do, its flight is quite rational, if I may use an expression that, in this sense, is rather metaphorical. A part of mankind—primitives, savages, barbarians—once trembled and still tremble before a number of imaginary dangers that are superimposed on real ones and sometimes conceal them: spirits, the dead, sorcerers, magic spells, omens, evil gods. Take crocodiles, for instance. The testimony of a great many travelers who have lived near the great African rivers teeming with crocodiles —M. Levy Bruhl has collected it in his book, *La mentalité primitive*—proves that the crocodile is considered a harmless animal. The people have no fear of bathing or even of sending their children to bathe within a few meters of some of these horrible creatures. Furthermore, up to a certain point they are quite right. Like all animals, the crocodile is extremely timid; the noise made by a group of bathers is enough to frighten him. He goes away or he remains quiet. Thus, people may bathe in the river right beside him without anything happening—which is proof to the natives of his harmless nature. But then why is it that from time to time the crocodile will attack and devour a man? The explanation is the same everywhere: the crocodile attacked the man because a witch doctor who wanted to harm the man put a spell on the animal. The man is completely unafraid of the crocodile, who is perfectly substantial, but is deathly afraid of the witch doctor, whom his imagination has conjured up. The latter, to the native, is the real culprit; he hates him, fears him, and wants to expose him.

But man is not only afraid of real and imaginary dangers; he is frightened of his own power to frighten others. A terrible dilemma therefore confronts him: he is the most feared creature because he is the only one who can make weapons, but just for that reason he is the most frightened creature. The weapons should give him confidence in his strength and soothe his fears, for they are his protection against beasts and against his fellow men. But weapons may also be used for attack. The more men arm themselves for safety's sake the more frightened they become, because they constitute a greater danger to each other. The sages who, at Geneva in 1932, sought the definition of a purely defensive weapon probably did not suspect that, if they had found it, the discovery would

have completely changed the destiny of man by bringing
to the world an age in which he would have lived without
fear.

In this way man lives surrounded by countless terrors,
some natural and others self-created, some real and others
fictitious, the latter being more terrifying than the real
ones. Government is the highest manifestation of that fear
in man that he himself inspires by his attempts to free
himself of it. That is possibly the most profound and most
obscure secret of history. A rudimentary authority is
present even in the poorest and most ignorant of human
societies. The schema on which every state, large or small
has been organized has always and everywhere been the
same: rulers who govern, policemen and soldiers who
forcibly impose the will and the decisions of the rulers,
and the masses who obey, either voluntarily or not. Mankind has lived, does live, and will live only under such an
arrangement, and for a very simple reason: men distrust
and fear each other, especially because of the weapons they
have made to defend themselves.

Every man knows that he is stronger than certain of his
fellows and weaker than others; that, living alone in a state
of complete anarchy, he would be the scourge of the
weaker and a victim of the stronger, and would live in
perpetual fear. That is why in every society, even the
crudest, the majority of men give up terrorizing the
weaker so as to be less afraid of the stronger—such is the
universal formula of social order. Add to this the fear of
war. As soon as two groups of human beings come in contact, they distrust and fear each other as do individuals,
and for the same reason—the weapons that each group possesses. The other group may not have evil intentions, but
supposing it did? It may not have them today, but supposing it did tomorrow? Precaution is required: the first
group must arm itself and obey the rulers who organize
the defense. But these defensive precautions always appear
as a threat to the other group. Their mutual distrust

reflects fear, as two mirrors placed opposite each other reflect images *ad infinitum*. It is in this reflecting game of fear that we find the true origin of war. Cupidity and ambition come later; they are justification or recompense sought for the struggle, consequences and not causes of war, which was originally caused by fear.

Government, like the weapon, is fundamentally a defense against the two greatest fears of mankind—anarchy and war. And at the same time it springs from universal fear and from the dual race—masters and serfs, if I may be permitted to use the term preferred by a mediocre philosophy, fashionable during the last half century—into which mankind is divided. The majority of men are timid, modest, and submissive creatures, who form the plastic material of government because they are born to obey. The race of masters is a minority with a stronger vital spark, and consists of those who are ambitious, active, and imperious, who by deed or thought must prove their superiority. The enthusiasm of superiority is often so strong in this type of man that he hurls himself against the most dangerous obstacles with the inevitable alternative of knocking it down or being knocked down in the attempt.

If one is to believe a solitary translator who, at the beginning of the nineteenth century, made a study of the Bible at its original and purest source, the two races of man would be symbolized in the fourth chapter of Genesis by the two great allegorical characters, Cain and Abel. Cain would be a symbolic name, the root of which would betoken in general that which is dense, compressed, active, absorbent, and, applied to human nature, that which is strong, powerful, rigid, vehement, which is central, which serves as foundation, as rule, as standard, which agglomerates, which adapts, which grasps, which understands, which assimilates to itself. The name Abel would come from a root which would mean, in the physical world, that which is dilated, tenuous, soft, inconsistent, and, in the moral world, weakness, mildness, resignation, and surrender. Summing up, in the political world, Cain represents the men destined to rule, Abel the men destined to obey.[1]

This polarization of mankind into masters and serfs would seem to fit in perfectly with the plan of a pre-established order in the very nature of man. Since there are men predestined to rule and men predestined to obey. . . . Since the latter are more numerous and the former a minority. . . . Since neither the former nor the latter can subsist by themselves . . . the minority, therefore, would merely have to recognize their strength and put themselves at the head of the masses: the relationship being complementary and integral, it should be easy to establish and maintain it. And so it would be, except for a tremendous complication—the nature of the means of coercion that the masters must use in order to make themselves obeyed and that have the same effect as weapons: they repress fear and they create it. Coercion can bend men to its will, but it can also lead to revolt. The two effects are always possible and are never completely foreseeable; they depend on circumstances that are often mysteriously hidden and impossible to find—temperament, the mood of the moment, the real or assumed strength of the resistance, the nature of the coercion—whether it is more or less just, more or less intelligent, more or less severe. This uncertainty of effect and reaction, inherent in all acts of force, is the fundamental cause of one of the most mysterious and important complications of history and life: that, if the subjects are always afraid of the government to which they are submitted, the government is always afraid of the subjects which it governs. Cain is afraid of Abel: that is why he ends by killing him. In those strongly constituted states at the center of great civilizations, this fear can dwindle to a last faint residue, but it is ever present, at least potentially. A single incident can always awaken it.

[1] Fabre d'Olivet, *La langue hébraïque restituée* (Paris, 1922), Vol. II, pp. 122ff.

There has never been, there never will be a government that is absolutely certain of exacting complete obedience at all times. Every government has known and knows that revolt is latent even in the most submissive obedience, and that it can break out from one day to another under unforeseen circumstances; every government has felt and feels itself on precarious ground, to the extent that it has been obliged to use force in order to gain power. The sole authority that is not afraid is that which is born of love: paternal authority, for instance. In order that this dual relationship of reciprocal fear should not exist between men and government, the latter would have to be recognized and obeyed in full and absolute freedom, with respect and sincere love. As soon as threats and strictures intervene, fear is born: the men are afraid of the government, which is oppressing them, the government is afraid of the men, who may revolt.

But fear of its subjects is not the only fear inherent in the government; to that must be added the fear of its agents and collaborators. As long as these serve with fidelity, they form the invincible strength of the government, but they, too, are men with changing moods; and what becomes of the government if they revolt? Shorn of its strength, it ceases to be a government. It does what it can to ensure the fidelity of its collaborators, with money, honors, privileges, gratitude, interest, admiration, and fear. But the result is never one of complete, absolute, and unconditional security. The danger of a revolt persists, at least as a possibility, even in the better-constituted states. All history is only a succession of abortive or successful revolts against government and of attempts to prevent these revolts. The government is never secure but always tottering; it frightens itself as much as it frightens the others. Because of a contradiction inherent in the very nature of man, every government constantly lives in permanent fear of its subjects and of the coercion it must exercise on them to obtain obedience, because it realizes that mankind is everywhere and always in a state of potential revolt. That is the mysterious and awful fear of government. If Fabre d'Olivet's translation of Genesis has profoundly penetrated the meaning of the Scriptures, the allegory of Cain and Abel would explain this great mystery of life. The violence of Cain toward Abel would be the coercion exercised by the government on the docile and resigned masses of mankind. But the consequence of this coercion is that Cain, the government, lives in perpetual terror, though destined to be the stronger and the invincible.

10. And Ilôah said unto him: what hast thou done?

11. Now art thou cursed. . . .

12. Troubled by uncertainty and terror, thou shalt wander over the face of the earth.

13. Then Cain said unto Ilôah: how great must be my sin, according to the purification thereof. . . .

14. Behold, Thou hast driven me out this day. . . . I must conceal myself from Thy presence with care; troubled by uncertainty and terror, I must wander over the face of the earth: and so, therefore, every creature who finds me will be able to overcome me.

15. But Ilôah made known his will, speaking thus to him: every creature who tries to overcome Cain, the strong and powerful transformer, shall, on the contrary, be he who shall exalt him sevenfold. . . .[2]

"Nequaquam ita fiat: sed omnis qui occiderit Caïn, septuplum punietur," is the Vulgate translation. I am not in a position to decide which of the two translations is closer to the original; but it seems obvious to me that it is easier to discover a profound meaning in the French translation of this enigmatic chapter than in the Latin. Here it is, in clear and simple language: Government is condemned to live in terror because, in order to govern, it makes use of physical force and violence; yet, despite its fear, it will always be stronger than all the revolts that will

[2] Ibid., II, p. 322.

break out against it, because its existence, like its fear, is conformable to human nature. The Bible, many centuries ago, may have proclaimed in esoteric language an obscure and difficult truth that only today is beginning to dawn upon man's intelligence, revealed by a long succession of tragic experiences.

V

THE FEAR OF BONAPARTE

Man is, then, the most timid of all creatures. He is born full of fear, and he lives a prey to terror. But, though he does live a prey to terror, he is different from the animals because he wants to be brave. Among all the contradictions of human nature, the basic one might well be this: man is a timid creature who wants to be brave and vanquish his fears—both the real and the imaginary ones.

It is by means of this contradiction that civilization and progress may be defined. Civilization is a school of courage and is measured by the results of the effort man makes to vanquish his chimeric fears and to understand the real dangers that threaten him. Progress is everything that is of help to man in vanquishing his imaginary fears and discovering and eliminating the real dangers. Civilization is the result of progress so understood.

Science and religion? Let us return to the fundamental question: are they, and to what extent, forces of progress? According to current belief, every discovery and invention of science would be progress, while no religious advance would. According to our definition, science and religion are forces of progress in the extent to which they help man vanquish his fears.

The great semitic religions—Judaism, Christianity, Islam—were a tremendous progress. They purged the Mediterranean basin and the classical world of a crowd of evil gods that had infested it, and substituted a single God, who is not, like the deities of polytheism, the embodiment of a fear. Instead of tormenting men, he helps them. We no longer realize what these religions of terror, under which mankind lived until the advent of monotheistic religion, were like, nor how the oppression of these monstrous ravings of the imagination, crystallized into sanguinary gods, crushed the mind of man. When one thinks how people no longer barbarians were accustomed to sacrifice their children to the gods by throwing them into crematory furnaces, one feels almost ashamed to belong to the human race. The God of the Bible freed a part of mankind from a great many of its imaginary terrors and increased man's courage, that profound and obscure source from which has come the progress made by the Christian peoples in the last twenty centuries, including the progress made by science.

For at the beginning of all our knowledge there is an act of courage. We began to uncover nature's secrets the day we lost our fear of them. And man's struggle against his fears also gives meaning to progress in the sphere of politics, by allowing us to distinguish between civilized states and primitive states. Government, too, like religion, becomes humanized and civilized with the passing of time insofar as it sheds its active and passive fears; and it sheds these fears insofar as principles of legitimacy multiply, are defined, and become necessary. The real nature of these principles is to exorcise fear, the mysterious and reciprocal fear that always rises between the government and its subjects. That is why they have the right to be venerated as Genii of the City.

This is a point that must be thoroughly understood. We

have seen that a government frightens its subjects and is afraid of them because it is obliged to impose its authority on them forcibly. But force is never certain of obtaining obedience; it can also lead to revolt, which is why, if it inspires fear, it is always afraid. We have seen that principles of legitimacy are principles that establish the right to govern and the duty to obey. Now obviously, if in a society those who govern and those who obey are agreed upon one of these principles, acknowledge it to be just and reasonable, and undertake to respect it, their relations will become smoother, more favorable, more secure, and exempt from fear, insofar as respect for the principle, continuing down through generations, increases mutual confidence. The government will be far less frightened of its subjects and of their revolting, knowing that it can count on their voluntary and sincere consent. Being less frightened of its subjects, it will not have to terrorize them nearly as much; less terrorized, the subjects will obey willingly and cheerfully. The principles of legitimacy humanize and alleviate authority, because it is in accordance with their nature to be accepted sincerely, as just and reasonable, by everyone who rules and by the majority, at least, of those who obey. The acceptance of the principles is not always active, willed, conscious of their deeper meanings. It can be—and frequently is in the masses—a habit more than a conviction, a slothful legacy from the past, a kind of resignation to the inevitable. An individual has been born and has found a certain government established, he has been accustomed since childhood to considering it necessary and irreplaceable, he accepts it as he accepts so many other things in life that do not depend on him, without question, with the conviction that it has aways been that way and always will. But, even when it implies this crude form of passive consent, a principle of legitimacy is able to free the government from its fears. It is sufficient that a majority of its subjects have been plunged for several generations in this passive state of acceptance for the government to feel itself widely recognized and accepted; feeling itself widely recognized and accepted, it will be less frightened of its subjects and have less need of frightening them. Therein lay the great strength of the old legitimate governments.

That is why we must not think of the absolute monarchies that existed before the Revolution as regimes of terror and force. The historians and political parties of the nineteenth century often made this mistake, whence many false notions of the Old Regime that have prevented us from understanding the nineteenth century and its revolutions. Everything depends on acceptance. If a people become convinced that one family has been chosen by God to govern them, that this family knows what is good for them better than they do, that they must accept its will and its actions with respect and confidence and without too much criticism, then an absolute monarchy is legitimate. It will benefit from the advantages common to all legitimate governments; it will not be too afraid of its subjects and will be able to govern them without frightening them too much. Italy, before the revolutionary invasion of 1796, was governed by an absolutely totalitarian regime that allowed no criticisms of the government in any form whatsoever. But the regime was mild and knew none of the horrors and violence through which totalitarian states impose their rule today. Why? Because it was legitimate. The great majority had accepted it for two centuries, at least passively, through habit, but also with sincerity. As we shall see later, arbitrary and violent despotism is always the result of illegitimacy.

In short, a legitimate government is a power that has lost its fear as far as possible because it has learned to depend as much as it can on active or passive consent and to reduce proportionately the use of force. The consent implied in all principles of legitimacy seems to be the kernel of truth in the center of the famous myth that Rousseau invented—the social contract. Society does not originate in a contract but in human nature itself: whatever his origin, whether divine or natural, man is man because he has a knowledge of good and evil and because he can only live in a gregarious state. But a kind of implied contract does exist at the very foundation of government, which is the most important organ of society, as soon as it becomes legitimate. The principles of legitimacy are only varying forms of this implied contract, among which the government and the governed of whatever country and epoch may choose. Every principle of legitimacy establishes a certain number of rules for the acquisition and the exercise of power; the implied contract bears on these rules and on the reciprocal agreement that as long as the power is acquired and exercised by those who govern according to the rules, the subjects will obey it. Every principle of legitimacy, then, carries with it, as soon as it is actively or passively accepted, an agreement to obey, conditioned by the observance of certain rules—in other words, a real contract. As soon as one of the two parties no longer respects this contract, the principle of legitimacy loses its strength and it no longer reassures either the government or the subjects. The fear returns.

There, now, is the explanation for the awful fear of dictators. It is the fear inherent in government, the primordial fear of revolt on the part of its subjects, which rises to the surface as soon as the government violates the principle of legitimacy that up till then has justified it. We have seen that principles of legitimacy are only defenses against the active and passive fear of the government—man's greatest dread after the sanguinary and cruel divinities that his imagination conjures up. Men struggled so hard to invent these principles and to put them into practice as they progressed and became more civilized because it became more and more repugnant to them to be tormented by governments that were afraid of them as well as to obey frightful deities who ordered them to throw their children into the fire. But, if by some chance the principle of legitimacy meant to eliminate fear is no longer respected, then primordial fear, the fear inherent in the nature of government, the fear of ever-possible and imminent revolt by the subjects, breaks out anew, with the violence of a sudden reversion to barbarism. No other phenomenon is so extraordinary and yet so simple, so easy and yet so difficult to understand.

The case of Bonaparte is an enlightening one. What was Bonaparte in 1799, when he took part in the *coup d'état* of the 18 Brumaire? The real flesh-and-blood Bonaparte, that is, and not the legendary hero of the Napoleonic myth, the nineteenth-century rival of Hercules. He was a young man of thirty about whom there had been much talk in Europe because he had been mixed up in some events that seemed incredible for the simple reason that they were incomprehensible, and that were incomprehensible because they were new, the Revolution being as yet an unpublicized phenomenon. The Italian campaign? No one in France or in Europe had understood anything about this spectacular and senseless adventure, including the protagonists—the Directory and Bonaparte. Moreover, this remained a mystery until about thirty years ago, when the first of the most secret dossiers in the Vienna archives were made public. People with vivid imaginations and various interested parties had built up a tremendous fiction about this incomprehensible phenomenon; the public had been completely convinced that Bonaparte, within a few months, had driven the Austrian monarchy out of the Po Valley, had conquered, liberated, and regenerated Italy; and it had gone wild with enthusiasm. This enthusiasm had calmed down somewhat afterward, during the hardships of war, but had flared up again in the second half of 1797, after the Treaty of Campo-Formio. Deceived by official propaganda, France had believed that Campo-Formio meant peace, real peace, lasting peace. And since she preferred peace to glory and power. . . . Of all this enthusiasm, admiration, and hope,

very little was left in 1799, at the time of the *coup d'état.*
The Treaty of Campo-Formio had lasted only a few
months, a great general war had resulted from this abom-
inable document, and with the general war had come the
tremendous burden of conscription for the masses. The
law of September 5, 1798, by which the Directory forced
conscription on France—and indirectly on Europe—was
the consequence of the situation created in Europe by
the destruction of the Venetian Republic and the partition
of northern Italy between France and Austria, carried out
at Campo-Formio. As for the expedition to Egypt, which
had followed the adventure of Italy, the public was not
yet aware, at the end of 1799, that France had lost half
her fleet and her best army as a result of it. But the oligarchy governing the republic were well aware of it; and,
when Bonaparte attempted to justify his return and the
abandonment of his army by his impatience to come and
save the republic, the cold reply was made that the republic had already been saved by Masséna at Zurich.

Many historians have said that Bonaparte would have
been swept into power at the end of 1799 by an irresistible
current of public sentiment. That is a myth. The *coup
d'état* of the 18 Brumaire was planned in a secret atmosphere of uncertainty, distrust, and general fright. No
warm current of feeling, no Gulf Stream of enthusiasm,
could have melted this frozen sea of fear. If the Directory
was unpopular, no one dared show any opposition. The
organizers of the coup were aware of the hidden discontent
of the people, but they also knew that this discontent
would not show itself until after the success of their coup.
This fact explains why the coup was so badly prepared,
explains the delays, the awkward complications, the contradictions that almost made it a failure. At the critical
moment the soldiers refused to march, and Bonaparte almost lost his chance for the blow against the parliament.
It was Lucien, as lawful president of the Cinq Cents, who
won them over by means of an incredible falsehood, telling

them that they were not going against the parliament but to defend it from a band of assassins in the pay of England who were going to dissolve it. The 18 Brumaire, from Saint Cloud to the Luxembourg and the Constitution of the Year VIII, was a series of coups carried out while public opinion remained inert, paralyzed by fear and despair. Everyone was utterly weary of revolutionary despotism, everyone wanted a liberation, a respite, some sort of change at least; but no one knew what form the liberation, the respite, the change would assume, or how they would be accomplished.

We can now understand this great mystery that has confused history for over a century: the mystery of why Bonaparte, after leaving the salons of the Luxembourg to apply the Constitution of the Year VIII, suddenly became terrified. He feared that a general revolt would be the answer to the secret meeting in the Luxembourg and to the artificial constitution that had been drafted. This fantastic constitution, whose framework we have already examined, was ingeniously constructed but was founded on nothing —neither on tradition, nor on a principle recognized and accepted at least by a part of France, nor on precedent, nor on foreign example. The Senate, the Tribunate, the Legislature of the Year VIII had nothing in common either with the States-General of the Old Regime, or with the English Parliament, or with the House of Representatives and Senate in Washington, which was believed by a number of people to have been the model; or with any of the hereditary councils that had governed the aristocratic republics of the eighteenth century; or with the elective assemblies that the Revolution had attempted to set up before, using the English or American constitutions as models. The three assemblies of the Year VIII were neither hereditary nor elective; in fact no one knew what they were. And whence came the authority of the First Consul, who was placed at the head of the State for ten years with more extended powers than those of any former king of

France, an authority unshared and unrestricted? By what principle, doctrine, precedent, model, or tradition could it be justified? It could only appear to both royalists and republicans as a scandalous tyranny, a sheer imposition of force without any legal justification. The laurels of the Italian campaign might be qualification for the supreme command of the army, but not for a sovereignty with scarcely any limits, such as the Constitution of the Year VIII conferred on Bonaparte.

This Constitution, then, was from beginning to end an adventurous improvisation and a complete novelty—the most dangerous possible weakness for a constitution. If, on the one hand, Bonaparte had been bold enough to approve it, he would have been astonishingly insensitive, on the other, not to have felt from the very start of his rule that this whole system of ingenious and unprecedented improvisations had no foundation but floated in space, and could meet with no serious, vigorous, or sincere acceptance from anyone, either from the republicans or the royalists, from the Catholics or the free thinkers, from the elite or the more or less inert and colorless masses; that the whole system could only be imposed by force, and by an enormous amount of coercion. But force can result in either submission or revolt, and the more pressure is applied the more difficult it becomes to foresee which of the two eventualities will come to pass. Let the machinery of coercion required to impose so extravagant a constitution be halted for twenty-four hours, and the latent revolt might everywhere break out from sheer despair over the innumerable evils of the Revolution: a third of France had been ravaged by civil war, there was foreign war on every frontier and the threat of multiple invasion, state finances and the wealth of the people were completely ruined, everywhere existed discord, hate, distrust, despair, fear of the present and terror of the future. Revolutions are like earthquakes; we live in constant dread of a new tremor. Being in this position, it was only natural for Bonaparte to be frightened of any opposition, no matter how innocent—newspaper articles, parliamentary discussions, grumbling in private, pretended advice from Mme. de Stael to Benjamin Constant. "If I should give the press a free hand, I would not remain in power three months"—a sincere confession of this fear of opposition, inexpressible but justifiable, which the dictator feels because everywhere he senses a latent revolt that might explode at any moment. No longer feeling himself supported, shielded, protected by a principle of legitimacy that would guarantee the consent of his subjects, he is afraid of everything: the most reserved and prudent criticism, the most innocent manifestation of the discontent simmering everywhere. Therefore, everyone must stop thinking; a too energetic move on some one issue might lead to a general revolt, just as a shout on a mountain can loose an avalanche.

Such were the beginnings of the Consulate, of the first totalitarian despotism of modern times. A brilliant assembly of illustrious French and foreign historians have described the First Consul as a superhuman individual who was utterly confident of himself and of his plans, who alone had the gift of seeing clear into both present and future. If he suppressed the right of opposition, it was merely because he was so far superior to his contemporaries: why should a prophet need the councils of an opposition? In short, if he suppressed all the liberties, it was in the sole interests of France, so that she might be saved more quickly. If the consular government is so described, then all nineteenth- and twentieth-century history becomes a complete enigma. The fundamental cause behind everything that happened between 1800 and 1814 is an access of fear, that fear which, from the very start, takes possession of all the powers created by force in violation of the principle of legitimacy, ancient or modern, that should justify them. The entire history of the Consulate and of the Empire is merely the growth of this access of primordial fear to enormous proportions. For the last century, history has made unprecedented efforts to transform this fear, which was to have so many consequences, into an act of strength and energy for the use of more or less authentic Nietzchean philosophies. I myself only discovered this tragic fact, concealed beneath the heavy cloak of historical falsifications woven during the last four generations, because I saw it repeated in Rome from 1922 to 1926 amid less tragic circumstances. The actual experience enlightened the past for me. After having understood this primordial fear, I was able to reduce the enormous disorder which devastated Europe from 1789 to 1815 to a few general formulas that would be clear and intelligible. A concentrated analysis of this disorder led me to discover, at its origin, the same phenomenon—the terror that overcomes the dictator at the very moment of his accession to power, because he has obtained it by violating a principle of legitimacy. Principles of legitimacy have the task of freeing the government and its subjects from their mutual fears and of replacing more and more in their relations force with consent. They are therefore pillars of civilization, since civilization is an attempt to liberate mankind from the fears that torment it. But, if in a civilized state a principle of legitimacy is brusquely violated and the power acquired by force, a people immediately relapses into fear and barbarism.

At this point a primary question obtrudes, one more important and more serious than any we have yet faced: why are these relapses into fear and barbarism possible? Why, of all the pillars of civilization, are principles of legitimacy the easiest to overthrow? That is the foremost question, the most puzzling enigma in the history of mankind. To solve it we must study the foundations of the principles of legitimacy.

VI

THE GENIUS OF THE OLD REGIME AND THE GENIUS OF THE REVOLUTION

Principles of legitimacy are born, grow up, age, and die; sometimes they come into collision and clash. Their life cycles and their clashes are the invisible foundations of history. Invisible because it is extremely difficult for mankind, though perforce submitted to them, to understand these cycles and clashes, which take place in the obscure depths of society. That is why our age completely fails to understand the nature of the tremendous drama that started with the World War and for a quarter of a century has been unfolding in a series of astonishing and unexpected catastrophes that appear to be inexplicable. They seem inexplicable because they originate in the struggle between the hereditary, aristocratic, and monarchic principle of legitimacy and the elective and democratic principle of legitimacy—a dark and mysterious struggle, with its roots in the dim past, that for two centuries has caused men to fight each other without knowing exactly why. Ever since the French Revolution, the aristocratic and monarchic principle has been attacked by men sincerely convinced that they were fighting in the name of world freedom and progress, and upheld by men no less convinced that they were defending the cause of order, family, religion, and civilization, savagely being attacked by the new barbarians. But both convictions were only antithetical manifestations of the same malady—the fever of political passion—too intermittent and capricious a fever to serve as an explanation for an event of such magnitude and significance. As we have seen, it is impossible to compare or set up a table of values for principles of legitimacy, since there is no standard of comparison. We have also seen that the two principles that have been clashing for two centuries—heredity and election, democracy and monarchy —are only partially rational and just, and that they can be equally criticized. And we have seen that it is impossible to make any sort of comparison, as to which has the better government, between a democracy and an aristocracy or between a republic and a monarchy, when the degree of civilization is the same. Those who fought for the Genius of the Old Regime and those who fought for the Genius of the Revolution, in the belief that one was better than the other, were blinded by passion and lost all objectivity. And there again, in this particular instance, we come to the same question that was asked at the beginning of the book in more general terms: Why do men struggle so hard and so frequently to bring about changes in laws and institutions when they have no practical means of telling whether the changes are good or bad? Why has so much blood been spilled for a monarchy or a republic, for an aristocracy or a democracy, when monarchy and republic, aristocracy and democracy, stand equal before the tribunal of reason, which is unable to judge between them?

We answered this terrible question at the beginning of the book, stating that "The struggle for power has played so large a part in history for a reason more profound than a desire to ameliorate the State: because of certain forces that act inside human societies and prevent them from crystallizing into definite forms." These forces are the principles of legitimacy or the Genii of the City. But this explanation was really only a provisional hypothesis, a thesis to be demonstrated. The moment has come to verify the thesis and the hypothesis by a study of just this particular case: The struggle between the Genius of the Old Regime and the Genius of the Revolution, how it broke out at the end of the eighteenth century, and in a century and a half set all Europe ablaze and later the whole world. It is a problem that dominates all Western history in the nineteenth and twentieth centuries. In order to solve it we must start with one fact of the utmost importance: that a principle of legitimacy is never isolated, never exists, acts, or is applied by itself alone. It always works in conjunction with the customs, the culture, the science, the religion, and the economic interests of an age—with the general orientation of minds, to use a term of Mme. Gina Lombroso's. When the customs, culture, science, religion, economic interests—in short, the general orientation—change, the principle of legitimacy is also modified. Thus, the aristo-monarchic principle held sway in Europe for centuries, because of a social condition that had its birth in the barbarous confusion of the later Middle Ages and attained its full growth between the fifteenth and seventeenth centuries. The concentration of the power, by hereditary right, in a small number of dynasties and noble families was at that time based on a parallel concentration of wealth; the subordination of the masses on a permanent inequality of property. Divided into a few large estates, the most important wealth—the land—belonged almost exclusively to the courts, the nobility, and the Church, to that part of society which governed; it was practically the appanage of the great military, political, judicial, and ecclesiastic bodies. The dominated masses were restricted to the subordinate offices of Church and State, the liberal professions, agricultural and industrial work, and store-keeping; commerce, especially in certain republics, and the higher positions of the Church in every State were shared between the dominant group and the dominated masses. But independent industry carried on by free artisans, and retail commerce were not very developed, for every great estate tried to produce everything it needed. Precious metals were rare and dear, interest was forbidden, credit nonexistent. Life was wretched and ostentatious at the same time. There were few necessities, and no comfort, even in the wealthiest classes, but what a profusion of luxury! Furs, laces, silks, brocades, pearls, rubies, diamonds, sapphires, gold, silver, horses, carriages, palaces, villas, banquets, balls, music, painting, sculpture—since the Middle Ages all the Muses had labored to surround the monarchy and the aristocracy with a sumptuous array of splendors, the remnants of which are now preserved in museums. Aristocracy and monarchy developed and attained the fullness of their growth in the qualitative civilizations of the Western world that preceded the great quantitative revolution of the nineteenth century, in those civilizations whose purpose was not to multiply the riches and increase the power of man, but to attain certain models of perfection. Moreover, art was only the most sensual and most popular of the perfections with which the Old Regime used to dazzle the masses and convince them of the superiority of the ruling power. There was also religion, with its monastic orders, its cathedrals, its ceremonies, its celebrations, its saints, its hierarchies, its charities, its doctrines. But Christianity is equalitarian, it acknowledges all men to be equally the sons of God. The inequalities inherent in the organization of society, the social strata and the principles of legitimacy that justify them, are to the Church merely material accidents, subordinate to the great archproblem—the welfare of the soul. How is it that an equalitarian religion was able to remain for so many centuries the sacred pillar of the aristocratic and monarchic regime? For kings and princes ruled Europe for centuries amid a fantastic swarm of churches, monasteries, priests, male and female saints, to the sound of bells ringing from dawn to dusk in every street of city and town. Up till the end of the eighteenth century, this was one of the most extraordinary puzzles of Western history. But Christianity superimposed on its doctrine of universal equality a philosophy of soul and body that exaggerated platonic dualism to the complete annihilation of the flesh, and a morality that, as Leo Ferrero said, exalted the love of God and men to the complete annihilation of egoism. A philosophy and a morality that were incomprehensible to the masses, that could only be understood and applied by an elite. Christianity is a religion for the people, surmounted by a resplendent superaristocracy of saints and sages. At the height of their glory, the aristocracy and the monarchy were wise enough to welcome this elite into their exclusive circle and keep them there. Thus, they increased their prestige, and created a solidarity between the institutions of the Old Regime and the Christian churches that, though without doctrinal justification and in spite of temporary conflicts, proved to be strong and deep, and endured for centuries. The test of that came later on in the midst of the tempest loosed by the French Revolution.

Supported by the hereditary principle, by landed wealth, by the Bible, by the Church, by the fascinating splendor of the bygone qualitative civilizations, the monarchies and aristocracies of the Old Regime had succeeded in making the people accept their rule as legitimate; a very few families ruled over vast numbers of people who were convinced that their subjection was just, reasonable, conformable to the will of God and to their own interests. Contrary to the practice of modern states, these hierarchies asked few sacrifices of the people: conscription was unknown, as also wars between peoples, taxes were light, and the government was cheaply run, since many of the public functions were performed gratuitously by the nobility. On the other hand, the dominant classes exacted a complete, absolute, and unconditional respect. Ceremonial was one of the sacred laws of the Old Regime—a meticulous, indisputable, and inviolable code of manners, destined to symbolize, on a small scale, at each moment of the day, the unalterable differences of caste. The Old Regime did not recognize the right of opposition such as we know it—the right of the minority to assume that the government is consistently wrong and to demonstrate the fact every day. But it recognized that organized social groups had the right to present their grievances, to declare their wishes, to consent or not to consent to certain laws. That was the task of the numerous assemblies that existed under different names in the republics and monarchies of the Old Regime: diets, parliaments, councils, estates, *staende*. If during the seventeenth and eighteenth centuries, monarchic absolutism encroached on the rights of these assemblies throughout continental Europe, it was through fear that the right of total opposition would result from the exercise of these more modest rights. In exchange for respect, the rulers provided protection: the defense of the weak, the administration of justice, the maintenance of order, the guarantee of the prosperity of the people and the middle classes, even while they were engaged in commercial warfare and ruining themselves. The noble and reigning families were expected periodically to sink up to their ears in debt, because their wealth made commerce prosper and secured work for the people.

As long as this orientation was universal and sure of itself in Europe, the hereditary, aristocratic, and monarchic principle of legitimacy remained as solid as the Alps. The generations followed each other, accustomed to the hierarchies of the system as they were to the rotation of the seasons or the phases of the moon. But the orientation and the system that it had created began to totter as a result of the great geographical explorations of the fifteenth century and the Reformation. At the Council of Trent the papal legates allowed no opportunity to pass without saying to the Protestant German princes: "You are supporting the people against the pope. But take care; after their revolt against the pope, the people will revolt against the princes, kings, and emperors!" Beginning with the sixteenth century the flow of gold and silver from America brought about the first signs of inflation in Europe; Calvin permitted the charging of interest; merchants became wealthy, industries expanded, and artisans multiplied. At the same time the Renaissance of the classics brought about the secularization of learning. The first discoveries of scholarship and science, the astronomy of Copernicus and Galileo, the colonization of America, the increase of wealth, the growth of armies, augmented the confidence of men in the strength of their will and of their intelligence. A critical spirit was born; already in the seventeenth century it was being whispered in the salons that the government could do better, and reforms were timidly being suggested. In particular, men were concerned with improved methods of agriculture, with increasing the number of industries, with the expansion of commerce. The great science of the Middle Ages—theology—began to decline, while mystical fervors began to pall—a forewarning of the general incredulity shared by the upper classes in the eighteenth century. In the middle of all these changes appeared the idea that a government needs the sanction of the people to be legitimate. At first this did not take the aggressive attitude of an enemy of hereditary legitimacy, determined to supplant it; instead it showed itself timidly, modestly, as an improvement of the dominant principle, a remedy for its ever-possible abuses. More and more the sentiment arose in every class that, no matter how well disposed the aristocracies and the courts are toward the masses, the destiny of man cannot be confided exclusively to the good will or good intentions of the mighty; that all men, even the most humble, have souls, and rights that a government must respect.

Moreover, England stood as an example of the idea that the government, at least to a certain extent, must be controlled by the governed. In England, monarchic absolutism did not triumph, as in France and the rest of continental Europe during the seventeenth century; the right to consent to taxes, the fundamental task of all parliaments, estates, or diets of the Old Regime, developed into a collaboration between the House of Commons and the House of Lords under the guidance of the State. Though the power of Parliament was not justified by a specific principle of legitimacy, opposed to the aristo-monarchic principle, but by a Charter and by tradition, the Commons were a new governing power, non-hereditary, elective, separate from and independent of the aristocracy and the Crown, which controlled and limited the two traditional powers, transforming the opposition, with all the liberties that go with it, into a fundamental right.

All over Europe, but especially in France, observers were studying events in England, and with each succeeding generation there was an increase in the number of people who argued that a similar system of controls and checks might be useful elsewhere as well. At the same time the prestige, the cohesion, and the idea of caste were gradually being weakened in the nobility. Some of the old families died out or were ruined, and their places were taken by merchants, lawyers, and doctors who had become wealthy. The various governments increased the sale of titles, money widened and at the same time shook the ranks of the aristocracy, which became more fluid, less respectful of both divine and human laws, more eager for knowledge, for pleasure, for money, and for power. Political struggles broke out everywhere, involving the problem of limiting the power of the aristocracy and the courts. These were especially bitter in the republics, where the elective principle was widely followed; this was particularly true·in a tiny republic—about twenty to thirty thousand inhabitants at the most—on the hills bordering the western shores of Lake Leman. This little town had for two centuries been the refuge of the Calvinist heresy. It was governed by a hereditary aristocracy divided into two parts: on top were the citizens, who alone could hold the most important offices; below them were the bourgeois, who, with the citizens—about fifteen hundred altogether —made up the General Council or the Sovereign Council, which had the legislative power, the right to declare war and make peace, and the right to approve taxes. But this dual aristocracy was further divided into those with wealth and those without. Although the majority of the General Council consisted of artisans and merchants who were comfortably off, a superaristocracy of wealthy families, in control of the top positions, the Small Council, and the Council of Two Hundred, really governed the republic and attempted to dominate the General Council by appropriating the sovereignty to themselves. Not, however, without meeting resistance, leading to some violent clashes, in the course of which the problem of the respective rights of the assemblies began to arise.

This general ferment of ideas only increased during the eighteenth century. Meanwhile agriculture continued to make strides, commerce and industry expanded further, precious metals abounded, and the subjection of the lower classes—especially the artisans and merchants—diminished in proportion as their numbers, their comfort, or their wealth increased. The third estate, especially in France, became larger as wealth and culture increased; the idea of tradition weakened in the nobility; intellectual curiosity and skepticism took hold of the upper classes, including the clergy. Science began to encroach on the mysteries of nature; pantheism and empiricism attacked the old Aristotelian philosophy, which had been crystallized into Thomism by the Church; the critical mind launched a general attack on the State, on morality, on law, on all society.[1] The new ideas pierced the general effervescence in every direction, like shooting stars on the night of Saint Laurent; sometimes they even seemed to fall like meteors, from an unknown corner of the sky. One of these apparent meteors fell into the midst of aristocratic and monarchic France in 1762—the *Contrat Social*. For instance, where does the distinction between sovereign and prince, between State and government, come from? What significance does it have in the aristo-monarchic society of the eighteenth century? The sovereign or the State—the two expressions were synonymous for Rousseau—would be the whole people united in one body to make the law of the land, the law that, according to Rousseau, was the true expression of the general will on a subject of common interest. But what is the general will, the source of law and consequently of authority, too? It is the sole will, indivisible from the social body as a whole, that aspires after order, justice, security, when it determines subjects of common interest. In its most perfect form it becomes unanimity. It does not admit of different interpretations by parties; it is unique. When individual wills—interests we would call them today—prevent the general will from manifesting itself in unanimous approval, people may agree to try to find it by a majority vote. But this convention will have no value unless it is accepted unanimously; and a majority vote will not involve any guarantee that the general will so expressed is authentic, in spite of its claim to express it. A majority can be wrong. It is legitimate only when it expresses the general will. But how is this to be recognized? Rousseau leaves this question out of his reasoning. The general will is an absolute, religious in character. It can be discovered only by the mind, when the latter is in a state of grace, to use a religious term. And the political state of grace required to discover the general will consists in freeing ourselves of specific desires

[1] In connection with this intellectual and moral transformation, see Paul Hazard's great work: *La crise de la conscience européenne, 1680-1715* (Paris: Boivin & Cie., 1935).

that each of us may possess as an individual, in order to preserve only the general will he possesses as a citizen.

Consequently, the legislative power is the sovereign and is to be identified with the people. The people, then, who alone can express the general will and make the laws, are the one and only sovereign. But it is not sufficient to make the laws: they must also be applied; furthermore, if the laws themselves are of general prescription, their application is always concerned with specific cases. The sovereign legislative power—the people—cannot apply them without confusing the general with the particular. Their application necessitates a new organ—the prince or the government, as Rousseau calls it—the executive power. But the executive power is not a sovereign power; the legislative power and the people are the sovereign power, to which the executive power must be subordinated, because whoever makes laws has the right to supervise their execution.

The legislative power [says Rousseau (III, 11)] is the heart of the State, the executive power is its brain. . . . The brain can be paralyzed and the individual continue to live. . . . But as soon as the heart has ceased to function, the animal is dead.

Consequently (III, 13):

It is not enough that the assembled people should have once determined the constitution of the State by giving their sanction to a body of laws; it is not enough that they should have established a perpetual government, or that they should have provided once and for all for the election of civil officers. Besides the extraordinary assemblies that may be required by unforeseen circumstances, there must be those that meet regularly and periodically and that nothing can abolish or prorogue, so that upon the appointed day the people may be legitimately convoked by law, without there being the need for any other formal convocation.

Revolution then? A frontal attack against the Old Regime? It is evident that the doctrine of democratic legitimacy, as put forward by the *Contrat Social,* completely refutes the hereditary, aristocratic, and monarchic principle, on which the Old Regime was based for so long. In France, for example, the sovereign was the king; the legislative and the executive powers were combined in his person and administered by a council appointed by him that assisted him in his gigantic task. Applied to France, the *Contrat Social* would have acknowledged the king of France only insofar as the people had chosen him and for as long as he had retained their confidence. But Jean-Jacques, in his humble position as a stranger and guest, as a writer living on the outskirts of French society, could not even dream of such a challenge. He himself confesses, in the sixth of his *Lettres écrites de la montagne,* that he did not have France and Europe in mind when he wrote the *Contrat Social,* but his own country, Geneva, and the struggles between the St. Gervais quarter and St. Pierre, between the wealthy and those with only modest means, between the two councils dominated by the great families and the General Council. It is easy to recognize, in the sovereign and legislative people of the *Contrat Social,* instrument of the general will, the General Council of Geneva, and in the author a Genevan of modest circumstances, a member of this Council, little satisfied with his illusory sovereignty, who is seeking to justify on philosophical grounds the claims of his class and the struggles of the General Council against the tyranny of a wealthy oligarchy.

Thus, the *Contrat Social* is not fundamentally an attack against the aristo-monarchic system that dominated Europe, but a pamphlet on Geneva politics, a philosophic assault on the oligarchy of the Rue des Granges. He feared the Rue des Granges less than he feared the palace of Versailles. But the genius of Rousseau was a strange mixture of contradictory virtues. Believer and skeptic, poet and jurist, dialectician with a periodic tendency toward lyricism, realist and dreamer, timid and rebellious, desirous of tranquillity, of peace, of protection, yet always at war with society and its ideas, he could not resist the temptation to find a universal and eternal formula for legitimacy; to make, for himself, finally, the greatest of all discoveries, one that would enable us to create the perfect government and then retire from our duties as citizens to have a good time and enjoy the blessings of peace. And what did he do to find this formula? He took the institutions of the tiny republic of Geneva as an illustration for a far wider meaning, giving a universal value to the doctrine of popular sovereignty that he had discovered and formulated for Geneva. He glides from the local to the universal, from the particular to the general, from political pamphlet to philosophical treatise, almost without noticing it, by a chain of reasoning that may be summarized as follows: What makes the State one? The union of its members. Where does this union spring from? From the obligation that binds its members. Upon what is this obligation founded? Force? No, because force, being transitory, can create neither a right nor a duty. What is a right or a duty that disappears when force ceases? Since no one man is invested with natural authority over his fellow, and since might does not make right, only agreements remain the basis of all legitimate authority among men. A form of association which defends and protects with all its resources the person and the property of each associate, and in which each, though united to all, nevertheless obeys only himself and remains as free as before—such is the Gordian knot that the *Contrat Social* must sever. And it will sever it by a pact of union between individuals, which creates an ethical body composed of as many members as the assembly has voices, the latter receiving from this same pact its unity, its common "I," its existence, and its will. Each party contracts his obligation at the same time as he receives that of the others, all being absolutely equal at the moment of contract; and each engages himself to accept as law the general will, that of all the contracting parties, which is the supreme order and law—that is, the sovereign or the State. But how does this abstract sovereign act? By means of laws—public and solemn declarations of the general will on matters of common interest. The sovereignty being the exercise of the general will, it is inalienable: the power may be transferred but not the will. For the same reason it is indivisible. Rousseau also attempts to prove that it is infallible, but the proof is complicated, confused, and rather sophistical.

Obviously, the "social contract"—the spontaneous and free agreement among all members of a society to obey their general will—can be interpreted in two ways: either as a point of departure or as a culmination, as an actual historical event, preliminary to the formation of any governments, or as a perfection toward which all governments tend. Whatever interpretation is accepted, we are a long way from Lake Leman, from the hill of St. Pierre and its struggles; we are in the presence of nothing less than a doctrine of legitimacy that aspires toward a universal and eternal value and that completely denies hereditary, aristocratic, and monarchic legitimacy, the foundation of the Old Regime. In fact, if the social contract is a preliminary and actual historical fact, then all the regimes that, in the course of history, have moved away from it, including the aristocracies and monarchies, have become delegitimized and must be guided back to their origin. If the social contract is a goal for government, then a government, to be fully legitimate, must approach ever closer to it. In both cases, princes, kings, and emperors should be deposed from their thrones; the aristocracies and monarchies replaced by regimes in which the people are the sovereign and the government the instrument of the general will.

Was Rousseau, then, carried away by the latent power of his genius to take up an aggressive stand against the principles of legitimacy that for so many centuries had justified government in the Western world? Not at all. He resisted, at almost every step, the revolutionary spirit of his doctrine. He never made up his mind between the two interpretations of the social contract—the historical and the philosophical—which permitted him to examine neither thoroughly and to leave his doctrine in a cloud of uncertainty wherein its revolutionary character is eclipsed and becomes obscure. Sometimes it flashes out in a sentence, like the following from the eighteenth chapter:

When it happens that the people institute a hereditary government, whether monarchic in the form of a single family or aristocratic in the form of a class of citizens, it is not an engagement into which it enters: it is a provisional form that it gives to the administration, until it decides to give it another.

It would be impossible to state more clearly that there is but one principle of legitimacy—the will of the people; that aristocracies and monarchies have a right to govern for only as long as the general will of the people recognizes that right. But it is only a flash: the horizon is revealed for an instant, and then darkness blots it out. Rousseau does not insist.

In the same way, though he makes the people sovereign, he never defines his terms. Undoubtedly, when Rousseau talks about the people, he means the citizens and bourgeois of Geneva, who made up the General Council of the republic—the General Council, which was not a parliamentary assembly consisting of representatives elected by the people, but the entire body of Genevan aristocracy of fifteen hundred individuals who governed the republic like an absolute monarch, without having to render any account to their subjects; their only duty was to protect themselves from the wishes of individual members, which might disturb and corrupt the general will, that mystical unanimity which is the fountainhead of legitimate power. This conception of the sovereign people, based on the General Council of Geneva, explains Rousseau's statement that the sovereign people can never be represented. Pure democracy, therefore, if the doctrine is to be carried to the limit, is the only legitimate government, while representative government is a form of tyranny. But then, if the people is so conceived, what meaning will the word take on in nineteenth-century France, England, or Germany? Rousseau gives us no light on this major question. The sovereign he creates is never easy to identify, always vague, secret; we know that it must be somewhere, but cannot tell where. Rousseau did not dare to follow his train of thought to its fulfillment, to clear up things for himself so that the path he trod would be illuminated for him; he preferred to grope through a fog toward an uncertain goal, lose himself in confusing and tortuous explanations, because otherwise he would have ended up by discovering for himself and making others see that by wanting to uphold the rights of the General Council of Geneva without saying so in so many words, he had succeeded in formulating an ultrarevolutionary doctrine that made all hereditary and elective governments out of the question. The general will of the sovereign people, that religious absolute, whose revealing sign was a spontaneous unanimity, did not agree either with the monarchic absolutism then dominant, nor with future regimes based on the right of opposition, the first model of which England was already elaborating; while it was difficult to realize, accidental, and not very sincere in the aristocratic republics that had suggested the idea to Jean-Jacques. Rousseau made desperate attempts to conceal from himself and from others the revolutionary spirit of his book—whence all the confusion and contradictions that smother it. But at least he succeeded in having his little book read in France with curiosity and without fear by a small elite that never dreamed of the dynamite with which it was loaded. At Geneva, on the other hand, the dominant oligarchy was not fooled by the philosophical clouds with which Rousseau had half-concealed his sovereign, and it consigned the revolutionary pamphlet to the flames.

Fourteen years later, in 1776, a tremendous event took place: the English colonies in North America revolted and created a federation of republics, in which for the first time the hereditary, aristocratic, and monarchic principle was suppressed and completely replaced by the elective and representative principle. For the first time the West was to see a great state and a great civilization develop without kings, emperors, princes, or nobles, on the principle that all men are created equal. In the Declaration of Independence, drafted by Franklin, Jefferson, and John Adams, and proclaimed on July 4, 1776, the influence of the *Contrat Social* is apparent. It reads in part as follows:

We hold these truths to be self-evident, that all men are created equal, that they are endowed, by their Creator, with certain unalienable rights, that among these are life, liberty, and the pursuit of happiness. That to secure these rights, governments are instituted among men, deriving their just powers from the consent of the governed, that whenever any form of government becomes destructive of these ends, it is the right of the people to alter or to abolish it, and institute new government, laying its foundation on such principles, and organizing its powers in such form as to them shall seem most likely to effect their safety and happiness.

Then comes the account of the grievances that oblige the American colonies to make use of this supreme right, and the document closes:

We, therefore, the Representatives of the United States of America, in General Congress assembled, appealing to the Supreme Judge of the world for the rectitude of our intentions, do in the name, and by authority of the good people of these Colonies, solemnly publish and declare, That these United Colonies are, and of right ought to be, *free and independent States*; that they are absolved from all allegiance to the British crown and that all political connexion between them and the State of Great Britain, is, and ought to be, totally dissolved; and that as *free and independent States,* they have full power to levy war, conclude peace, contract alliances, establish commerce, and to do all other acts and things which *independent States* may of right do. And for the support of this declaration, with a firm reliance on the protection of Divine Providence, we mutually pledge to each other our lives, our fortunes, and our sacred honour.

But in this declaration the consent of the governed is assumed to be possible in all regimes; every regime, then, can be legitimate as long as it respects the inalienable rights of man. The American colonies are not revolting because the principles of legitimacy of the Old Regime are contrary to reason and justice, but because the government has ruled badly. The *Contrat Social* is still interpreted in its less revolutionary meaning; it is only a bastion built to protect the peoples against the abuses of power, not a point of departure for an attack on a tottering world destined to perish. The revolutionary dynamite that Rousseau had put, without wanting to, in his little book, would have remained quiet for a long time, like lightning in the heart of a cloud, if a tremendous historical accident had not set it off. What was this and how did it affect the charge? That is what we are going to see now. We are facing the crucial point of all Western history.

VII

A CRUCIAL TURNING POINT
IN HISTORY

We know that after 1780 all France was in a ferment and that the immediate and tangible cause of this ferment was the revolutionary position held by the court from 1614 on in not convoking the States-General. Like all revolutionary doctrines, absolute monarchy had both its strong and its weak points. By no longer convoking the States-General, the court had freed itself of any control that the nobility, the clergy, and the third estate might exercise on its policies; but it had no longer dared to tax the wealthy orders without their consent, which would have necessitated the convocation of the States-General. As wars were costly and expenses were mounting up, the monarchy had been forced to maintain an ever-increasing pressure on the poorer classes and to resort to the most ruinous expedients—such as loans and the sale of titles, offices, and exemptions. These abuses had been made easy by the fact that the budgets were kept in the utmost secrecy; and the public debt had been rising for a century and a half, while taxable property had diminished or had become more resistant. So dangerous a state of affairs could only lead to bankruptcy.

This must have been recognized at the close of the American war, which had cost half a billion. The impossibility of continuing to balance the budget with loans had become so obvious that, in 1786, Calonne decided to subject all landed property to taxation, including that which belonged to the nobility and the Church. But he did not dare to make such a drastic reform with only a royal decree, without obtaining the consent of the estates, required by the constitution of the monarchy, which, though it was not applied, had never been abolished. The only solution was to convoke the States-General. As for the court, though it did not feel strong enough to impose fiscal reform on the nobility and clergy out of hand, it refused to acknowledge that, by convoking the States-General after a lapse of 174 years, it was turning back to the constitution in despair because absolutism was no longer able to rule. Calonne resorted to half measures: on December 29, 1786, he summoned an assembly of 144 notables for February 22, 1787. But everyone protested that only the States-General could consent to fiscal reform; the assembly of notables unanimously supported this opinion, and Calonne resigned. Then began a fierce struggle between the court, which under no condition wanted to convoke the States-General, and an increasingly aroused public opinion that demanded its convocation as a legal right and as a requisite of the country's salvation. We are familiar with the dramatic events of that struggle and its outcome: finally, on August 8, 1788, the court gave in and agreed to convoke the States-General for May 5, 1789. After 174 years!

A reversion to the past or a leap into the unknown? Behind the agitation for taxes and for the rights of the States-General, a far greater restlessness was concealed, which originated in the Genii of the City, those intangible arbiters of man's fate: in the aristo-monarchic principle of legitimacy, which was growing old, and in the democratic principle, which was gradually gaining strength. France was being torn between these two forces without knowing why. As the Revolution drew nearer, the new orientation that for the last thirty years had been gradually wearing down the attachment of the people for the aristo-monarchic legitimacy, no longer bore any resemblance to the ageless falling of individual drops on an underground rock but had grown to the proportions of a subterranean torrent forcing its passage through a mountain. A torrent of ideas, of aspirations and hopes, of hate and enthusiasm, was gathering strength in the minds of writers and thinkers, in the presses that published their books, in the salons where they were discussed and passed from hand to hand, in the academies, literary societies, lecture halls, masonic lodges, and in those societies devoted to thought or philosophy, as M. Augustin Cochin has called them, whose vast network spread all over France. A torrent rushing through French society, carving out its bed in the midst of the traditions, institutions, interests, and orders—the clergy and nobility—which had been the backbone of the aristo-monarchic legitimacy and whose resistance was becoming weaker and weaker. A torrent that carried along with it a number of individuals even from these circles, but was especially swelled from year to year by the enthusiastic support of that part of the third estate which was most discontented and least dependent on the nobility or clergy—doctors, lawyers, notaries, large and small property holders, well-off merchants, intellectuals. This torrent upset a great many delusions—all those delusions that the first gropings of rational thought, the first successful ventures of science, the growth of middle-class wealth, the conquest of the globe, the greater knowledge of geography and of history, the example of the United States, the doctrine of Illuminism, and the work of the Encyclopedists, had spread through the upper classes all over Europe.

Must we, then, like M. Cochin, see in the tremendous passion for philosophy that took hold of France after 1750, only a capricious revolt on the part of reason and pride against the laws of reality? An attempt to build an imaginary city in the clouds modeled on that of Aristophanes, a "strange city whose birth and existence, contrary to every law, are based on principles by which others would perish"; a city "whose inhabitants are, by force of circumstance, possessed of a different point of view, situated on a different plane, given a different aim, than those of reality?"[1] No, the generation that prepared France for the Revolution did not want "to play at being a philosopher and a citizen"; the game that M. Cochin believed he had discovered at the bottom of all this fever and unrest was really a tragic ordeal, the causes of which lay deeply concealed. The history of France after 1750 offers a superlative example of the effect that the invisible Genii of the City produce upon the life of a people, without anyone's dreaming of their existence: of the mysterious agitation they occasion when they quarrel and come to blows. This period of French history is unintelligible and resembles nothing so much as a general attack of insanity, if one fails to penetrate the visible effects to seek out the invisible causes—the subterranean struggle between the aristo-monarchic principle of legitimacy and the democratic principle. After 1750, the Genius of the Old Regime fell into decrepitude; there was no one who clearly perceived this and admitted it to himself, but everyone felt it. France began to fall victim to a sort of restless apathy because, without realizing it, she began to have doubts about the venerable pillar of ancient social order—aristo-monarchic legitimacy; there were complex reasons for these doubts, some of which—we have already examined them—had to do with the general orientation of thought in Europe; but there were others that must be sought

[1] A. Cochin, *Les Sociétés de Pensée et la Democratie* (Paris, 1921), pp. 8, 9.

in the evolution of French society and government during the two preceding centuries. What with the privileges of the nobility, the clergy, and the religious orders, the monopolies of corporations, and the cumbersome welter of bought offices and exemptions, group interests had become crystallized to such a point that they interfered more and more with the flow of national existence, until France was threatened with serious internal congestion. At the same time the legislative and executive power had become completely concentrated in the Royal Council—a small committee, consisting of the king himself and four or five ministers chosen by the king as best he could from the tightly closed court at Versailles, whose idol and prisoner he was. Half a dozen individuals, over whose choice the country had no influence, who were bound only to the king and responsible to him only, who worked in a vacuum, completely out of touch with the nation and her interests, and were supposed to make all the laws, conduct the administration, the finances, the domestic and foreign policy of the most important state in Europe, a kingdom of twenty-five million inhabitants, a monarchy with tremendous responsibilities! Never before had the legislative and executive branches of government been so restricted in membership for so great a state, never had there been so frail an instrument for so gigantic a task. To understand what a monstrosity this government was in eighteenth-century Europe, it is not even necessary to compare the France of the Old Regime with England; it is sufficient to compare it with Venice. In the eighteenth century, Venice was a small state with a population of five million and very few responsibilities. Yet the legislative power was in the hands of an assembly—the Consiglio Maggiore—on which sat by hereditary right about fifteen hundred persons, the representatives of five hundred noble families; while the executive power was shared among a great many commissions and committees, all selected from the dominant aristocracy by varying methods of choice—a far larger and firmer representation than that existing in the French monarchy.

In the second half of the eighteenth century, France was no longer firmly enough attached to the old aristo-monarchic legitimacy for a docile acceptance of this situation: one must start with this primary fact if one wishes to understand the Revolution. France desired a general sweeping out of all these groups and their interests, a more closely knit unification of society, a reorganization of the government that would permit the cultured and comfortably off classes to have some influence in it. And she was quite right. It was in order to pave the way for this vast reform of the social structure and the government, and not to build a city in the clouds, that, after 1750, France gave herself over with such zeal to discussions on the nature, the origins, the transformations, and the justifications of government. She discussed them insofar as she was able, searching everywhere for the right solution, sometimes losing her way in the process. Is that anything to be astonished at? Life would indeed be easy if, in the great crises of history, human intelligence could always read the future. And in the crisis at the end of the eighteenth century, it was impossible for France to see into the future. If, on the one hand, the aging Genius of the Old Regime was plunging France into a restless apathy, on the other, the Genius of the Revolution, the new principle of legitimacy standing on the threshold of history, instead of calming and reassuring people, was aggravating the restlessness. The new principle was neither clear nor precise, its justifications were muddled and variable, and even the most intelligent people were not always able to understand it or else interpreted it differently; the majority, both attracted and frightened, neither accepted nor repulsed it and remained undecided; only a resolute minority opposed it. Thus, France, torn between these two Genii, had become a prey to restless anxiety. We cannot understand this state of mind better than by comparing the *Contrat Social*, which appeared in 1762, with the famous pamphlet of the abbé Siéyès, *Qu'est-ce que le Tiers-Etat*, published anonymously at the beginning of 1789, immediately after the royal decision to convoke the States-General. It is easy to see that Rousseau's ideas had made great strides in twenty-five years. Siéyès accepts his doctrine of the general will, but he states it more precisely, develops it, pushes it to decisive conclusions. The people, the obscure and badly defined term as used by Rousseau which, in the *Contrat Social*, conceals the General Council of Geneva, have disappeared. In their place appears the nation, the French nation—a well-defined entity bearing no equivocal meanings. The French nation is the sum of all the Frenchmen who share in "the *private* work and the *public* functions" by which society subsists (p. 4). Every class is a part of it, the third estate as well as the clergy and nobility; in fact the third estate has a better claim to it than the clergy and nobility because it is by it-self "a complete nation." It could govern society by itself, without the other two orders, whereas they could not even subsist without the third estate. The general will of the nation, that is, of all Frenchmen, is therefore the original source of every legitimate power, even that of the king; the light that had momentarily illuminated Rousseau's mind has been caught and harnessed to a doctrine that is both clear and exact.

The Nation exists before everything, it is the origin of every-thing. Its will is always lawful, it is Law itself. Before and above it there is only *natural* law. If we wish to form a just conception of the order of *positive* laws, which can emanate only from its will, we find at the top *constitutional* laws, which are divided into two categories: those that regulate the organization and functions of the *legislative* body and those that determine the organization and functions of the various *active* bodies. These Laws are called *fundamental*, not in the sense that they may become independent of the national will, but because the bodies that exist and act through them are

unable to harm them. In every plan of government, the constitution is not the work of the constituted power but that of
the constituent power. No delegated power can change the
conditions of its delegation in any way. It is in this sense that
constitutional laws are *fundamental*. The first, those that
establish the legislature, are *founded* by the national will
before any constitution; they are of the first degree. The next
must be established by a *special* representative will. Thus, all
parts of the government correspond to each other and in the
last analysis are dependent upon the Nation. We offer here
only a fleeting thought, but it is accurate.[2]

We can no longer have any doubts. For Siéyès, the
States-General, which is a constituted power, is incom-
petent to solve the problem of the legislative power and
the other fundamental problems that France must solve.
What France needs is an unlimited constituent power, to
which all the constituted powers, including the monarchy,
must be subordinated. If he accepts the States-General
as a temporary expedient, he does so on three conditions:
that the representatives of the third estate be chosen only
from among the citizens who really belong to it, that the
deputies from the third estate be equal in number to
those from the privileged orders, and that the States-
General vote by head and not by order.

Up till now Siéyès does not wrap himself around with
a mantle of obscurity and confusion, as Rousseau had
done; he is lucid, indeed even aggressive; he denies the
sovereign right of the monarch and replaces it with the
sovereign right of the nation and its general will. He is
still precising Rousseau, yet with less incision, when he
defines the general will and its legitimate manifestations.
The general will is not, as in the *Contrat Social,* an absolute, religious in character, whose two requisite perfections
are direct expression and unanimity. For Siéyès, too, direct
expression is the perfection of the general will; but it is
only possible in the smaller states; in the larger, the gen-

[2] Siéyès, *Qu'est-ce que le Tiers-Etat?*

eral will must be expressed by representatives. Representative government is therefore accepted as a legitimate form of power. Similarly, Siéyès no longer seeks the general will in Rousseau's unanimity, but is satisfied to find it in a "plurality"—we would say a "majority." According to Rousseau, a majority means nothing by itself, and has value only when it expresses the general will. For Siéyès a "plurality" is in itself the lawful expression of the general will. The right of majority rule, the cornerstone of representative government, is recognized. But there Siéyès comes to halt. He breathes not a word about the minority, or its relations with the majority, or the respective rights and duties of both majority and minority; he makes no allusion to the right of opposition. He confines himself to saying that elections must be free and general.[3] Finally, he does not consider the English parliament and the party system as a model, far from it.

The government in England is the subject of a constant struggle between the Ministry and the aristocracy of the Opposition. The Nation and the King seem almost to play the part of simple spectators. The King's policy consists in always adopting the stronger party. The Nation fears both parties equally. Its welfare requires that the struggle go on; therefore it supports the weaker to prevent it from being altogether crushed. But if the People, instead of letting the management of their affairs become the prize in a gladiatorial combat, wished to take a hand in it by means of real Representatives, does one honestly believe that the importance today given to the *balance* of powers would not disappear with a system which alone necessitates it?[4]

The English delegates are therefore not the real representatives of the people. Where are they to be found, and how are they to be chosen? Siéyès does not explain. Siéyès was a pathfinder, a leader of the vanguard, who at random attacked the bastions of the past, the defenses of

[3] Siéyès, p. 65.
[4] Siéyès, p. 65-66. Note (1).

the Old Regime, who was weak on some points and who did not inquire too closely into what would happen if the bastions did fall. He was widely read, and he had a disturbing effect on people's minds, but he failed to win the adherence of large sections of public opinion. Caught in the obscure struggle between the Genius of the Old Regime and the Genius of the Revolution, the majority, even in that part of the third estate most independent of the privileged orders, still hesitated. They were attracted and yet frightened by Siéyès' ideas. This could be seen when, at the beginning of May, the deputies arrived at Versailles, bearing with them the famous *cahiers*—thirty-six folio volumes full of demands, delusions, and chimeras. France was asking nothing less than to be made over completely with one wave of a magic wand. Spurred on by this general enthusiasm, the States-General should have gone immediately to work on its gigantic task. It did nothing of the sort. Hardly were the members assembled than they seemed to have had a paralytic stroke; for a month they did nothing, absolutely nothing: they were held up until June 10 by a question of procedure, which the government had not dared to solve and had passed on to the States-General—the question of whether they should vote by head or according to estate. The significance of this delay on the threshold of the new world is obvious. The States-General was an ancient institution dating back to the Middle Ages, part of the densely overgrown system of the aristo-monarchic legitimacies in the Old Regime. Its legitimacy depended on the will of the king, who alone might convoke it, and on the laws which for centuries had governed its composition and powers. It had no legislative power, which was the prerogative of the king; it could only draw the king's attention to abuses, ask for an explanation, insist that he adopt a certain policy or promulgate certain laws, give or refuse its consent to certain taxes. The thirty-six folios with their hopes and dreams could only be deposited at the feet of the king with a rec-

ommendation to his good will. But the king had convoked the States-General because he no longer had the
strength to balance the budget by himself; you can imagine whether he would have had the strength to transform thirty-six folios of demands into laws of the realm!
There was only one way for the States-General to get
around this obstacle: follow Siéyès' recommendation and
demand not only the legislative power, but also the unlimited constituent power before which all constituted
powers had to give way. It was this momentous choice—
to be or not to be—that was concealed behind the question
of procedure the States-General had been fumbling with
ever since May 5. Voting according to estate would be according to tradition, titular rights, written law, the ancient constitution of the monarchy, the Genius of the
Old Regime; voting by head would mean revolution and
its Genius, the new principle of legitimacy proclaimed by
Siéyès.

It was because of this, too, that the third estate hesitated. It wanted to satisfy France, regenerate society, open
a new and happier era in the history of mankind. But to
demand the constituent power, or even the legislative
power, signified a revolt against the king, against an ancient power that was the source of the legitimacy of the
States-General itself. It meant revolt for a principle of
legitimacy that was new, little known, vaguely defined,
badly understood, that hovered between Rousseau's general will and the sovereign right of the nation, as stated by
Siéyès. The two Genii of the City, the old and the new,
were for the first time meeting each other face to face,
neither of them very sure of itself, the first because it was
too old, the other because it was too new. But the States-
General was certainly getting nowhere by wasting away its
time in confused uncertainty, while all France was waiting
with bated breath for a miraculous palingenesis. Something
had to be done. Finally, on June 10, Siéyès proposed that
the third estate turn itself into an "active assembly" and

"summon" the members of the two privileged orders to
the hall of the estates "to be present at, concur in, and submit to a general examination of powers." This proposal
was hardly a frontal attack; by the expression, "active assembly," it merely hinted at the chief question—a demand
for the constituent power—the real revolution! And yet
the third estate continued to hesitate; a long discussion
ended uncertainly: 247 votes for the resolution as it stood,
except that in place of the word "summon," the word
"invite" was substituted; 246 votes for the resolution
amended; 51 against. Did this mean that the resolution
was approved or not? For a long time the members
wrangled over this; the decision had to be postponed to
the evening session, and finally that evening the first revolutionary motion was approved. But, as the invitation of
June 10 did not succeed in overcoming the resistance of
the privileged orders, in the session of June 15, Siéyès
proposed that the third estate proclaim itself the sole
representative of the French nation. That was the conclusive act of revolution, the substitution of the new Genius
for the Genius of the Old Regime. And once again the
third estate hesitated. It discussed the matter for three
days; it examined numerous resolutions, and listened for
three days to a magnificent speech that revealed the secret
of the Revolution with truly astonishing prophetic insight.
Its author, Mirabeau, had been capable of it because he
alone, for some mysterious reason, was in secret touch
with the invisible Genii of the City. This is what his prophetic speech announced to the third estate, to the States-
General, to all France: The legitimacy of the States-General was established by convocation of the king and by the
ancient laws of the realm; it would fall on the day that
it revolted against the king and the constitution of the
monarchy. On that day, would it be possible for the national will to establish a new legitimacy in place of the
old one? The third estate should not be deluded: the general will of France, which had sent the twelve hundred

members of the assembly to Versailles, was certainly fervent, but it was also muddled, contradictory, disorganized, and lacked firm foundation. It was not yet recognized as a permanent constitutional power with an exact role; its manifestations were vigorous, but sporadic and precarious.

At last, on June 17, the assembly of the third estate came to a decision; by a vote of 490 to 90, it decided to call itself the National Assembly and to inform the other two estates that a constitution would be established with or without their help. This time at last the Rubicon had been crossed. The rest is familiar. The court tried forcibly to impose its will on the Assembly; the Assembly resisted, met in the tennis court next door, took the famous oath, and defied the royal power to its face and, behind it, the Genius of the Old Regime. Frightened by the inevitable collapse that would have followed any new attempt at violence on its part, the court capitulated on June 28. The king ordered the nobles and clergy to join the National Assembly. If not the constituent power dreamed of by Siéyès, at least the legislative power had been transferred from king to Assembly; a great revolution, and a necessary revolution, had taken place. We have already seen why it was necessary. Though there were a great many dreams and delusions in the hopes held by the people, there was one issue on which they had plenty of cause for complaint. The country had become too complex, too vast, too civilized for all the laws it needed to be made by a hereditary king and four or five ministers chosen by him from an airtight court where he was a prisoner as well as a god. France needed a legislative power with a wider foundation, in more direct and immediate contact with the nation. How else were the reasonable claims of the *cahiers* to be satisfied? With the decisive step thus taken, the Assembly should have had a clear path to travel. But again it was held up. The three weeks following this preliminary revolution were no more active than the preceding ones had been. Everyone was uneasy. The Assembly was as uncomfortable about its victory as the court was about its defeat. Why? Mirabeau had prophesied truly in his great speech on June 15: the National Assembly, after its revolutionary action, could no longer, like the States-General, either justify itself by royal convocation and the ancient laws of the realm, or find support in the traditional division of society into classes, which it had denied. But neither could it justify itself by the doctrine of the general will of the nation, as formulated by Rousseau and Siéyès. This was understood and accepted as yet by only a very small minority, and was too new, too abstract, too confusing; it was not supported, as in modern parliamentary states, either by old laws and traditions, which would have established without any question its powers and methods of action, or by a solid organization of parties and opinion. The National Assembly was still an apprentice assembly, whose powers and rights were uncertain.

These uncertainties might have been clarified if they had been embodied in the Old Regime system of aristo-monarchic legitimacies—by means of a regular and definitive cession of the legislative power on the part of the king. That was how the role of the parliament in England had grown up beside that of the royal power. Since the king was able to cede his own powers, the royal transmission would have been the sanction that would have legitimized the new legislative power, in the same way that the delegation of his authority by the king legitimized all the executive and judicial organs that administered France in his name. Moreover, that is what Louis XVI and the Assembly were preparing to do, after June 28, by transforming France into a constitutional monarchy and adapting, as in England, the outmoded system of aristo-monarchic legitimacies to the new spirit of the times. And then, sixteen days after the revolution of June 28, an extraordinary event that no one had foreseen or desired, an event without precedent, unique in human history, almost supernatural, took unfortunate mankind by surprise in the midst of its dreams, and transformed the miraculous palingenesis awaited by so many into a revolutionary apocalypse, which has already lasted for more than a century and a half.

VIII

THE FIRST DAY OF THE REVOLUTIONARY APOCALYPSE: JULY 14, 1789

—◆◆◆◆—

Government is always an organized minority that has to do only with isolated individuals or small groups. That is why it is imposed without too much difficulty. The strongest government would fall in a few hours, police and courts would be completely and instantaneously paralyzed, if all the subjects came to a simultaneous agreement to withhold their obedience. Man's existence is relatively ordered, and every state succeeds in making itself obeyed because a general refusal to obey is an impossibility.

At any rate we are entitled to call it impossible, since it is so difficult. But it is not altogether impossible because there has been one example of it—so far as I know, unparalleled, as was the emotional contagion out of which it sprang. On July 14, 1789, the Bastille was stormed and taken in a tremendous rising of the people, under circumstances familiar to everyone. It is less familiar that this victorious uprising was followed, for the first time in history, by the event which we held, not without reason, to be impossible: All over France, for six weeks, as soon as the news from Paris was heard, all the people—peasants, workers, lower middle classes, officials, upper classes—as at a signal after a secret agreement, refused to obey. An immediate and irresistible correlation was thereupon established: the masses revolted because they sensed that authority was paralyzed; authority ceased to exist because it felt that the masses had freed themselves. The majority was carried away by an unaccountable frenzy, the minority followed willingly or unwillingly, convinced up to a certain point only; but the fact remains that everyone revolted. Barracks and monasteries were emptied as soldiers and monks deserted, the army scattered to the four winds, the administration was dislocated, neither courts nor police functioned any longer, taxes and seigniorial dues were no longer paid, everywhere monasteries and castles were stormed and pillaged. The aristocratic and monarchic hierarchy was not thus attacked and overthrown by a revolution so that it could be replaced by new powers; in a few weeks it vanished into nothingness, disappeared into an enormous crevasse of history that all at once opened up beneath its age-old foundations. The monarchy did not fall on August 10, 1792, but during the six weeks that followed the fall of the Bastille. On June 28 the king had been deprived of his legislative power as the result of a constitutional conflict between the Crown and the States-General, the meaning of which was clear and definite; during the weeks that followed the storming of the Bastille, Louis XVI became a king without an army, without a police force, without courts, laws, or money; he was despoiled of all his powers, not by right but by deed, without any constitutional conflict and without advantage to a new power. Never in Western history had there been so unexpected and so tremendous an emotional contagion; one of the most grandiose among all historical edifices built by mankind unexpectedly crumbled away within a few weeks in the middle of a peaceful Europe; one of the most ancient and cultured civilizations was stripped completely bare from one day to the next before the eyes of the whole world, woke up one fine day to find no army, no courts, no police, no administration, no law, not even a shred of order with which to cover itself.

Was there an analogy between the revolution of June 28 and the disaster of the next month? Obviously the victory of the third estate must have encouraged the spirit of revolt and discredited the court. But it is also obvious that there was a great disparity between the humiliation of the king on June 28 and the complete collapse of the aristocratic and monarchic legality a month later. The former event was far too insignificant a cause for so tremendous a catastrophe; it was only the final burst of gale that topples a withered tree whose roots have been weakened for a long time by an invisible disease. What disease? How may we recognize it? What are its immediate causes and its primary origin? I believe that we can only understand nineteenth- and twentieth-century history up to the present insofar as we are able to answer this tremendous question, which raises itself on the threshold of the modern world. I shall attempt to answer it later on to the best of my ability; for the moment we must devote ourselves primarily to discovering the nature, the scope, the importance, and the consequences of an event that is so difficult to understand because it was unique. But this is a necessary preliminary to the discovery of its origin and causes. No, the six weeks that followed the capture of the Bastille were not, as they appear to be in the histories written during the last century and a half, one of the numerous and more or less analogous outbursts of disorder that marked the course of the French Revolution. The six weeks that followed the capture of the Bastille were the real beginnings of the French Revolution. If by the French Revolution is meant the sum of the events that upset France and Europe from 1789 to 1814, the decisive initial event that unleashed it was neither the agitation of the philosophical societies and the masonic lodges, nor Siéyès' pamphlet, nor the deficit in the budget, nor the convocation of the States-General, nor the revolt of the third estate, nor the Oath of the Tennis Court, nor the king's capitulation on June 28: it was the crumbling of the monarchic and aristocratic order after the Bastille, the gigantic cataclysm that surprised everyone because no one had either wanted or expected it. After the Bastille, the Revolution abandoned the grandiose initial program with which it had come to Versailles, and it concentrated all its efforts on a single aim: the establishment of a government that would be acceptable to France and reconcilable with the peace of Europe. But it took twenty-five years and oceans of blood to rebuild what six weeks had sufficed to destroy! That is the underlying philosophy of the French Revolution. Let me add that the capture of the Bastille and its immediate consequences were a phenomenon with even greater significance from a universal point of view, perhaps the most serious, the most mysterious, the most extraordinary phenomenon in history. In Paris, the memory of the Bastille is still celebrated on July 14 when the people dance in the streets under the lamps. The pity of man's ignorance! Every year on that day we should give ourselves over to meditation, and reflect upon man's fate, understanding the true significance of that event. It may be defined thus: because, toward the end of the eighteenth century, one of the foremost peoples in Europe refused for six weeks, only six weeks, to obey, a sort of revolutionary apocalypse was thereby brought about, which has lasted for a century and a half and now, after having devastated Europe, threatens to spread over all the world and destroy everything. That is what I shall attempt to prove.

Let us begin by a study of the immediate, general reaction to this unprecedented cataclysm. This took the form of a frightful panic, the first "great panic" of modern history, which in a few days broke out all over France. It began in the rural and urban masses. In the country and in the small towns the most alarming rumors were spread:

that bands of robbers were coming to burn the forests, cut
the grain, and pillage the towns: that the king's troops, led
by princes of the royal blood, were approaching; that foreign troops were invading France to punish, enslave, or
exterminate the people. The people armed themselves, bar-
ricaded the towns and villages, beat the countryside for
these imaginary enemies. For the first time in history the
masses had revolted in France with complete success, and
the first effect of their victory was that they became frightened of their revolt. What a lesson for all revolutionaries,
whether by word or by deed! Together with the great
panic of the masses, frightened of their revolt, there began
the great panic of society in general, frightened by the
revolt of the masses: the great panic of the court, the National Assembly, the nobility, the Church, and the third
estate. Great and humble, rich and poor, wise and ignorant,
all were seized at the same time by the same terror, that,
since there was no more law, no one was secure, and that
anything was possible. If, on the one hand, the masses were
afraid of a nonexistent conspiracy on the part of the aristocracy to mobilize imaginary bandits and troops, on the
other, the aristocracy began to flee before a danger that did
not yet exist and that their flight would create. At the very
moment when the deluded masses were imagining him in
various sections of France at the head of an army marching
toward Versailles to subdue the National Assembly, the
comte d'Artois was crossing the Alps with a few secretaries
and servants to take refuge in Turin. He had been the first
prince of the royal blood to flee after July 14: he was not
to return for a quarter of a century.

The "great panic" is the beast that rises from the sea of
the revolutionary apocalypse; the beast that resembles a
leopard and has the mouth of a lion; the beast to whom "it
was given to make war with the saints, and to overcome
them"; the beast who has "power over all kindreds, and
tongues, and nations." As the invisible protagonist in the
drama of the Revolution, the great panic was to play the

principal part until 1814 and force an entire generation to cut each other's throats, by throwing them into a fierce delirium of bloody hallucinations. It was to disappear suddenly in 1814, as though by a miracle, and the subsequent generations, grown up in order and peace, were to forget it, their imaginations no longer conjuring up its invisible and terrible form, and were not to understand the great drama, which, deprived of its protagonist, would have no more meaning. Because they were unaware of the "great panic," the generations of the peace that followed were likewise not to understand the incredible audacity of the National Assembly and were to regard it as the first great folly of the Revolution. Anarchy was abroad all over France, there were no longer any army, justice, police, money, or administration; but in Versailles there were twelve hundred men who assembled every day to make laws. Drops of ink on scraps of paper—that was all these laws were. But with its drops of ink, this extraordinary Assembly destroyed the whole of the old aristocratic and monarchic organization of France and constructed a new and unprecedented organization on metaphysical foundations. On August 27, 1789, the Assembly finished the discussion and approved the last articles of the Declaration of the Rights of Man. In a sublime flight of prose, it declared that men are born free and equal; that the aim of every political association is the preservation of the natural and imprescriptible rights of man—liberty, property, safety, and resistance to oppression; that the principle of every sovereignty resides in the nation; that law is the expression of the general will and that all citizens have the right to concur in person or through their representatives in its formation; that it must be the same for all; that every citizen may speak, write, and publish in freedom, the free communication of thoughts being one of man's rights, except in certain cases covered by law. The sovereignty of the people, the right of opposition, the political freedoms that the latter implies, juridical equality, were all recognized as foundations of the State.

All the aspirations toward a new orientation of government and State that had been proclaimed by the philosophy and literature of the eighteenth century in France and England were translated into the fundamental law of the new France. Voltaire, Montesquieu, Rousseau, the Encyclopedists, the Physiocrats, Locke, Hume, the doctrinaires of natural law—all were present, distilled and condensed, in this astonishing document. One can well understand the tremendous impression it made on the whole world. Was this the beginning of the reign of reason, of liberty, of equality, of justice? The world had never seen a greater revolution! But what condition was France in at the time she made this great constructive effort? We are enlightened by a speech made by the archbishop of Bordeaux, the Lord High Chancellor, before the Assembly on August 7: "Property has been violated in the provinces; incendiaries have ravaged the dwellings of the citizens; forms of justice are disregarded and are replaced by violence and proscriptions; license without bounds, laws without force, tribunals without any work, commerce and industry suspended. And yet, gentlemen, it is not only poverty that is behind all this disturbance: it is the total subversion of the police and all regular authorities that is the cause of all the evils." At the same session Necker announced that payment of taxes and imposts of all kinds had almost completely ceased throughout France. In his speech appears this textual sentence: "Relief offices have been pillaged, their books scattered, their receipts stopped or suspended in a multitude of places the enumeration of which would take up too much time."

It seems obvious that such a situation should have called for the proclamation, not of a metaphysical charter of the rights of man, but of martial law throughout France. Moreover, the king did not fail to call the Assembly's attention to this inconsistency. In September the Assembly laid the foundations for the constitution of the realm by approving nineteen articles, which it sent on October 1, with the Declaration of the Rights of Man, to the king for his august sanction. These articles gave France the new legislative power she needed by creating a permanent assembly; they recognized the king as the head of the executive power with the right to appoint and dismiss ministers; they granted him the right of a suspensive veto on the resolutions of the Assembly. In a letter that was read to the Assembly on the morning of October 15, the king, after having said that "new constituent laws cannot be well judged except when taken as a whole," added:

I grant my consent to these articles, in accordance with your wishes, but on certain positive conditions from which I shall never deviate: that is, the general outcome of your resolutions is to place the executive power in the hands of the monarch. A series of facts and observations, which I shall put before you, will show you that, in the present order of things I can protect neither the collection of taxes, nor the distribution of grain, nor the individual liberty of citizens. Nevertheless, I wish to fulfill this essential duty of the Crown. And so I ask that we act together to remove all these different obstacles.

"Treason!" the leftist historians have been crying for a century. But, in substance, what was the king saying to the Assembly? He was saying: You send me a declaration of the rights of man and the first articles of the new constitution. Very fine, but I beg you not to forget that at this moment in all France there is no longer any justice, order, or State; that everywhere people are pillaging and killing with impunity; that imposts are no longer being paid; that commerce has everywhere ceased and that Paris is threatened with starvation. You confine yourselves to stating that the executive power belongs to me; that is not enough: it is extremely urgent that you also give me the means to exercise it: an army, a police force, a judiciary, an administration. I no longer have anything.

From his point of view the king was right. The National Assembly was making laws that, though very fine on paper, were inapplicable because France was sinking into anarchy. But the National Assembly received the king's letter in bad grace and boldly continued to destroy the old France and build up the new. Royal authority had always hesitated to interfere with acquired rights, crystallized interests, and traditions: the Assembly, in a few months during the second half of '89, abolished the last vestiges of the feudal regime—discrimination between classes, venality in public offices, all exemptions and financial inequalities, church tithes, the privileges of corporations, boroughs, and provinces, the parliaments, which the kings had made so many futile attempts to abolish. It remade the whole judicial system from top to bottom, introduced the jury, reformed criminal law. On October 10, Talleyrand proposed that all church property revert to the State, and that the latter should have charge of all religious expenditures; and, on November 2, the Assembly passed by 568 votes to 346, with 40 abstentions, a motion of Mirabeau's to put the entire fortune of the Church at the disposal of the nation. In three weeks an institution even more ancient, more ramified, more enveloping than the monarchy—monachism—was overthrown.

We have seen that Rousseau constantly talks about the people and never defines them. In November, the Assembly confronted the important question of who the people were. Or, to employ the phraseology of the Declaration of the Rights of Man, what is the sovereign nation? The Assembly made a distinction between passive citizens and active citizens. Passive citizens were those that had a right to the protection of their property and liberty, but that did not have a right to participate in the formation of political bodies: women, children, and men who either had nothing or whose possessions were below a certain level. Active citizens, able to contribute to the making of laws and the exercise of power, were those that possessed some material wealth. They constituted the sovereign nation and were divided into three categories according to the extent of their property. The first category, the poorest, had only the right to meet in primary assemblies to choose the electors who would elect members to the different assemblies; the second, more wealthy, furnished the first with a choice of second-degree electors and members of departmental assemblies and municipal districts; the third and wealthiest was eligible for all offices, including the National Assembly.

There were about 4,300,000 primary electors, two thirds of all men over twenty-five—a very large suffrage if not a universal one. But it is evident that the real sovereign nation was represented by a comfortably off and cultured minority, the only group from which members of all the elective assemblies might be chosen. A bourgeois constitution, therefore—as M. Aulard has stated? In my opinion this should go down in history as a reasonable constitution, at least theoretically reasonable. It admitted enough of the people into the City so that the democratic principle of popular sovereignty was not a farce; and it secured the power to the classes possessing wealth and culture. One could not, in 1789, ask for a more democratic constitution from even the boldest individuals. De Maistre wittily ridiculed the constitutions that men pretend to produce from a few drops of ink. A political constitution is not made by writing down some constitutional phrases on a few sheets of paper: a constitution is the slow and accumulated work of a way of life and of a certain age—laws, customs, traditions, all superimposed, adapted to each other, sometimes even contradictory. The English constitution, for instance, or the constitution of the French monarchy at the height of its glory. The noble Joseph [De Maistre], from a rational point of view, was quite right. But the Revolution was justified in doing what it could with the possibilities so limited. The old monarchic constitution having crumbled, what could the new power do, suspended as it was in an immense vacuum, except write constitutions that would only be futile scratches of ink? The vacuum was there, and had swallowed up the work of centuries; it was imperative to try to fill it, and what else could one throw into it but legal treatises, made as perfect as possible? And so the Assembly, as though spurred on by an inner demon, went from one constitutional law to another, surrounded on all sides by ever-increasing anarchy. After having defined, recognized, and crowned the new sovereign, the nation, the Assembly, in December, passed a great law on the legislative assemblies that were to reorganize the executive power in accordance with the elective principle. It was the nation, that is, the whole body of active citizens, which, in first- and second-degree elections, were to select, from the well-to-do elite of a qualitative regime, civil and criminal judges, officers of the national guard, that is, of the force charged with the maintenance of order, in fact all administrators charged with conducting public affairs of every kind. Through a complex system of self-government, based on Anglo-Saxon models, the greater part of the executive power was bestowed on the members of departmental and municipal assemblies elected by the people. Although the law placed all these magistrates under the control of the king, the king and his ministers had in reality nothing to do under the new constitution. Of the old executive power, the king kept only the command of the army, which, moreover, was completely disorganized, without the power to declare war and make peace, which had passed to the Assembly. The hereditary principle had been completely ousted in favor of the elective principle; it survived only in the king, who had become a mere shadow. The people now had to administer their own interests with the help of representatives elected by them.

Thus, a structure centuries old was destroyed under an avalanche of laws. Siéyès seemed to triumph beyond his wildest dreams; the nation came into its own, with an unlimited constituent power over the past, the present, and the future. And yet this Assembly, which seemed to have become the great arbiter of man's destiny, was just as frightened of the people's revolt as the court, the Church, and the nobility. The great panic had taken possession of it as well as of all the other organs of society. We know what happened on October 5: A huge crowd of women from Paris arrived in Versailles and invaded the National Assembly, which did not dare to have them driven out by the bayonets of the soldiers, and there proceeded to denounce the imaginary conspiracies of the court and Church and to demand bread. The Assembly, completely overawed, decided to send a deputation to the king, in which a dozen women would be included and which would demand the ratification of the Declaration of the Rights of Man and of the other laws still in suspension. At ten o'clock that evening the king announced his consent to all ratifications demanded; everyone thought that was the end of it. But the female rioters spent the night in Versailles and the next morning, reinforced by more rioters from Paris, invaded the castle and parliament, seized the royal family, and carried everyone off to Paris. It was the rape of a court and a parliament by a mob of women—an episode without parallel in history. The Assembly, the demiurge that was remaking the world, did not dare to raise a hand against these poverty-stricken furies, submitted docilely, like the court, to being taken to Paris by a mob in skirts.

How are we to explain this paradox of an almost superhuman omnipotence and an almost ridiculous impotence? It was the unique case of an Assembly that found itself, after July 14, swinging in a vacuum, with no resistance to overcome and nothing to support it. King, court, princes, nobles, high clergy, high bureaucracy—everyone, after the Bastille, was so terrified by his own impotence that no one dared make any serious resistance, even to the most absurd ideas and acts. Since all opposition was paralyzed, it required only a little nucleus of resolute deputies, the vociferations and squallings of a few pamphleteers, and a popular demonstration to secure a majority in the Assembly for the most daring proposals. For instance, it is not certain that the Assembly was in favor of the law secularizing the wealth of the Church: a few popular demonstrations sufficed to have it passed by a large majority. Under such conditions, the forces that wanted the destruction of the Old Regime became irresistible. But this Assembly, against which nothing or no one could offer any resistance, had nothing to support it. The tremendous authority that clothed the States-General at Versailles during the month of May, sprang from two sources: the ancient laws of the realm, and the somewhat confused but ardent enthusiasm of the national will of France, which had sent it to Versailles with thirty-six hope-laden folios. In June, the States-General had renounced the prestige and support of the traditional legitimacy. After the Bastille, during the second half of '89, the unanimous enthusiasm in France vanished. The court, the nobles, the high clergy, the plutocrats of the third estate were not at all satisfied to be stripped of all power. The demolition and reconstruction carried out by the Assembly injured a great many interests; gave rise to a great many fears, suspicions, and hates; envenomed the discord that lurked in the Assembly and in all France. The great dualism of the invisible Genii sprang from the heart of the great panic: the aristo-monarchic legitimacy was old but far from dead as yet; the democratic legitimacy had the enthusiasm of youth, but it was still vague, incoherent, badly understood. By the end of '89 the enthusiastic unanimity of May had already broken up into two parties that were arguing in a vacuum: one was afraid of the Revolution and wanted to stop it but couldn't; the other was persuaded by the lack of any real opposition to develop its program beyond all reasonable limits. The frightened classes grouped themselves behind the two parties in the Assembly; the nobles, the wealthy, and the clergy, became more and more suspect to the middle classes and the populace in general; and the more the latter accused them of imaginary conspiracies, the more the upper classes regarded them as barbarian hordes that were trying to put civilization to the sword. Though the National Assembly had its admirers who did not hesitate to declare the divinity of the constitution that it was preparing, the skeptics who condemned its work and denounced it as a disaster were increasing both in and out of the Assembly in the upper classes. The emigration of the aristocratic families, which had begun after the fall of the Bastille, was accentuated during the following months: the nobility fled before the increasing agitation of the masses, who were already, in the fall of '89, cruelly suffering from poverty and enforced idleness. There was no bread, due to a bad harvest and the obstruction of transport by the prevailing state of anarchy. But the people had another explanation for their poverty: the court, the nobility, and the clergy were preventing the arrival of the convoys of wheat in order to chastise the people for their support of the Revolution; the archbishop of Paris was paying the millers to stop their mills. An even greater danger was that fanatics capable of exploiting the persecution complex and the spirit of revolt in the masses were setting to work in the shadow of the Declaration of the Rights of Man and the freedoms which it granted. Papers and clubs mushroomed everywhere. On September 13, Marat published the first issue of *Le publiciste de Paris*, which later became the *Ami du Peuple*. The next month, October, the Society of Friends of the Constitution, founded April 30, 1789, followed the Assembly to Paris, settled in the Rue Saint Honoré, in the library of the Jacobin Convent, and began to cover all France with a great network of Jacobin clubs.

With such chaotic conditions, the danger of a new constitution based almost completely on the elective principle was obvious. France was in need of a vigorous executive who would restore the law that had been overthrown after July 14; in order to create it by means of a system of self-government, she would need an organized, experienced, and capable electorate. Would it be possible, even for a nation as civilized as France, to create a capable electorate in a few months, at a time when the entire people were in revolt and a great panic covered the land? In any case, the Assembly did not waste much time over this possibility, and it attempted to help the new executive power by means of committees that corresponded directly to the new authorities, giving them their orders and treating the ministers like clerks. The Committee of Investigation, instituted on July 28, 1789, at the beginning of the great panic, controlled the political police, getting its information directly from the new municipalities, ordered inquiries, and issued writs of arrest. The Diplomatic Committee, established July 29, 1790, took over the conduct of foreign affairs and had the credentials of ambassadors transferred to itself. The Financial Committee, after December 19, 1789, had its own special funds, called extraordinary funds, distinct from the royal treasury; it was particularly concerned with assignats and the national wealth; the Feudal Committee, created August 12, 1789, did not confine itself to facilitating the redemption of seigniorial dues but corresponded directly with the local authorities to help them overcome the obstacles involved in applying the various laws. The Military Committee, set up on October 1, 1789, was in close collaboration from the very start with the War Minister and supervised all military administration.

This was a third executive power, which was added to the power of the king and that of the self-government, created by the great law of December, 1789. But the only result was that the weakness of the State and the internal chaos increased from one month to the next. The three powers, by competing with each other, weakened and neutralized instead of helped each other, and this at a time when there should have been a single strong power. A single unified policy might have spared the Western world the apocalyptic catastrophe in which the anarchy was to end; if only the court and the Assembly could have come to an understanding, hurriedly reorganized the army, the police, the courts, and the finances, and re-established order. After that the constitution could have begun to function and the new age would have opened. How was it that the National Assembly, which had so many superior brains, was unable to see the obvious and urgent need of a single strong power? The answer is that the great panic blunted their perspicacity. As the Assembly buried itself deeper in its great reformatory work, as the disorder caused by the disaster of July steadily increased, and as the currents of opposition in the court, the nobility, and the clergy became strengthened, the panic increased to tremendous proportions. The court, the aristocracy, and the clergy were afraid of the Assembly; the Assembly was frightened of the court, the aristocracy, and the clergy: the most innocent acts were interpreted by both sides as indicating hostile intentions; these tendentious interpretations were backed up on both sides by fantastic accusations. Everyone was living under the constant shadow of imaginary conspiracies. How, then, could the Assembly ally itself to the court, the aristocracy, and the clergy, which it distrusted more and more, in order to suppress the revolt of the masses? The masses were well-disposed toward the Assembly because they saw in it a protection against the imaginary conspiracies of the court, the aristocracy, and the clergy; they were always ready to stage demonstrations in its favor—demonstrations which, in the absence of all authority, rapidly acquired the significance of a decisive force.

It was then—between 1790 and 1793—that the revolutionary apocalypse, begun on July 14, and the great panic which it brought about combined to produce the decisive event: the final rupture between the Genius of the Old Regime and the Genius of the Revolution, the war of extermination between the principles of legitimacy—aristo-monarchic and democratic—which caused and were yet to cause blood to flow. Before then the two principles had fought in England, but without ever having come to a final rupture. The Commons had defended the rights of the people, as empirical rights, established on paper by laws, that limited but did not deny, on the basis of a superior and absolute principle, the rights of the Crown and the aristocracy. That is what had permitted and was to permit the English freedoms to develop through successive compromises and result in understanding and collaboration between the two invisible Genii, between the Crown and aristocracy and the people. After 1790 the French Revolution took a different path from that of the English; it became a metaphysical revolution that proclaimed the new democratic principle of legitimacy as an absolute, almost religious in character, like truth, happiness, good, or salvation. The other principle, the Genius of the Old Regime, became nothing but error, evil, perdition, which had to be exterminated by pen and sword in every institution and in every mind. The Genius of the Old Regime accepted the challenge; and the revolutionary apocalypse revealed itself to the world in its first manifestation—a rain of blood and fire that lasted for a quarter of a century. On one side there was the frightful sanguinary despotism of the Terror—the pitiless proscriptions, confiscations, legal murders, *coups d'état,* delations, laws on suspects, deportations. The Old Regime countered with permanent revolt and civil war, crime, conspiracy with the enemies of France, invasions prepared abroad. On both sides it was to be an implacable war of systematic calumny and extermination, an ideological war, more deadly than the old religious wars. Must we then agree with M. Cochin and lay the blame for this revolutionary apocalypse on eighteenth-century philosophy, which seems "to have made its dwelling in the City of the clouds, with its center over the void," and succumbed to "the rapture of leaving the earth and taking to flight . . . over the steeples of cathedrals"? No, the cause is still the beast of the Apocalypse, daughter of the Bastille—the great panic.

The National Assembly had managed to find a certain

measure of support in the memory of the national enthusiasm that had created it, a certain prestige in the great reforms it was legislating. But the Legislative Assembly and the Convention, which followed it, had no foundations at all; they were suspended in a vacuum. They could not be legitimized by the aristo-monarchic principle, which they denied, nor by the democratic principle, which the majority did not understand and which the elections made even more unacceptable by the incoherent and contradictory manner in which they applied it. Furthermore, neither of them could count on a single stable organ of government to carry out its will: neither a police force, nor a gendarmery, nor courts which would ensure their independence and safety; nor an army capable of defending the land; nor a treasury provided with enough funds for the more necessary public expenditures. The Legislative Assembly added war to the horrors of so desperate a situation. The situation of the Convention, after the fall of the monarchy and the decapitation of Louis XVI, is one of the most appalling in history. With absolutely no support from the nation, with no principle of legitimacy to justify it, with no police, justice, army, or money, and at war with half Europe, it was also torn internally by struggles between factions that were eliminating each other in their hate and fear. It is impossible to understand the Legislative Assembly and the Convention without realizing that the members of these two governments were all mad with fear, that they saw enemies everywhere, in Europe, in France, even in the midst of their assembly, of their government, of their own party. Fear led individuals, as it did groups and governments, to commit acts of violence; violence increased the fear, which in turn more and more aggravated the cruelty of men. It was thus that, from one violence to another, the Convention proceeded to the massacres, mass exterminations, legal murders, drownings, and shootings of the Terror.

But the more blood these unfortunate victims of the

great panic shed the more they needed to believe in their
principles as absolutes. Only the absolute might still ab-
solve them in their own eyes and sustain their desperate
energy. The Jacobins did not spill all that blood because
they believed in popular sovereignty as a religious truth;
they tried to believe in popular sovereignty as a religious
truth because their fear made them spill so much blood.
Without this inversion, the French Revolution would be
nothing but a senseless tragedy played by drunken actors.
Marat, who demanded 200,000 heads every day in his
paper, could not bear to see an animal tortured. The contradiction is a weird one; and it has been attributed to
the idiotic fallacies in the philosophy of the age. But there
is a simpler explanation. Marat could suffer when he saw
a dog being tortured because he was not afraid of the
dog. When he was demanding 200,000 heads, he was a
man crazed by fear, who from morning to night, night
to morning, was terrified of being imprisoned, assassinated,
or guillotined by the enemies he wanted to exterminate.
Fear made him a wild animal, and the wild animal sought
justification for its excesses in the absolute. It was fear and
the need for the absolute that led the Revolution to make
the *Contrat Social* its Bible and Rousseau its Moses. Suspended in a vacuum, unable to lean on a clear and precise principle of legitimacy, the Revolution clutched at a
book, at a philosophy—a book and a philosophy that lay
within easy reach. The *Contrat Social* had many advantages for becoming the Bible of the Revolution: it was
short, it seemed clear and precise, though it was far less
so than it seemed at a first superficial reading; it swarmed
with contradictions that justified the most varying interpretations. Finally, it gave the theory of the general will
the value of a religious truth, as M. Cochin has very well
brought out; it went into no details on the juridical and
political procedure by which the general will, the source
of legitimate power, could or should be expressed. Which
was very convenient for a Revolution obliged to pack the

prisons in the name of liberty, and to chop off so many heads in the name of humanity!

Thus it was that the Genius of the Old Regime and the Genius of the Revolution, the aristo-monarchic principle of legitimacy and the democratic principle of legitimacy, declared war on each other. And so began the restlessness of a world.

IX

A RESTLESS WORLD

————◆◆◆◆————

The French Revolution will remain a complete mystery, as long as it is not understood that it could not, and why it could not, either apply or deny the doctrine of popular sovereignty. A frightful contradiction which is the key to the great mystery. We have seen that no principle of legitimacy is so just and reasonable that it imposes itself immediately and irresistibly upon man's consciousness. The majority of Frenchmen, in '89, had never heard of the general will or the sovereignty of the nation; they were still attached to the monarchy, the Church, the past, unaware of their sovereignty and unwilling to exercise it. The first applications of the new principle still further increased their repugnance. The result was that as soon as the Revolution delivered over to the people the instruments of the new sovereignty, the people used them to demolish the institutions of the Revolution. It was this contradictory situation that, more than the crimes and mistakes denounced by its detractors, was the undoing of the Directory. After the the fall of Robespierre and the end of the Terror, the Revolution for the first time tried to subdue its fears and return to the grandiose plan it had originally started with. The Directory in the beginning did its best faithfully to apply the formula of democratic legitimacy, by granting the freedoms implied—those of speech, press, assembly—and by respecting the right of opposition. But it soon perceived that the right of opposition and its freedoms were of particular advantage to the royalists and Catholics because the majority of the people were behind them. In a fair struggle between majority and minority, the adherents to the aristocratic and monarchic principle would have carried off the honors, legally possessed themselves of the power, and exterminated the Republic, together with all its champions.

Since it was impossible to deny and just as impossible to apply the principle of popular sovereignty, what was to be done? Siéyès was not the fool that Napoleon's apologists have painted. He had a proud and strongly speculative intellect, and he was apt to become infatuated with his ideas, partly because they were never banal and partly because they were his own; he was brave and aggressive, avaricious of wealth and avid for the glory that came with the playing of a great role in history, yet impatient with the daily cares and worries that are the natural appanage of power; more enterprising in exceptional circumstances than active in the normal course of events; both farsighted and clear-headed, he was capable of acting with great courage when driven by passion, deviating neither to the right nor left of the line first chosen and followed—to sum up, a man who, in his own way and in certain respects, was a profound thinker, but was false in everything else, a man who had become possessed by the Genius of the Revolution, the principle of democratic legitimacy. He believed sincerely, passionately, with all the strength of his convictions and his pride, in the doctrine of the general will and sovereignty of the nation; and at the crucial moment he had known how to act. It had been he, in 1789, who had started the Revolution by leading the third estate in the assault on the Old Regime. He had chosen to make a direct frontal attack, which had seemed the most likely to bring success; the attack had succeeded, and he had replaced the royal sovereignty with the sovereignty of the nation, the king's Council with the National Assembly. A tremendous revolution! In short, he had been the protagonist of the promising prologue to the Revolution, its guiding light— but only for a moment. He had no more idea than anyone else that three weeks after his victory the whole front, one point of which he had attacked, would fall to pieces by itself; that the aristocratic and monarchic order would melt completely away; or that the sovereignty of the nation, which he had established in place of the king's, would be swept away with the rest by the tremendous wave of a great panic. What was to be done? Like so many others, he disappeared during the great panic, and did not reappear until the advent of the Directory to give it his assistance in the serious and sincere organization of the nation's sovereignty. It was only natural; in helping the Directory, the fearless leader of '89 was doing no more than resuming the work that the great panic had interrupted. And then came his second and most frightful disillusionment: the country he had proclaimed sovereign in 1789 ten years later abdicated in favor of the old powers. And so it happened that the leader of the third estate and its revolt in 1789 reappeared in 1799 as the organizer of a second revolution, which, in spite of him, ended up as the antithesis and negation of the first—the 18 Brumaire and the Constitution of the Year VIII. We have already seen that the latter was ingeniously constructed but that it had no foundation, neither of tradition, nor of a principle acknowledged and accepted, at least by a part of the country, nor of precedent, nor of foreign models. From start to finish it was an adventurous improvisation and a complete novelty. It had sprung from nowhere, drawn by the power of the intellect that had created it. Was it, then, as so many historians have said, the work of an idealist accustomed to nourishing himself on chimeras? But the man who had opened the breach in the Old Regime on June 18, 1789, was too mighty a demolisher of old walls and builder of new ones to amuse himself blowing soap bubbles. If he ended by thinking up a completely novel constitution, without historical precedent, without past or experiential foundation, based on sheer imagination, it was because he wanted to solve a problem that had appeared for the first time in human history; a problem that was insoluble, but that Siéyès had to believe soluble and wanted to solve at any price because his life, his work, the whole Revolution, depended on a solution. It was a titanic effort, which involved nothing less than an attempt to justify, by the sovereign will of a nation, a regime that the majority of the French people, rightly or wrongly, did not want. After long and solitary reflection, Siéyès thought he had found the magic formula that would free the Revolution from its contradictions. It was the formula "that confidence should ascend from below and authority descend from above"; and it was to be realized, as we have seen, by a government that was superior to the people and independent of it, but rested firmly in the hands of the revolutionary oligarchy, which would select the representatives of the popular will among 6,000 persons, to be indicated by the people with the help of a graded elective system.

Indisputably, this was the work of an extremely vigorous speculative mind. Siéyès only wanted to continue where he had left off in 1789, to save the Revolution, and the national sovereignty it had established, by the freedoms with which the new sovereignty had to be surrounded. But the man who conceived this unique constitution had neither the desire nor, perhaps, the requisite qualities to apply it. It was necessary to seek among the revolutionaries for a less speculative man, a man who was used to action and would be able to stand the daily struggles and annoyances that accompanied the exercise of power. And the man of action, in applying it, partly falsified the formula. To be sure, we may ask whether another would have applied Siéyès' formula with less falsification of the author's intentions. But, since fate chose a man called Napoleon Bonaparte to apply the formula, the best we can do is to determine what he did with it. Siéyès was a brave man. He had proved it in 1789; he was to prove it again in 1799, when, at his own risk, he confronted the insoluble problem that was confounding the Revolution. But the strange fate that his courageous attempt met was that of being constantly baffled by the fears of other men. In 1789, it was the great panic of France that destroyed his work; in 1799, the fear of Bonaparte was to distort the Constitution of the Year VIII. We have seen how Bonaparte, charged with its application, became frightened of a Constitution without precedent that gave him tremendous powers but no support. Driven by that fear—the awful fear of illegitimate governments—Bonaparte, in the space of four years, managed to distort Siéyès' Constitution into a government that sought justification, at one and the same time, in both principles of legitimacy at war with each other. After having proclaimed himself the head of a hereditary dynasty, Napoleon had himself consecrated by the pope, acknowledged by his crowned cousins, and admitted through marriage into the inner circle of their families. But at the same time he had himself elected emperor by a national plebiscite, obtaining a total of 3,572,329 votes as against 2569 on a proposal presented by the government and conceived as follows: "The people desire the hereditary transmission of imperial dignity in the direct, natural, legitimate and adoptive descent of Napoleon Bonaparte; and in the direct, natural, and legitimate descent of Joseph and Louis Bonaparte, as ruled by the Senate council organic 28 Floreal, Year XII." Furthermore, the Empire, like the Consulate, recognized, as state organs, certain assemblies that were supposed to be the expression of the national will and to provide the imperial authority with democratic legitimacy.

If the revolutionary generation, never having either seen

nor felt them, was unaware of the invisible Genii, which it had so unconsciously set at variance in 1789, Bonaparte surpassed all his contemporaries in his insensitivity. He believed he could couple the two principles, almost harness them, like two docile horses, to the chariot of his fortune, by means of a few ceremonies, spectacles, marriages, and subterfuges. Neither the pope, nor Marie Louise, nor the recognition of the legitimate dynasties could supersede the ancient state of possession, as Talleyrand put it, the sanction of centuries—ancestral legitimation—which had been the essential element of monarchic legitimacy under the Old Regime. Whatever he did, Napoleon remained the son of a lawyer from Ajaccio, a parvenu, a mock emperor, a revolutionary counterfeit of monarchic sovereignty. But neither could his power be justified by democratic legitimacy. The plebiscite that had proclaimed him emperor had not been the free and sincere expression of the people's will, but a mere formality imposed by coercion of the government and by the absence of any alternative. Similarly, the assemblies that should have obtained popular consent for the regime were only puppets whose strings were pulled by the emperor. Appointed indirectly by him, they had no contact with the country and were incapable of opposition or resistance; their duties were confined to stammering yes or no as the emperor wished. The pretended reconciliation of the two principles resulted in a monster: a government born of a fantastic constitution conceived out of time and space, a government that was neither a monarchy, nor a republic, nor an aristocracy, nor a democracy; no one knew what it was, even those who had created it. This indefinable monster terrified France and Europe because it first terrified itself. That is the secret of Napoleon's career. As we have seen, no sooner had he been elected First Consul than he suppressed all the freedoms that Siéyès had hoped to save, because the least opposition terrified him—the incurable vice of a power that was the first to be frightened by its own unjustified and unjustifiable crime. His foreign policy was the result of the same fear. Napoleon's inordinate ambition and grandiose plans existed only in the minds of his historians. After having been fortunate enough to make the treaties of Lunéville and Amiens, which made France the foremost power in the world, why should he have attacked Switzerland, the Italian republic, and, finally, Piedmont—all violations of the two treaties, which resulted, in 1803, in the rupture with England and an eleven-year war, at the end of which France was to lose everything she had gained in the Revolution? Because he wanted to seize the lines of communication that led from France to northern Italy across Piedmont and Switzerland; and he wanted to seize these because he was afraid of Austria. Supported as she was by the elements favorable to the Old Regime, Austria was more solidly entrenched in Italy than France; Bonaparte was afraid she would overthrow the delicate structure that the Revolution had set up on the peninsula, if France were not in a position to send prompt aid. After Austerlitz, with the treaty of Pressburg, he expelled Austria from Italy, and made the latter a French protectorate. Was he satisfied then? Not at all; he merely transferred his fears to Germany; at this point he feared that Austria might seek revenge. In order to weaken Austria, he destroyed the Holy Roman Empire, created the Confederation of the Rhine, and began to arm and unify Germany under the impression that it would be of help to him against Austria and Prussia. He ended up by breaking off relations with Prussia; he conquered her at Jena, invaded her, annihilated her. As a final triumph he managed to conclude an alliance with Russia. With Germany and Italy subdued, with Russia as an ally, he had become the master of the continent. He should have felt secure: what could England do, alone and without allies? But, instead, he became more uneasy than ever: he disarmed Prussia and intrigued to disarm Austria; everywhere he was obsessed with fear of Germany, even in Spain. Spain was bleeding from a hundred wounds. No matter, he was afraid of her because she might ally herself to Germany when the latter attempted to revolt. Furthermore, he trusted his ally only up to a certain point. Yes, the Czar of All the Russias called himself his friend and admirer, and was not sparing of both spoken and written compliments on every occasion. But Napoleon knew that the alliance with the revolutionary empire was repugnant to the Russian court, the aristocracy, and the high bureaucracy. He knew that the court of St. Petersburg was constantly in touch with the courts of Vienna, Berlin, and London. He was just as frightened of Russia as he was of Prussia, Austria, and Spain, of all the states he had conquered; he saw in every one of them a future enemy because he was uncertain of his power and knew that he would fall at the first battle he lost. "Do you imagine that your master could enter Paris in this fashion after having lost such a battle as I have lost?" That was the question Francis II, entering Vienna after Austerlitz amid the acclamations of his people, put to the French ambassador.

As France was militarily stronger than any other continental state, she was always the one to attack. Her fear was an aggressive one—which fact, in the eyes of contemporaries and of posterity, transformed it into insatiable ambition or into extraordinary prowess. Nonsense! Napoleon was the aggressor in so many wars for only one reason, and always the same one: that he might avert the danger of a future attack, a danger which was either completely imaginary or very exaggerated. But, if all the courts of Europe trembled before him and if the coalitions that interfered with his sleep were difficult to establish, it was he himself in the end who brought on the coalition that defeated him, by his frightful panic and by the insane blows that this panic caused him to rain upon Europe in every direction.

His reign, both internally and externally, was nothing but a terrible paroxysm of fear that terrified Europe and

set it on fire. For ten years Europe trembled and was unable to rest under the incessant threat of war because the
emperor Napoleon was afraid. But why was he afraid?
We may now give a conclusive reply to the important
question with which we began our investigation and to
which we have already given a provisional answer. The
all-powerful emperor, the master of Europe, the Nietz-
schean superman, shook with fright from dawn to dusk
and from dusk to dawn because the two invisible Genii,
which alone are able to inspire a government with courage, did not support him—neither the monarchic legitimacy nor the democratic legitimacy. Both had deserted the
Tuileries and its new master because neither he nor his
government took either of them seriously. The head of
a great army, of a great administration, of the most powerful state in the world, he nevertheless sat alone in his
palace, living in constant fear of his solitude.

In 1814 a great king came home to the Tuileries, bringing with him the two Genii that the Revolution had put
to flight after having set them at each other's throats—
divine right and the Charter. And he, too, tried to bring
them together, this time to serve the cause, not of ambition, but of order and peace. He had found the theoretical
formula for his plan in Montesquieu and the first practical example of it in the youngest of the Western powers—
the United States. The old French dynasty was not afraid
of the new era since it found its inspiration and its model
in eighteenth-century philosophy and across the Atlantic.
How was he to accomplish the task of bringing back to
France and reconciling the two invisible Genii, guardians
against fear, which the Revolution had first set at variance
and then banished, precipitating France into all sorts of
terrors? By a division of the two powers—executive and
legislative. Chosen by God to govern man, the king would
keep the executive power; he would choose, appoint, and
direct the ministers, who in their turn would appoint and
direct the officials. Of the old legislative power, which,

together with the executive power, the kings of France had held until 1789, the king would keep the initiative of proposing legislation and the right to promulgate it; the right to discuss laws and approve them, together with the right to fix and vote budgets, would be reserved to the parliament. But this would be a real parliament, which, to a certain extent, would represent the other invisible Genius, the democratic principle, because it would recognize a chamber elected by a restricted but free electoral body, and the right of opposition, with some of the freedoms—press, speech, assembly—that the right of opposition includes. The greatness of Louis XVIII consisted in his understanding that a parliament is not a serious institution, capable of guaranteeing to a state the securities inherent in the democratic principle, unless it possesses and exercises the right of opposition. After all the magnificent blunders that fear had made the Revolution commit, in the almost hopeless situation of France in 1814, real genius was needed to recognize that truth and have the courage to apply it.

The Charter and the policy that applied it were a great attempt to put an end to the conflict that had been started between the two principles of legitimacy in Europe, first by the decay of the ancient aristo-monarchic legitimacy, and then by the mistakes and calamities of the Revolution. A great idea and a great attempt, which the nineteenth century, too busy inflating the false grandeurs of the Revolution, failed to understand. But, if the idea and the attempt were great, they still failed to help France recover the lost sleep, to which the rest of Europe returned after 1815, and even aggravated her sleeplessness toward a final convulsion. As soon as the executive power and the legislative power are separated in accordance with Montesquieu's theory, conflicts may break out. If they do break out, then a legal solution is quite possible and even easy in a democratic republic—in Washington, in Berne, in Geneva, or in Zurich. The two powers are not sovereign; each is equally the instrument and representative of the people, who alone are sovereign. The two powers are in conflict because the sovereign—the people—contradicted itself when it chose the two powers. Since each power is equally legitimate and representative of the sovereign will of the people, it follows that both have the right to maintain their positions while waiting for the sovereign people to decide which is right and re-establish harmony between them, thus abandoning its contradictory stand. As long as the two powers are in conflict, the administration will be paralyzed and public affairs will suffer; but the people, the sovereign, will not be able to complain, because it is they who are at fault. The contradiction is their doing and can only be undone by them.

But in the French monarchy of the Restoration, the king and parliament were not two organs representing a single superior sovereign, but were two equally sovereign powers, one making the laws and the other applying them. As there was no superior power to make final decisions, any conflict between the two sovereigns meant a clash of strength. Transplanted into a monarchy, Montesquieu's theory created a permanent rivalry between the king and parliament, between the executive power and the legislative power. In France, the rivalry between the two forces began immediately after the restoration of Louis XVIII and the promulgation of the Charter, in a fierce battle of tracts, pamphlets, and newspapers, which suddenly came to a climax in 1830, over the famous decrees of Charles X against the press, and led to a battle of the barricades in the streets of Paris. Paris became the arena for a revolutionary tournament between the two invisible Genii, both of which had been intended to cure the government of its fear but neither of which wanted to co-operate. The tournament lasted three days, and in the end the aristo-monarchic principle acknowledged defeat. Charles X abdicated and went into exile. The Charter of Louis XVIII had the misfortune of being a dualistic solution, which, instead of mitigating the conflict, aggravated it. A conflict between two spiritual forces can only be resolved by a unitarian solution, a return to unity either through fusion or the extermination of one of them; or by a trinitarian solution, the appearance of a third, mediatory force.

Louis Philippe, who succeeded Charles X, was another figure in European history who was as significant and as misunderstood as Louis XVIII. He invented a method to reconcile the two inimical principles and a system of government that lasted for a long time after him, until 1914. His secret consisted in recognizing, both in theory and in public, the superiority of the legislative power; while in actual practice invisibly controlling it by means of the executive power and royal authority, insofar as it was necessary to prevent it from deviating either to the left or right. Without altering the text of the Charter, Louis Philippe accepted the principle that no minister could stay in power against the wishes of the parliament, that every minister or ministry that received a minority in the Chambers had to resign, as in England. In theory, France was governed like England after 1830. Actually, the new king maneuvered secretly from the very beginning to ensure that the parliament gave its confidence only to ministers and ministries that accepted the larger outlines of his policy. The influence of the court, still of great weight in France during the first half of the nineteenth century; the personal authority of the new king, which was guaranteed by his intelligence, his strength of will, his experience, his career, his political aptitude, and his courage; the intellectual and moral confusion into which France had been plunged since the Revolution; the weakness and disputes of political groups and parties; the antipathy that democratic principles and representative institutions inspired in a large section of the country; the ignorance of public opinion, which, not seeing the conflict of the two principles, was not even cognizant of their existence and knew nothing of the profound truths concealed under the constitutional issues of the regime—all these factors ensured the success of this subtle, secret, and hermetic policy for several years, that is, for as long as it could be kept secret in an age in which all great affairs of state were becoming more and more public property. But this success was neither immediate nor easy. During the first ten years of his reign, Louis Philippe had to overcome the noisy discontent of the salons and the streets, which every day seemed to threaten the security of his throne; there were endless ministerial crises, general elections with doubtful results, attempts on his life, bitter polemics in newspapers, political and financial scandals, and popular riots. The king did not really succeed in imposing his system on France until 1840, after having found in Guizot the conscious and intelligent collaborator that his policy required. Upheld by the secret influence of the king and aided by a political group of which he was the leader, Guizot managed to stay in power without a single break. The parliament became a docile instrument of the executive power, which on the surface seemed to emanate from it. The electoral body, restricted to 300,000, was easily won over by the dominant group and always gave a majority to the latter's candidates, and the stability of the ministries was ensured. Floating on the turbulent seas of a public opinion that was restless, uneasy, pulled this way and that by opposite ideas, the government followed the middle course, between right and left, which the farsighted old king and his able minister steered for it—the minister in full view of the public, the king invisible.

Fundamentally, Louis Philippe adopted, but with more resources and at a more favorable moment, the idea from which the Constitution of the Year VIII had sprung and which fate had caused to come to grief on the contradictions and totalitarian terrors of the Napoleonic regime. We have seen that Siéyès wanted to give France a representative government, with the right of opposition and its necessary freedoms, but to submit it to the control of a superior and independent organ that, without shackling the popular will, would prevent it from verging too far either to the right or left. We find the same idea at the bottom of Louis Philippe's system. Was he directly influenced by Siéyès? He may possibly have known the abbé during his youth. Be that as it may, Louis Philippe adopted, willingly or not, Siéyès' theory, but replaced, as the organ controlling the legislative power, Siéyès' constitutional jury and the Brumaire Senate—a revolutionary assembly without authority or prestige—with the king and court, still a power in France during the first half of the nineteenth century. The king was no longer the consecrated power, the divine representative who personally directed the State, as under the Old Regime; under Louis Philippe's system, his role was to harmonize the old and new forces that, upheld by the two principles of legitimacy, disputed for the direction of the State—the mediatory and conciliatory force whose task was to co-ordinate and confine their too often contradictory and violent efforts. This solution was not a dualistic one, like that of Louis XVIII, but a trinitarian one. The king was no longer identified with the aristo-monarchic principle, as under the Old Regime; he detached himself from it as far as possible to be able at times to support the democratic principle against the other, against the very principle from which his own power had sprung.

But royal authority could only become the mediatory and conciliatory force by concealing itself behind the democratic principle and pretending that it had no power and was at the mercy of parliamentary majorities and the will of the people, in short, by deceiving France and the rest of the world. In the "Philippist" regime, the democratic principle was a reality because the right of opposition and its freedoms were recognized and admitted to the extent of their being able to restrict, embarrass, and impede the government. But the democratic principle, by seeming to be the principal power when actually it was only a controlling power, also became in part a deception. Now a principle of legitimacy cannot become a deception, even in part, without giving rise to a general state of confusion. The invisible Genii, whose task is to free the government from its fears, become angry when they are distorted, and change into enemies and scourges of the men whom they should protect. A power that is active when it pretends not to be, and a power that pretends to rule when it is ruled, become corrupt and discredited. The inevitable outcome of Louis Philippe's system was that the aristo-monarchic principle was discredited and the democratic principle became an object of scorn. The aristocracy, the high clergy, the wealthy classes, the intellectuals, the masses, who for centuries had venerated the aristo-monarchic principle in the person of the king, gradually lost their respect as the king became an enigmatic and equivocal figure in the shadow where he had concealed himself the better to act as mediator. Furthermore, what monarchy lost was not gained by democracy; in representative government, as it functioned under Louis Philippe, there was something deceptive, incomplete, incoherent, which failed to satisfy either theories or aspirations. In short, Louis Philippe's solution was a false trinitarian solution.

France's restlessness was aggravated. In order to calm it, Louis Philippe's regime began to drug the people's minds. It was under Louis Philippe in France that the narcotics were first prepared—cocaine or others—with which political groups and parties were to poison the whole of Europe for the next century: the Napoleonic legend, the romantic myth of the liberating Revolution, imperialistic nationalism, humanitarian equalitarianism, and socialism. The taste for these opiates spread all over Europe, which, toward 1840, began to arise from its slumber as it became infected with France's restlessness. But in France the use of these drugs only precipitated the crisis latent in the false trinitarian solution found by Louis

Philippe. The factor that provoked it was the logic inherent in every principle of legitimacy. A principle of
legitimacy is only partially just and rational. But, insofar
as it is just and rational, it carries with it certain applications and deductions that are imperative and categorical
because they are in the logic of the principle. The ones
that suffer from the incoherencies with which the principle is applied, are usually the ones that make an appeal
to logic. The Philippist regime pretended to apply the
doctrine of democratic legitimacy, by identifying the sovereign people with 300,000 electors. Could the theory be
supported that these 300,000 citizens were the only sovereign, and for the sole reason that they possessed a certain
amount of wealth? That all the others—thirty or more
million—could only be the subjects of a tiny oligarchy of
wealth? Under Louis Philippe, to be an elector and enjoy sovereignty it was necessary to pay 300 francs in taxes.
If someone paid only 295 francs, all the rest—culture, intellect, respectability, capability, civic zeal—counted for
nothing; a difference of five francs meant that the most
capable and devoted citizen passed from the category of
sovereign to that of subject. Was it either just or reasonable to make the doctrine of popular sovereignty into a
sovereign privilege for 300,000 fortunate citizens in a
country of thirty or thirty-five millions overflowing with
all kinds of ability and zeal?

From a logical point of view, a qualified franchise was
a manifest weakness of the Restoration as of the July
Monarchy. After 1840, as soon as the power was firmly in
the hands of Guizot, his coterie, and the king, the opposition, seeing that a majority of the tiny electorate were
definitely and permanently attached to the dominant party,
began a flanking attack by raising the question of electoral
reform. The severely qualified franchise of the July Monarchy was an injustice, they claimed; the democratic principle could not be taken seriously unless the franchise
were popularized! The more daring began to talk of uni-

versal suffrage, and the demand for the sovereign rights of the people became the subject of tremendous agitation. All historians admit that the masses in general—rural and urban—paid little attention to this fuss. But the logic of the democratic principle, the decadence of the aristo-monarchic principle, the turbulence and unbalance of the age, led to the concentration of all the discontent and uneasiness in the movement for electoral reform. Thus, electoral reform, which in itself really interested very few people, became the symbol of a great change that many people desired, without exactly knowing what it should be. Louis Philippe and Guizot knew that a widening of the suffrage would put their system out of commission, and they opposed any reform. But feeling ran high, and once more, as in 1830, the two invisible and hostile Genii fought it out in the streets. And once more, as in 1830, the king was defeated.

The July Monarchy had fallen on the question of electoral reform. There was no acceptable successor in the royal family. There was no sovereign from another family who was capable of ruling. For the second time it was necessary to proclaim a republic, and for the same reason as in 1792: there was no other possible solution. No one wanted a republic, yet everyone was obliged to accept it. But this time the logic of the democratic principle made itself felt: since there was no longer any other sovereign but the people, it was impossible to identify the latter with a small fraction of France; the people could only be the sum of male citizens who had reached the age of reason. At this time, women were still only flowers in the gardens of the City! The logic of the democratic principle tended, in 1848 as in 1792, toward universal suffrage. France and all Europe turned pale with fright when they learned that the republic had invited every French citizen, rich or poor, wise or ignorant, to elect a national assembly on April 17. Was France to be governed by the democratic principle alone? Was the red flag to be unfurled and the power given over to the revolutionary parties? It was in 1848, after the February Revolution, that the socialist party, which up till then had led a semiclandestine existence, began to show itself openly and draw the attention of the public, in the midst of the somewhat confused agitation of the more or less extreme leftist parties, all of which declared themselves champions, spokesmen, and zealous servants of the new sovereign—the people. Monarchic and aristocratic Europe, weakened but still alive, trembled with fear. Universal suffrage appeared to it in the guise of permanent revolution and complete subversion.

And finally, on April 17, to the sound of Easter bells and before the eyes of a quivering Europe, the people of France carried out their first act as sovereign by electing the assembly that was to organize the republic. Seven million Frenchmen voted freely, without any official pressure, as real sovereigns. How did the new sovereign treat its power on the first day of its reign, which was to be the reign of the Revolution? Did it decree the universal destruction of society, the overthrowal of all existing values, the sublimation of the lowest orders, or any similar outrages? No, it elected an assembly half of which consisted of avowed monarchists, Orleanists or Legitimists, and the other half of republicans converted since February. The real republicans, those who had proclaimed the sovereign rights of the people before the revolution and wanted the complete exclusion of the other principle, received only a small minority. The revolutionary parties had hardly any representatives in the assembly. The sovereign people opened their reign with what amounted to an abdication. Embarrassed by their rather unexpected sovereignty, they declared their willingness to retrocede it to the former authorities, or at least to share it with them.

And then the first great tragedy of universal suffrage broke out: the June Days. What were the June Days? The armed insurrection of the extreme leftist parties, the cham-

pions of popular sovereignty and the principle of democratic legitimacy, against the National Assembly, which
they accused of being too conservative and too attached
to the other principle. But the National Assembly was the
free and sincere expression of the sovereign will of the
French people. In June, therefore, the parties of the extreme left launched an armed revolt against the sovereignty of the people, because it had proved to be too
conservative. This signified that they were the champions
of popular sovereignty only on condition that the sovereign people voted for their program, for their doctrines,
and for them. In that case, they were the sovereign, not
the people, since the latter were forced to give them the
power under pain of being dispossessed of it by violence.

The result was catastrophic. By June, the February
Revolution had already failed, and in the most lamentable
way. Universal suffrage was the most immediate, coherent,
and sincere application of the democratic principle; but
was it possible to found a state on universal suffrage, if
on one hand the upper classes feared it as a revolutionary
force, and on the other the democratic parties rebelled
against it because it was too conservative? Threatened
from both sides, in a country where the people were sovereign against their will, universal suffrage was unable to
govern the State. Though the monarchy had fallen, a republic could not be substituted for it. How was this frightful impasse to be overcome? Toward the end of the year,
in December, France attempted the solution of electing
Prince Louis Napoleon, nephew of the Emperor, as president of the republic, by five million free votes. The election of December, after that of April, was the second
authentic, because free, act of the French people's will,
declared sovereign by the February Revolution. Historians
have been repeating for a century that France voted for
the Emperor's nephew because he represented the two
principles of Bonapartism—equality and authority. It must
be confessed that in 1848 the French must have been a

nation of fools if they had identified these two principles
with the son of Queen Hortense. Equality? But he was a
prince, a member of a sovereign family, which, though of
bastard origin, had finally been recognized by monarchic
Europe under the Old Regime. Good or bad, it was the
aristo-monarchic principle of the Old Regime, and not
the equalitarian ideal of the Revolution and of democracy,
that Prince Louis Napoleon represented. Authority? But
up till then he had distinguished himself only by attempts
at sedition and revolt against the established order, and
by a book full of subversive revolutionary absurdities: *Les
idées napoléoniennes.* If the French people had wanted
to put a champion of equality and authority at the head
of the State, they should have voted for General Cavaignac. He was a bourgeois of humble extraction whose rise
was due not to birth but to his ability and accomplishments; instead of fomenting sedition or writing revolutionary books, he had suppressed the June insurrection
with an iron hand. There, at least for the partisans of
equality and authority, were more authentic claims than
the bastard title, the conspiracies, and the imbecilic book
of his rival.

No, in December, 1848, the French people preferred
Prince Louis Napoleon to General Cavaignac as chief of
State, in spite of the superior claims of the latter, because
Napoleon's nephew, being a prince and belonging to a
family whose sovereignty was recognized, resembled a
king of the Old Regime more than General Cavaignac,
the son of a bourgeois family and known only through his
accomplishments. The prince was, if you wished, a second-
rate sovereign, compared with a Hapsburg, a Hohenzollern, a Wittelsbach, or a Bourbon, but he did belong to
the sovereign clan; and, for lack of a better, he might
give France the illusion of a monarchy. In 1848, a bourgeois on a king's throne still seemed monstrous to the
French people. The election in December was, after that
of April 17, the second proof of the deeply conservative

tendencies of universal suffrage, of the repugnance that the populace still felt in 1848 for the Genius of the Revolution and for their own sovereignty. The parties of the extreme left were hoodwinking themselves in their belief that universal suffrage would be a revolutionary force.

What was to be done? The problem of 1814 and of 1830 had risen again. Napoleon's nephew attempted in his turn to find a new reconciliation between the invisible Genius of the Old Regime and the invisible Genius of the Revolution. He could not act otherwise. On one side he tried to revive the monarchy, from which France had such difficulty in detaching herself, by re-establishing the Empire. The Empire was merely a substitute for the monarchy. But monarchic sentiment, toward the middle of the nineteenth century, was no longer as strong, as sensitive, as suspicious as it had been at the beginning. It had become more accommodating. People had become accustomed to considering the Bonapartes as a sovereign family, and the Napoleonic Empire as an acceptable imitation of the dynastic sovereignties established in the rest of Europe. Literature, by narcoticizing all Europe with the Napoleonic legend, had greatly contributed to throwing everyone into confusion, in France and elsewhere. In short, the Second Empire was accepted—or submitted to—by France and by the rest of Europe more easily than the first. But in France the tradition of the Old Regime was still too strong, especially in the upper classes, for Napoleon III to be accepted as the legitimate heir to the throne of France without aversion and a weakening resistance. At the same time the Empire had borrowed too heavily from the monarchy to escape the hate of the republicans. Though the Empire was too revolutionary for the real monarchists, it was still—despite its origin—a hereditary monarchy to the republicans.

The Genius of the Old Regime could not be of much assistance to the new Bonaparte in legitimizing his power. The Genius of the Revolution still less so. Napoleon's nephew restored universal suffrage, which had been distorted by the conservative majority of the Assembly, but only to shackle it once more. In resuscitating and adapting to his own age the political system of his uncle, he again suppressed, together with all the freedoms that were an integral part of it, the right of opposition, which the Restoration and the July Monarchy had recognized and respected to a sufficient extent so that the democratic principle should not become a complete parody. As in the first Empire, he turned the government into a corrupt and terrifying machine charged with transforming universal suffrage, the pretended sovereign, into a slave of the government. He made a farce of the elections and a fable of the legislative assemblies, which became supernumeraries instead of living organs. But this farce of a democracy deprived of the right of opposition and freedom of franchise, could only discredit, instead of uphold, the government in power.

Napoleon III, like Louis Philippe, sought a trinitarian solution of the great problem, with the revolutionary dynasty of the Bonapartes as the mediator between the two Genii in conflict—a mediator this time no longer hidden, as in the July Monarchy, but self-proclaimed and acting in full sight of everyone. But the new trinitarian solution was even more false than its predecessor had been. What it pretended to conciliate was not the two struggling Genii but two lifeless counterfeit copies, for the two Genii had again deserted the Tuileries, fled the nephew as they had fled the uncle. Abandoned by the two Genii, doubly illegitimate as a monarchy and as a democracy, the Second Empire was, like the first, a prey to fear. The new emperor feared the people he ruled as much as had the first. If he was less afraid of the rest of Europe, it was because Europe was completely at peace and because he could not upset it. But, in order to justify the twofold illegitimacy of his government by means of a great exploit, he tried to alter the treaties of 1814-1815, revenging himself on Austria, who, beaten so frequently in his uncle's reports, had ended up with the continental hegemony in 1815. If he favored the national movement in Italy and Germany, it was in order to chase Austria out of Italy and Germany, and not to satisfy his pretended morbid taste for chimeras, as too many historians have repeated. He succeeded in diminishing Austria, but to the advantage of Piedmont and of Prussia, without any benefit to France; in 1870 his revenge even resulted in a catastrophe that toppled his absurd and incoherent regime.

This time France turned to a unitarian solution: that of founding a republic in which the government would be made legitimate by the democratic principle alone; of terminating the feud between the two principles by the complete elimination of the aristo-monarchic principle. Switzerland, after 1848, had been the first and only example of a democratic republic, but Switzerland was a small state, with a special international position. To launch a democratic republic founded on universal suffrage in the midst of a monarchic Europe was a daring enterprise for a great state such as France. But France had to take the risk: it was time for the hour had struck. The monarchies of Europe had also awakened, had also begun to suffer from the same restlessness that had attacked France, because the struggle between the two invisible Genii had broken out in their midst in 1848. After 1870, Europe followed two plans in search for the final solution of the great problem: ahead, France boldly advanced toward the unitarian solution; half a century behind her, the continental monarchies struggled with the dualistic solution of Louis XVIII or the false trinitarian solution of Louis Philippe. Monarchic Europe, two generations behind, followed the same path that France had trod, but without the rapidity and clarity of the conflicts that had characterized the latter's progress, with a confused sluggishness that seemed to perpetuate the struggle of the two principles in the stagnation of an incurable disease.

Prussia and the greater part of Germany after 1848, Austria after 1866, attempted to take over, in spite of its failure in France, the dualistic theory of Louis XVIII. Among all the influences that French thought has exerted on the Germanic world during the last two centuries, the Charter of Louis XVIII was one of the most occult and powerful. By a division of the legislative and executive powers, conceived and applied in accordance with Louis' dualistic model, the monarchies in Germany and Austria succeeded in maintaining intact, until 1914, the sovereign rights of the Old Regime, at the same time calling in the help of parliaments, elected with a certain amount of freedom, which could offer a measure of opposition within limits, criticize and make reservations regarding the broad domestic and foreign policies of the State, without ever seriously disturbing the policy of the court and the top administration, which completely escaped their control. In the Germanic world the monarchy succeeded until 1914 in preventing the disaster that had ruined the work of Louis XVIII in 1830, but the incompatibility, held in check by the partly open and partly concealed political game of the two courts, simmered inside, constantly provoking strange and unexpected upheavals without any visible cause, which the other peoples failed to understand. The dualism, which in France had exploded in a convulsion of freedom, secretly lurked within the two Germanic empires, like a dread disease which the patient is unfamiliar with and from which he would prefer to die rather than be enlightened.

Similarly, the Philippist regime, which lasted only eighteen years in France, had a longer life in the countries that imitated it. They were numerous: Italy from 1878 to 1922; Spain after 1870 and until the 1931 revolution; and the Balkan countries. All these states were governed, like France under Louis Philippe, by the sovereigns and the executive power, with the collaboration of supposedly sovereign parliaments. These parliaments theoretically had the right to assist the ministries in weaving and unraveling the Penelopean web of high politics, but actually they had only a modest, though very useful, power of criticism and control; and they could only make use of that power within certain limits determined by the monarch and the high bureaucracy. The latter were the real Penelopes of high politics and governed the country as they wished, whether the people and its putative representative, the parliament, liked it or not! At all events, the people could console themselves with the rather arbitrary conviction that the king ruled but did not govern.

I have never been able to discover who had the idea of introducing "Philippism" into Italy, which is the invisible key to all the puzzling events in our history for the last sixty years or more. One thing is certain, and that is that it was introduced after the accession of King Humbert, who succeeded to the throne in 1878. His father, Victor Emanuel II, had governed by means of another system, closer to that of Louis XVIII. Was it on the personal initiative of the king? Or was it the secret influence of clandestine advisers? I have no idea. I have often wondered whether Philippism might not have been imported by Urbano Rattazzi, the great boyhood friend of King Humbert, his favorite adviser, and for many years his Minister of the Royal House, that is, administrator of the dynasty's property. But that is a mystery that will probably never be cleared up. Italian statesmen are not accustomed to writing their memoirs; and, when they do, it is not to reveal but to conceal essential truths. For instance, take Signor Giolitti. Read his *Memoirs,* wherein he relates all the important incidents that marked his parliamentary career up till his long presidency of the Council. A reading of it gives one the impression of an English premier raised to power by a parliamentary majority. He was careful not to relate that, when elected deputy for the first time in 1882, he was presented several weeks later by Urbano Rattazzi to King Humbert, in the salon of the

Duchess Letta Bolognini, Piazza Esquilino No. 2, where every evening the king would encounter several friends, such as General Pellou and the engineer Brin. He was careful not to relate that he began to curry favor with the king in the duchess's salon and that he curried so successfully that ten years later, in 1892, the king suddenly appointed him president of the Council, to the great stupefaction of the parliament, which was taken completely aback. That was the real cause of Signor Giolitti's political fortune. But everything is a mystery about the powers that governed Italy after 1860. The mystery has been so thick, so well-planned, so carefully guarded, that its perpetrators and beneficiaries ended up by becoming the dupes of their own dissimulations and falsifications. I am certain that Signor Giolitti would have been very much surprised and would not have understood if someone had told him that he was the Guizot of Victor Emmanuel III and that Victor Emmanuel III was a numismatic Louis Philippe.

But in Italy and in Spain Philippism did not fall to pieces after eighteen years, as it had in France. It would be futile to look for the same rapidity and logic in Italy and Spain with which the weaknesses of the system were made manifest in France, thereby causing the catastrophe. In Italy and Spain the crisis of the Philippist system was delayed as that of Louis XVIII was delayed in Germany and in Austria, discrediting at one and the same time the institutions of monarchy and the institutions of democracy, filling people with confusion, unsteadiness, and cynicism, which made it more and more difficult not only to understand the essence but also to realize the existence of a principle of legitimacy. More and more the government took on the appearance of a sleight-of-hand act, planned to deceive the people with fallacious formulas and obtain as much money and obedience from it as was possible.

Thus, while in France, after 1900, the struggle between the two invisible Genii seems to have been appeased by the permanent elimination of the aristo-monarchic principle to the advantage of the other, in the rest of Europe it was secretly aggravated by mysterious upheavals, whose origin and danger were unknown to the patient peoples. There was one exception—England. Only England, between the fever that was dying down in republican France and the fever that was mounting in the continental monarchies, led a normal existence. England was the only one among the great states of Europe in which the two antagonistic principles of legitimacy bickered without ever coming into actual conflict; in which representative institutions ended up by amicably sharing the power with the aristocracy and the monarchy; in which the Old Regime was able to reach an understanding with the nineteenth century and survive, without trying too stubbornly to live. That is why the course of England, after 1789, was so different from that of the continent. She was spared the lacerating struggle between the two invisible Genii. And that is why, in the midst of the world's restlessness England went to sleep; Leo Ferrero saw and understood her while she slept.

Then suddenly, for a while, the feverish restlessness of mankind seemed to come to an end with the permanent and universal elimination of the Genius of the Old Regime and the victory of the rival principle. The World War broke out in 1914; in 1917 the Russian monarchy was overthrown; the following year the Hapsburg, Hohenzollern, Wittelsbach, and all the other German dynasties toppled one after another—an inextricable tangle of bodies. Republics were proclaimed in Moscow, Berlin, Vienna, and Budapest; universal suffrage became the general rule; the revolution of '48, which had been thought dead and buried, came triumphantly to life after seventy years. Only two monarchies survived among the great continental states—the Italian and the Spanish—both weakened and tottering, powerless to continue Louis Philippe's system any further. The Spanish monarchy was soon to fall.

For a while France seemed to dominate and show the way to Europe as the state that had broken the trail, stated and solved the archproblem; that of founding a great state in Europe that would be governed according to the democratic principle alone. This unitarian solution, discovered after a century of violence, of sacrifice, and of restlessness, seemed to be the model and example for all the new republics. It even seemed to be the climax of the revolutionary apocalypse begun on July 14, 1789; the end of the great conflict, the final pacification, which wiped out and absorbed, by justifying it, all the blood spilled during the apocalypse. There could be no comparison between that and the mausoleum full of anachronisms and modernisms in which England had been interred ever since 1689. France, which up till 1918 had been the only republic among the great states of monarchic Europe, had become the leader of a new crop of republics, which steadily increased after 1917. She seems to dominate nineteenth-century history as the heroic explorer of the hidden paths of the future.

But this illusion did not last for very long. It was not long before revolutions were breaking out everywhere, revolutions that rejected the solution of the great problem discovered by France after a century and a half of struggle and sacrifice, and proclaimed new solutions that were better and more fundamental. Russia was the first, and she was followed by Italy, Germany, and Spain, to mention only the larger states. The Western world was caught completely off guard; stupefied by the deluge of phrenetic imprecations against democratic legitimacy, it understood nothing of all this, and, after 1930, lost itself in a cloud of false doctrines and evil passions in which its vision was distorted. Where were we and where were we heading? Nobody knew. Then, all at once France disowned a hundred and fifty years of her history as a deplorable mistake, and joined the company of the peoples and states that had rejected her solution of the great problem.

After this event none of the history of the nineteenth century makes any sense. The confusion becomes general. We must go to the bottom of the problem, distinguish between legitimate governments and illegitimate governments by means of fundamental definitions, study immediate forms and clear up the mental chaos we have been wandering in by a true understanding of its nature. The only European model of a legitimate state that remains and that will help us understand, is England, but an England that has been awakened by a shower of bombs and flames falling on her from the skies.

X

LEGITIMACY AND
PRELEGITIMACY

Legitimate government, good government, is that which does what it has to do, which does it well, which succeeds in achieving the public good. Its legitimacy is confirmed by its utility. It is considered useful when its means of action, by their vigor and by their structure, appear to be appropriate and proportioned to its aim. Just power is born so that it will provide men with what they need when they are gathered into a community; its existence is determined by the conditions that create it. It exists when this necessary good exists. The absence of this good reveals the absence of the power, that it has been abolished, or diverted, or distorted. The harm that a power does is a sign and a confession of its evil nature or of its bad structure, and is proof of its inability to do that for which it was created.

Naturally, the good and the harm done by nations cannot be compared with the good and evil in human beings. Human beings have an average life of thirty-five years to make use of; nations, which count their age in generations of mortals, are a species of immortal. By public good and public harm is meant good that lasts and harm that is protracted. The degree of good attained or of harm done must also be noted. Every rung of the ladder raises possibilities of doubt or dispute, which the next rung either increases or diminishes. But there is a stage at which discussion ceases. This is the criterion before which there can be no doubt. It is called public welfare. A government that does not ensure it is a government whose incapacity removes it from power. A government that ensures the protection of society and the State acquires an incontestable claim to permanence. It is only a claim, but one that counts. This majesty that surrounds the welfare of the nation and the country is sufficient to create a discipline. This discipline existed at the origin of both transitory governments and lasting governments.

Public good. Public harm. Because the Carolingians did not ensure the security of the land and the people against Bulgars and Normans, they were forced to give way to our Capetians. Because the Capetians provided efficacious protection, they logically came to be the consecrated rulers. If democracy had furnished the most important of these advantages, it would have earned the same consecration. Its mistakes, aggravated by the memory of its ostentatious promises, all bearing on vital issues, rationally and inevitably lead to its disappearance. The characteristic of generating public harm is a proof of illegitimacy that no popular vote can remedy. Condemnation results from facts.[1]

That is the answer with which the nineteenth and twentieth centuries remained content, when, as infrequently happened, they stopped for a moment between revolutions to ask themselves, *stans pede in uno,* what a legitimate government was. Legitimate government, then, should be efficacious government, good government. This doctrine is expounded in the passage we have quoted from a distinguished man of letters. It may be found, in more learned guise, in the books of eminent philosophers and jurists—M. Hans Kelsen, for instance, one of the greatest exponents of constitutional and international law of our time.

What are we to think of this doctrine? Let us put the argument into dialogue form.

[1] Charles Maurras, *Enquête sur la monarchie* (Paris: Hachette, 1928), pp. CVII-CVIII.

"The legitimacy of a government is confirmed by its utility."

"Very well, but by whom and by what is its utility confirmed?"

"It is considered useful when the means of action, by their vigor and by their structure, appear appropriate and proportioned to the aim."

"Right again; but who will be the judge of this, as Richelieu used to say? Is a government legitimate only when everyone agrees that the means employed by the government are appropriate and proportioned to the aim? In that case there would be only one legitimate government in the whole world every one or two thousand years. Whether a government succeeds or not, the public good is the most controversial problem in history. Must the right to judge be reserved for a particular section of society—either personal authority or a selected group? If so, its supreme competence must be justified; the question of legitimacy will be transferred to that authority or group. Must we then finally acknowledge that the majority has the right to judge? It would then be necessary to know by what signs the true majority opinion would be recognized, and what should be done if the majority either did not know how or did not want to express it. That is still a possibility."

"But there is a stage at which discussion ceases. This is the criterion before which there can be no doubt. It is called public welfare. A government that does not ensure it is a government whose incapacity removes it from power. . . . Condemnation results from facts."

"Is that absolutely certain? The most conclusive proof of a government's not ensuring the public welfare is that it allows itself to be dispossessed. And yet take the case of Louis XVI, which is decisive. On May 5, 1789, the date on which the States-General assembled at Versailles, he was venerated by the whole of France as her legitimate king; the famous *cahiers* are an irrefutable proof of this.

After the fall of the Bastille, the whole of France ceased to obey him; within ten weeks he had become a completely inefficacious power—a king without an army, police force, courts, administration, or treasury. Had he or had he not, in less than three months, attained that 'criterion before which there can be no doubt'? If so, the events of August 10 drove from his throne a king who had already been deprived of it by his incapacity, at least since July 14, 1789. In that case, how are we to explain the fact that for several generations a large part of France denounced and that a part still denounces the deposition of Louis XVI as an inexpiable crime? That at a certain moment Louis XVIII was able to ascend the throne and exact obedience as the successor to his brother? The latter's rights, the legitimacy of his power, had not, therefore, been vitiated by the inefficacy that seemed to have deposed Louis XVI as early as 1789. According to the doctrine of efficacy, every government is legitimate when it has the strength to exact obedience and loses its legitimacy when it no longer has that strength. Might would then be right, and every government in power would be as good as the next. The question of legitimacy would be solved by ignoring it. Such was the method widely applied by the epigoni of idealistic philosophy. But problems are not solved by ignoring them. The efficacy of a government is not a 'constant' since it is continually subject to variation. Greatness and decline, that is the cycle traveled by all human powers. But the right to govern, like all rights, is by nature a 'constant'; it extends immovable and unchangeable over a variable period of time, during which the efficacy of a government may increase or diminish. Therefore it is impossible to identify a 'constant' and a 'variable.' Legitimacy can only be established by a clear, fixed standard of comparison, bearing the same meaning for everyone and incontrovertible in its application. Where is this standard to be found? There is no difficulty about a choice: it can only be found in principles of legitimacy."

Here we are back again, after a voyage through history lasting two centuries, to the modest reflections with which we began our inquiry. "What are principles of legitimacy?" That is the question we raised at the beginning, after having learned from Talleyrand's *Mémoires* of the rather mysterious, semiclandestine, and esoteric existence of these principles. The first answer we gave was that they were justifications of power, capable of immunizing it against the most terrible evil from which it can suffer— the fear of its subjects. And we then established that in Western civilization they are reduced to only four altogether: the elective principle, the hereditary principle, the aristo-monarchic principle, and the democratic principle. From these four principles a certain number of rules were drawn, which must be strictly observed in the conferment and exercise of power if the government is to be legitimate. A power is legitimate when the methods used, first to establish it and then to exercise it, are conformable to these principles and to the rules drawn from them. It is that conformity, and not the degree of efficacy, that establishes the right to govern, for it is a "constant" easily verified. One may argue whether it be just and reasonable for the supreme power to be transmitted by heredity from father to son, or for the right to govern to be established by the majority of an electoral body. But once the principle of heredity or the principle of the majority has been accepted, the succession or the majority are easily and incontrovertibly verifiable facts. The son will be the legitimate king; those selected by the majority will have the right to take the government into their hands.

A government is therefore legitimate if the power is conferred and exercised according to principles and rules accepted without discussion by those who must obey. There are still peoples who, without knowing the abstract theory of legitimacy, yet recognize in the respect for these rules and principles the source of the right to govern.

Before 1914 and the great flood of revolutions that swept over Europe, all the Western peoples possessed, unawares, this simple and yet profound science of government. We remarked on the fact at the start of our inquiry:

> If you should ask a Swiss why the state council of such and such a canton has the right to govern, he will reply that it has been elected by a majority of the people. The same reply would have been given before 1939, by a Frenchman, an Englishman, a Belgian, a Dutchman, or a Scandinavian, if you had put to each the same question about his country's parliament. If, at the close of the year 1763, a Venetian had been asked why the Serenissimo Doge, Alvisio Mocenigo, was acknowledged to be the head of the republic, and obeyed as such by everybody, the Venetian would have answered that he had been elected on April 19 of that year by the Consiglio Maggiore, to which belonged, by hereditary right, all male members of the four hundred and fifty families inscribed in the Golden Book of Venice. Similarly, fifty years ago, if a Prussian, Austrian, or Russian had been asked why such and such a minister governed the entire country in his own field of public administration, the reply would have been: "The King or Emperor appointed him." And all these explanations would have seemed absolutely pertinent and incontrovertible to everyone.[2]

These answers seemed pertinent and incontrovertible because they recognized the sole justification of the right to govern, which within its limits is clear and precise, comprehensible, and capable of guiding people instead of bewildering them. Efficacy is an apparent justification, which assumes that it is possible to establish a hierarchy of superior and inferior principles of legitimacy—a hopeless task, as we have seen. It originates in the confusion that the struggle between the two principles has been causing for the last century and a half in Western civilization; and it has only increased the confusion. The ordinary people who were content to identify the right to govern with the

[2] Pp. 22-23.

respect for a few clear and universally accepted principles and rules, without subjecting them to a too exacting criticism, penetrated the problem of human order more profoundly than the philosophers of efficacy. We may now affirm, after our historical excursion, that these principles are really and truly the invisible Genii of the City and the foundations of universal order. Whenever they grow old, or are destroyed, or come into conflict, fear comes upon those who govern and those who obey, thoughts become confused, feelings are distorted, war begins inside each City and between the different Cities. In order that a City may live without fear and prosper under human order, it must accept one of these Genii as sovereign, remain faithful to it, and apply it with loyalty, without guile or perfidy. A City may confide itself to two Genii and be happy, but in that case the two Genii must be in harmony and cooperate. Unfortunate is the City that has become the arena for a battle between two hostile Genii: Discord will plunge her bloody claws into its flesh and rend it to death.

But here a difficulty that we have already touched upon rises up once more, this time redoubled. That legitimacy of government depends on the respect for these rules and principles, that it is the sovereign remedy against fear, the foundation of universal order, and the source of the City's happiness, is a fact that can be verified both in the past and in the present. But it is a fact against which man is always in at least a potential state of revolt. The revolutionary spirit is a permanent force in history because it satisfies that obscure need for revolt which reason justifies. Is it possible that the everlasting hierarchy of man is supported by columns that are so fragile, by principles that have nothing of the absolute, of the transcendent, of the eternal? We have already confirmed it: the four principles of legitimacy that the Western world has in the past applied or is applying today, are limited, and the rules drawn from them are conventional; neither the ones nor the others are rational and just except up to a certain point and under conditions the existence of which is never guaranteed. Insofar as the egoism, the fickleness, and the ignorance of man intervene—and they are always present in great human affairs—the four principles, and consequently monarchy, aristocracy, and democracy, become equally absurd.

These objections are accurate, and the question they raise is perhaps the most serious of all those whose solutions are indefatigably sought by man. We shall attempt to answer it a little later, at the close of our inquiry. For the moment, we shall confine ourselves to inferring a few consequences from these just objections that will help us toward a better understanding of the nature of principles of legitimacy. The first is that legitimacy is never a natural, spontaneous, simple, and immediate condition. It is a condition both artificial and accidental, the result of a long struggle that may as easily end in failure. No government is born legitimate; a number of governments become legitimate by being accepted, and for this time is required. A people must become accustomed to their principle of legitimacy—as Talleyrand observed.

I speak of the legitimacy of governments in general, whatever their form, and not only of that of kings, because it must be applied to everything. A legitimate government, be it monarchical or republican, hereditary or elective, aristocratic or democratic, is always the one whose existence, form, and mode of action have been strengthened and sanctioned over a long period of years, I might even say over a period of centuries. The legitimacy of sovereign power stems from the ancient state of possession, as also, in the case of individuals, does the legitimacy of the law of property.

In order that a people may recognize a government as legitimate, a certain period of time is required, which is easily explained by the fact that principles of legitimacy are only partly rational and just. The hostility of those who do not wish to accept a new principle of legitimacy, either through misoneism, through fear, or through attachment to other governments, can always be explained by the occasional absurdity of the principle. A republican will always protest that it is irrational to attribute sovereign rights to a capricious accident such as heredity; a monarchist will always have a good time denouncing the encyclopedic incompetence of universal suffrage.

Legitimacy, therefore, is preceded by a preparatory condition, which may be called prelegitimacy. Prelegitimacy is legitimacy still in its cradle. Every government began by being a government that had not yet won, but was attempting to win, universal acceptance and had a good chance of succeeding; it became legitimate the day it succeeded in conciliating the opposition aroused by its advent.

During the period between 1920 and 1930, in discussing legitimacy and its forms, I was often asked this question:

"Is the Republic of Weimar a legitimate government?"

My reply would be along the following lines:

"No, the Republic of Weimar is not yet a legitimate government. Rightly or wrongly, there is still too large a part of Germany that refuses to accept republican institutions and the democratic form of legitimacy that justifies them—universal suffrage and popular sovereignty. A vigorous, passionate, vehement opposition by different groups and influences, blowing over the country like a tempest, prevents the crystallization of the general consent, whether active or passive, that creates legitimacy. The Third Republic in France held the same position from 1870 to 1900.

"The opposition to republican institutions was still too large for the Third Republic to be considered a legitimate government. It became so after 1900, when a new generation had grown up with its freedom. The latter accepted it. The Republic of Weimar may have the same fortune if it does not fall before the majority make up their mind to accept it or resign themselves to it."

The same remarks apply to the Spanish republic of 1931. It, too, during its brief and heroic life was a prelegitimate government. Prelegitimacy is the most difficult trial to which a state can be subjected. In a legitimate state the government and subjects equally respect the principle of legitimacy; their accord establishes a kind of balance, which renders the task of the government relatively easy and certain. In a prelegitimate state the government must respect the principle, since no government can hope to educate its subjects to respect something that it does not respect itself. But though the state must respect the principle, a large part of the population, sometimes even the majority, does not accept it and is at least in a state of latent disobedience. Consequently, during the period of prelegitimacy, the principle of legitimacy, instead of supporting the government, needs to be supported by it against the open or concealed opposition it encounters. The principle can only assure the government of the consent of a minority or a slender majority, insufficient to free the government from the burden of fear; the government, therefore, has good cause to be afraid, that is, to fear the opposition and the possible revolt of the majority or of a few powerful minorities able to turn the discontent of the majority to their advantage. But at the same time it must subdue its fear to the extent of not being led into using violence and strong-arm tactics to overcome the opposition, which would render impossible or extremely difficult a permanent crystallization of universal acceptance. It is the most dangerous situation in which a government with serious intentions can find itself.

The danger is particularly great for democracies; later on we shall see why. But how may a government pass from a state of prelegitimacy to a state of legitimacy? We have seen that the main requirement is time. But time alone is not enough, because it can only create habit, passive acceptance, ensure the consent of the people by their adherence, which is the most timid form of legitimacy. Generally the masses do not go beyond passive adherence: they accept a regime as being just and rational because they have found it already established, and are convinced that the world has been and always will be governed in the same way. But over and above this passive adherence there is one of the greatest forces in history—collaboration by active and vigorous consent. It is customarily found in the intelligent elite of a society. In order that a government may attain the full maturity of its legitimacy, it is necessary that at least a minority believe actively in its principle, with an almost religious fervor, which sublimates it by clothing it in transcendent splendor. And this sublimation of a principle of legitimacy can only be effected by means of a sentimental crystallization—of admiration, of gratitude, of enthusiasm, of love—which, forming around the principle of legitimacy, transforms its imperfections, its limitations, its lacunae as a conventional principle, into an apparent absolute to which devotion is due. Legitimacy attains its full maturity, its highest degree of efficacy in this fervor, in this complete, sincere, joyous, even if partly illusory, acknowledgment of the government's superiority, which transforms it into a sort of paternal authority.

How may this plenitude of legitimacy be realized? The means to be employed are numerous. Art has always been one of the most potent. Painting, sculpture, architecture labored not only in the monarchies and aristocracies of the Old Regime, but in all periods, in all latitudes, to actualize for the masses, in magnificent works, the grandeur of the government and its superiority over the habitual mediocrity of the world and man's commonplace existence. It was the same with gold, silver, ivory, diamonds, precious stones of every kind, furs, magnificent materials, laces. Today they are no more than the appurtenances of women and accessories in seduction—worn by women and offered by men. But up to the French Revolution these lovely objects had a far more important role to play: they were *instrumenta regni,* splendors with which the government surrounded itself in order to reveal to its subjects enchanting vistas of a hypothetically superior existence. Add to all that the parades, military reviews, triumphs, Maypole dances, and great public festivals; add the ostentatious splendors of the great religious or civil ceremonies and the ceremonial involved.

All these splendors helped the governments still wrapped in the chrysalis of prelegitimacy to attain their full legitimacy. Literature—poetry and history—performed the same function. In all periods of history, literature helped the government by placing its actions and its intentions in the best possible light. All this labor was beneficent and creditable so long as it was confined to polishing the rough edges of truth and embellishing it, in order to assist legitimate and sincere governments; but it was fatal and detestable when its purpose was to corrupt and pervert the truth so that illegitimate and violent governments could the better confuse their victims. Livy is a master of style and may be taken as an example. He stylized the Roman aristocracy of the great period and its virtues, which were real but rather uneven, upon a canvas of majestic perfection, in which the truth shines across the centuries, caught within the radiance of an eternal model.

And finally, religion, too. Government has been secularized only in a small part of the world, and that only during the last few generations. Everywhere formerly it sought justification in divinity for its ever doubtful and disputable claims. At certain periods kings and nobles dared to call themselves gods or descendants of gods. In Egypt and in the Asiatic monarchies of the past, the sovereigns were gods in the form of human beings, with temples, religions, and priests. The Romans were satisfied with attributing divinity to the founder of their race. Julius Caesar claimed that his family was descended from Venus; I do not say that he believed it, but be sure that he hoped others would believe it. The great semitic religions purged the nobler part of the earth of this sacrilege, but in Europe the aristo-monarchic regime always found its support in Christianity. I have already explained the paradox that lay in an equalitarian religion that, for centuries, rang the church bells in honor and for the salvation of emperors, kings, princes, dukes, and other titled powers. A contradiction that shows how little legitimacy is a question of doctrine, and to what extent it is a question of emotion.

Yet powerful as they are, all the splendors of art and all the prestige of religion are not enough to clothe legitimacy with an almost transcendent veneration, without the existence of a universal conviction that the government will render certain services particularly appreciated by those who have to obey. This conviction is necessary so that the affection which creates legitimacy may be born and endure. When a people accept a government as legitimate, they always imply that they are and will remain satisfied, as a whole, with its acts. The services by which a legitimate government gives proof of its efficacy may vary a great deal: order and prosperity within the nation, security without, victory in wars, prestige in every shape—colonies, empires, military, diplomatic, intellectual, and administrative superiority, the glorious memory of a great history, splendor of monuments, widely admired models of civilization. Among the many services it may render, every legitimate government attempts to select those that it knows will please the people most and that it is most capable of rendering; when the wishes of the people and the ability of the government coincide, the best combination and the least uncertain chance exist for an era of happiness in that country's history. When the people ask for services that are more or less beyond the power of the government to render, great difficulties may arise. The day that a people begin to have doubts about a government and its efficacy, that government's legitimacy begins to waver. Efficacy has a role in the eternal drama of legitimacy, but a different role from that assigned to it by contemporary thought. Though attached to it, legitimacy never depends directly on the efficacy of a government, which may increase or diminish over a long period of time without affecting the legitimacy. Legitimacy may even, to a certain extent, replace efficacy. The best governments are full of flaws, and no government would be obeyed if men were to exact absolute perfection. Legitimacy, and the affection that it engenders, veil, wash away, and help to tolerate the inevitable flaws and errors of government. How could a people consider legitimate and give their respect to either a monarchy or a democracy, if at each inconvenience or difficulty that arose, they felt an irresistible urge to denounce ancestral privilege or majority rule as intolerable?

These, then, are the fundamental reasons for which, as we have seen: "A principle of legitimacy is never isolated . . . it is always in harmony with the customs, the culture, the science, the religion, the economic interests of an age." But the conferment and the exercise of power to conform with the principle of legitimacy and the rules deduced from it, are the substance of legitimacy. The admiration, the gratitude, the affection that a legitimate regime succeeds in arousing, are its brilliant vestments. Because the vestments are brilliant and the substance is reduced to a conventional, uninteresting, and debatable principle, there is always the danger that a people or an age may confound the vestments and the substance. Serious disorders can then be produced. In order to arrive at a correct estimate of a state and its policy, we must know precisely by what signs a legitimate government can be recognized. We are going to study the problem for the two governments that for so many centuries have governed the western world—monarchy and democracy.

XI

LEGITIMATE MONARCHY

Never has legitimacy shown its hidden strength nor exorcised the demon of fear with such success as it did in Europe from 1814 to 1914, a great period that, though restless because of the struggle between the two Genii of the City, offered more security than other periods in history. The unquestioned legitimacy of the monarchic power guaranteed to a part of the world a security that had no precedent. My own generation—the generation born between 1870 and 1880—retains the unforgettable memory of that security, that unique moment of history when Europe seemed finally to be on the verge of freeing herself from the demon of fear. From 1870 to 1917 there were only two republics in Europe—Switzerland and France. In all the other continental capitals, great and small courts directed state policy, either openly or secretly, but everywhere with the active or passive consent of the peoples. Nowhere could a serious doubt on the legitimacy of their authority have been uncovered, in spite of the efforts made by the rival Genius, the democratic principle, to win over the masses. Up till 1917 we were all convinced that the reigning dynasties of Europe would govern for

centuries. If a European Jeremiah or Isaiah had prophesied in 1910 that ten years later the most powerful thrones
on the continent would have toppled, he would have met
with a storm of ridicule.

And then suddenly, in 1917, the Russians rose up
against their little father, deposed him, and massacred him
and all his family. A year later all the Germanic dynasties
collapsed one after another within two weeks, leaving a
tremendous pile of ruins behind them. Like the French in
1789, the other monarchic legitimacies of Europe disappeared suddenly into a vast crevasse of history that had
opened up beneath their ancient foundations. What is the
explanation for this double catastrophe—the one in 1789
and the one in 1917-18? Here we are confronting the chief
problem of Western history during the last three centuries.
We shall try to solve it by making a profound study of
legitimate monarchy.

King, kingdom, monarchy are polyphonic words that
have had many different meanings down through the centuries. The word king has been given to lifelong leaders
elected by the army, by the people, or by an assembly: for
instance, the seven kings of Rome, certain Germanic kings,
or the Jewish kings. Obviously these "kings" were very
different from Louis XIV, Frederick II, and the other
hereditary kings of Western monarchies, although they all
had in common the unicity of the supreme power and its
lifetime duration. Furthermore, there have been states—
the Roman empire during the first three centuries, for
instance—ruled by a single supreme power which, alone
or with the concurrence of other powers, chose its successor. One may, if one wishes, call these states monarchies,
but it seems clear that they, too, belong to a very different
category than that of the hereditary monarchies. Monarchic legitimacy, which we are going to study very
carefully, is that of the dynasties, of the "houses" (House
of France, House of Austria) which were the cornerstone
of European life from the Middle Ages up till 1918. We

are here concerned with a number of large states in which the supreme power was invested within a single individual, designated, to the exclusion of any form of choice or any consideration for personal ability, by means of biological heredity. We are going to try to discover how the hereditary legitimacy of monarchic government was able to establish and maintain itself for so many centuries at the heart of one of the greatest civilizations of history, and, if possible, how and why it vanished from the scene with such abruptness.

Let us put the question: What is required so that a hereditary monarchy may become legitimate, and thereby as free from the fear of power as it is possible for a monarchy to be?

It is before all necessary that the rule of succession be clear, precise, and strictly observed. Like the sovereign, the potential successor must be universally known and recognized without hesitation or difference of opinion. If he is not, it is always possible that conspiracies, attacks, and civil wars may result, in a contest for the succession; no sovereign would be sure of his rule but would live in the permanent fear of being assassinated or deposed by a rival, while the subjects would be unable to tell with any certainty which sovereign they should obey. Legitimacy would be in imminent danger of collapse. But to determine the rule of succession has never and nowhere been an easy task. Numerous dynasties have come to grief on that rock, especially in the ancient world, where marriage meant a continuous replacement of wives, made possible by the facility of divorce, and of concubines, who shared the sovereign couch with the legitimate wives. The fluctuations of marriage and the confusing number of births resulted in the continuous fluctuation of dynastic legitimacy; the wives who succeeded one another in the sovereign's bed, and the often ambitious and enterprising concubines who contended for the position of the wives, brought into the world legitimate and illegitimate children, whose respective rights were never clear and precise. Every child had his friends and backers who, through affection or interest, urged him to put in a claim for the power.

Alexander the Great, for instance. His mother, Olympia, had only been the second wife of King Philip and had been supplanted by a third. The first had had a son, and the third had had several. Alexander's rights to the succession were not incontestable. In order to stop all discussion, Alexander inaugurated his reign by a family massacre: the male offspring of the first and third wives of Philip were killed. Most of the sovereigns of ancient times ascended the throne by means of such massacres, although their tranquillity was not thereby ensured. In spite of these exterminations, they usually regarded their families as nests of vipers—full of rivals, pretenders, usurpers, conspirators, and rebels; and in their position what else could the unfortunate monarchs do except torment themselves with fear and tyrannize everyone else? I am almost tempted to state that in the ancient world the reason for the inability of hereditary monarchy, except in a few cases, to pass from the stage of prelegitimacy and attain its full legitimacy was that it almost never managed to establish a fixed and precise rule of succession. That would explain why, in the ancient world, the attempts to found a hereditary dynasty—in the Roman empire, for example, the efforts of Constantine and his successors—almost always resulted in the most frightful catastrophes—civil wars, invasions, flights in every reign.

Hereditary monarchy only became a potentially legitimate government, and therefore stable and relatively exempt from fear, because of Jesus Christ. By making marriage a sacrament, by sanctifying the eminent and exclusive right of the legitimate wife, Christianity stabilized the family sufficiently so that a rule of succession for the dynasties could be permanently established. Thanks to that stability, heredity was finally made acceptable as a principle of legitimacy to a great many peoples, though at the cost of countless fierce struggles and great hardships, even in Christian countries. It is not difficult to understand the reason for them. Heredity is the principle of legitimacy that gives the biggest role to chance and the smallest to intelligence, that is, it is the least rational and the most absurd of all principles of legitimacy. In spite of this weakness it came to be accepted in the West from the Middle Ages on, but only through a complicated process, constantly repeated before the eyes of the people, one of the chief aims of which consisted in making men worship the inequalities by which they were victimized. We must not credit human beings with an innate and invincible passion for equality. They may console themselves for the obscurity to which the greater part of them are condemned by either of two very different methods, first by making it a state of perfection in which everyone must share, secondly by admiring, in a few privileged individuals, the luxuries, the splendors, the pleasures, the superiority that are denied them. Admiration for the privileges of others is again an escape from one's own mediocrity toward a sort of superior existence. In order to become legitimate, the Western monarchies had to succeed in making the masses admire their privileges as their proper due.

We have already seen that in every country not penetrated by the semitic religions, the kings and nobles attempted to pass themselves off to the masses as gods or descendants of gods. "You are only men: we are gods," was a radical solution for the problem of authority. It offered no resistance to the revolt of man's consciousness, and in the West monarchy was forced to make use of more secular means of persuasion—especially of wealth. In every age monarchic legitimacy has been established by an alliance between iron and gold, by the marriage of power and wealth. The dynasty not only had to possess the greatest fortune in the state, except for that of the Church, but also had to be a great deal wealthier than the wealthiest families; and it had to spend this wealth without respite,

with an exhausting prodigality that was considered inex-
haustible, in all sorts of ways: wars, armaments, public
works, the welfare and protection of every class, public
display, court display, dynastic display, gigantic palaces
and castles with a thousand rooms, festivals and parades
of corresponding proportions. To dazzle the masses with
a glimpse of a superior life, give work to artists and artisans, make commerce prosper—that was the great aim.
When Moses prescribed that the king "shall not multiply
horses to himself," and that "neither shall he greatly multiply to himself silver and gold," [1] he condemned monarchy as the West has conceived it since the Middle Ages.

In every age and in every country prodigality has been
the fundamental sin of the dynasties. This is also true of
avarice, with its inseparable companions—cupidity and
rapacity. It was continually necessary to refill the treasury,
which always seemed empty. The financial worries of the
court were one of the most universal difficulties of legitimate monarchy, particularly before the Revolution, in the
era of its greatest power. But prodigality and avarice were
not enough; at the same time two just as contradictory
attitudes were required—display and isolation. In a hereditary monarchy the masses must be obsessed with the omnipresence of the sovereign, think constantly about him,
everywhere be conscious of his will and his deeds, without
his ever becoming one of them. Neither he nor his family
may ever be just ordinary individuals in any circumstance
or necessity of life; he is forbidden to be born, to grow up,
to eat, sleep, dress, talk, write, walk, amuse himself, marry,
and finally to die, like other people. Every act and gesture,
every desire and wish of the sovereign and his family are
regulated and fixed within a pre-established, solemn, and
ceremonial plan. Formerly, when they were no longer able
to stand the artificiality of their superexistence, and
wanted to lose themselves in the crowd for a while, live
like ordinary men for a few weeks, kings and princes were

[1] Deuteronomy, 18:16-17.

forced to lose their identity and travel incognito under a false name.

The greatest hardships were love and marriage. Kings and queens, princes and princesses, were men and women like everyone else: the flesh was weak! But they were obliged to live and reproduce without the danger-laden element of love—among all the obligatory hardships of ruling, surely the heaviest. In certain countries where the king was a living god—in Egypt, for instance—they had reached the point of creating sovereign couples out of brothers and sisters. A prerogative of divinity, incest was supposed to prevent the tainting of the dynastic strain. Cleopatra and her brother, Ptolemy Auletes, were never considered completely legitimate sovereigns by the Egyptians because they had been conceived in the mortal womb of a simple concubine. Christianity freed Western monarchy of this horrible custom, but in all monarchies, even in Europe and until recently, matrimonial selections were rigidly limited. Only marriages contracted within the circle of sovereign families had the mystical virtue of transmitting the right to rule—a tiny circle that state policy restricted even further, to the complete exclusion of the happiness and the health of the couple. If in the lottery of marriage every human being were given a chance to draw a good or a bad number, in the courts the lottery was fixed so that the players had nine out of ten chances of drawing a bad number. Whence all the tragic matrimonial disorders—bastards, concubines, favorites, morganatic marriages—that both great and small courts in every age have tried to conceal and stifle. In 1853, Victor Emmanuel II had become a widower at thirty-two; a new dynastic alliance would have been a trump card in the diplomatic game for the unification of Italy. A bourgeoise of doubtful birth, the "beautiful Rosina," snatched this trump from Cavour by a morganatic marriage. The last direct heir of the Hapsburg crown, the Archduke Rudolph, committed suicide to escape the twofold dread of an official marriage that was too repulsive and an illegitimate affair that was too fascinating. The elder brother of the present king of England preferred an American divorcee to the most powerful crown in the world.

The courts should have been splendid laboratories of eugenics, in which generations of healthy, intelligent, morally stable princes would have been prepared. Instead they were a repository for all the weaknesses of the generation: sterility, degeneration, infant mortality, hereditary insanity, impotence, or psychopathy. How many princes were born too late or died too early! With what sudden jolts the accidents of birth, of disease, of death, upset the order of succession and the continuity of power in all the courts! Louis XIII, Louis XIV, Louis XV, and their successors, to cite but one example. What perpetual fluctuation! One of the reasons for the success of the French Revolution was that by the second half of the eighteenth century the European dynasties had almost all become a prey to the most serious forms of mental and physical degeneracy. The Revolution diminished the number of dynasties, simplified and humanized the ceremonial, to some extent purified the courts. The monarchy took hold of itself and gained new life. But the fundamental weakness remained incurable.

In 1914, on the threshold of the First World War, most of the European dynasties were in a state of physical exhaustion; particularly in the case of those governed by direct succession, which is the most important, the accession of collateral lines was constantly weakening the dynasty. But the most serious complication of monarchic legitimacy was that all these weaknesses, although they were serious and continually tended to be aggravated, were completely ignored, as though they did not exist. We have seen that every legitimate government implies a sufficient efficacy, and that the respect for its legitimacy helps the subjects to endure the vices and errors inherent in every political system. In the case of hereditary monarchies, legitimacy must continually perform a sort of miracle in this field: it must convince the subjects that the sovereign is possessed of all the virtues, that he is wise, good, just, courageous, loyal, generous, farsighted; that everything he says and does is perfect; in short, that he is infallible and never makes an error. A hereditary power, not having been conferred by man, cannot be revoked by man; it is dependent only on God or on fate. Since it cannot be revoked and must last a lifetime, that is, for an indefinite period, it cannot therefore be subject to criticism; and, since it is not subject to criticism, it is considered infallible. There is no escape from these iron fetters. Criticism of a power may result in a general conviction of its incapacity; what would be the position of a state in which the supreme power is irrevocable, at the moment when everyone is convinced that the supreme power is incapable? The right of criticism and opposition always implies the possibility of sanction against the accused power. Every power open to criticism is revocable, ever irrevocable power must be exempt from criticism and acknowledged to be infallible. A frightening contradiction, but one that is inherent in hereditary government: the more weak, incapable, and mediocre the sovereign, the more complete, affirmative, and unreserved must be the official admiration. A very capable sovereign such as Louis XIV or Frederick II is protected to some extent from the grumbling of the people by his acts and deeds, while an incapable sovereign can allow no criticism: his actions would disclose his incompetence if they were appraised at their true value. *Parum de deo, nihil de principe*—a vital necessity for all hereditary monarchies, whether absolute or constitutional.

But this impossible yet necessary miracle, creates an insurmountable obstacle. A hereditary power is a departure from reason; but a hereditary power that is protected from any criticism or opposition is an utter absurdity. We can well understand that the ancients, in order to impose so monstrous a conception, had recourse to the desperate expedient of transforming their sovereigns into living gods. Ever since Christianity brought kings back into the human fold, absolute monarchy has been unable to find any justification. Bossuet supplied us with a curious proof of this highly important point in his book, *Politique tirée des propres paroles de l'écriture sainte*. At first intended for the Dauphin and handed over to the publisher after the death of the author, this book brings together everything in the Bible that could justify the authority of a French king and teach him the best way to make use of it. This collection is harvested with a truly impressive wealth of quotations and commentary, in long chapters that flow on like majestic rivers of eloquence. But the rivers shrink to a very tiny stream in the first article of the fourth book, which reads as follows: "The prince need not be accountable to anyone for the orders he gives." An excellent theme with which to justify absolutism, Bible in hand. But what did the Eagle of Meaux find in the Bible for this assertion? Two passages, which he disposed of in seventeen lines and which have an entirely different meaning. The first passage is taken from Ecclesiastics, 8: 2-5:

> I counsel thee to keep the king's commandment, and that in regard of the oath of God. Be not hasty to go out of his sight: stand not in an evil thing; for he doeth whatsoever pleaseth him. Where the word of a king is, there is power: and who may say unto him, What doest thou? Whoso keepeth the commandment shall feel no evil thing: and a wise man's heart discerneth both time and judgment.

It is the advice of a wise man who declares, alas with reason, that too often there is no redress or defense against the abuses of royal authority. From which he infers certain prudent counsels for whosoever desires to remain at peace; under no condition does he recognize the king's right, in God's name, to command whatever he wants without being accountable to anyone. The other quotation is still less pertinent; the passage is taken from St. Paul's Epistle to the Romans, 13: 3, and reads:

Wilt thou then not be afraid of the power? do that which is good, and thou shalt have praise of the same.

What relation is there between this otherwise reasonable advice and the monstrous powers that Louis XIV had usurped? [2]

Those two passages were all that the bishop of Meaux was able to find in the records of divine wisdom to sanctify the absolute rule of Richelieu, of Louis XIII, and of Louis XIV. Monarchic absolutism is an Oriental poison that the Christian West has always rejected, absorbing it only in stronger and stronger constitutional dilutions. A preliminary condition contrary to reason, such as that of uncontrollable and hereditary monarchy, may be developed in two directions, toward opposite extremities that are equally absurd. Even in the Middle Ages, Europe was covered with diets, states-general, parliaments, *staende,* public bodies variously formed, that had the right to present their grievances to the king, express their desires to him, concur with him in certain government acts that were subject to stronger criticism, taxation, for example. Those institutions were the first attempts to palliate the dangerous and absurd principle of infallible power by limiting it. They were the embryos out of which came parliamentary institutions, the right of opposition, and the principle of democratic legitimacy itself. After further development, they later came to a climax in England with constitutional monarchy, which was to save the principle of royal infallibility by giving up any idea of experimenting on the people with it and by confining the monarch's authority to acts in which it would be impossible or unim-

---

[2] See *Politique tirée des propres paroles de l'écriture sainte, à Monsigneur le Dauphin, ouvrage posthume de Messire Jacqes-Bénigne Bossuet, Evêque de Meaux* (Paris, 1709), pp. 118-119.

portant for him to make a mistake—in other words, by making a figurehead out of him.

This was an extreme solution, in itself irrational, for the absurdity of an irrevocable and uncontrollable power. An equally irrational but opposite solution was adopted by the French monarchy at the beginning of the seventeenth century—that of making the infallibility of the sovereign a complete reality. Since the king was infallible, he was to be accountable to no one for his actions. Starting with Richelieu, the French monarchy claimed infallibility not as a more and more enfeebled constitutional fiction but as a divine attribute of royal power, efficient in its completeness: the supernatural right of ruling over men and of being responsible only to God, a remote and convenient master who was not in the habit of demanding an accounting at fixed and stated intervals. The Orient had invaded Europe and its courts; England alone remained untouched. Committed as it was to this road, the French monarchy followed it to the very end and sought to justify its infallibility by an attempt to achieve extraordinary results. It threw itself into a series of exploits, one more grandiose than the other: that of attaining primacy in everything—military power, naval power, industry, commerce, art, literature; aggrandizing France in every direction and unifying her; weakening Europe by exploiting to the limit her religious and political dissension; disputing for the hegemony of the continent with the House of Hapsburg and the Holy Roman Empire and for the control of the seas with England and Holland; competing with Italy in the dazzling enchantment of royalty; colonizing Asia, Africa, America; playing off Protestantism and the papacy against one another; dazzling the whole world with the oriental splendors of the most sumptuous court in Europe. A magnificent program, but one whose magnitude was beyond the powers of the royalty and the country. One king, Louis XIV, was alone responsible for three wars that together lasted over thirty years! In order to achieve it, the monarchy carried its claims of infallibility to the most extravagant lengths—to isolation and venality.

First of all isolation. Beginning with Richelieu, as the monarchy undertook heavier tasks and was faced by greater responsibilities, it became more and more isolated. In order to sweep away all resistance, it lost any support it might have had from the nobility, the clergy, and the third estate if they had possessed the right, as did the House of Lords and the House of Commons in England, to collaborate in the royal state policy with a certain independence of opinion, desire, and will, and make their own contributions. But no, the king was infallible, all the initiative had to come from the court, all doubts or criticisms had to be excluded. The States-General, the most likely instrument for any possible collaboration by the nation, was suppressed, and the three estates became nurseries for clerks and officials that were capable of executing the plans of the court without contributing to their preparation. It was in this manner that the entire legislative and executive power of the most populous, the wealthiest, and the most powerful state in Europe became concentrated, as we have seen, in the king's Council: a clique consisting of six or seven individuals gathered together by the irresponsible will of the king, with no other bond between them. A clique that, although completely out of touch with France, her classes, her interests, and her desires, made decisions on war and peace; drew up legislation and made treaties; controlled the navy, the army, industry, agriculture, the police; determined the budget; and decreed taxes in secret—all without being accountable to anyone but the king, who more often than not was unaware of its manifold activities except through insignificant details.

And next, venality. So as to be able to spend money without stint on cannon, guns, wars, public works for both utility and display, in the seventeenth century the monarchy began to sell everything, including even church vessels and other sacred objects—titles of nobility, judiciary and military offices, the right to govern and administer the country. It set a price on honor, justice, and authority. In 1692, in order to meet the expenses of the war against the League of Augsburg, one of the greatest fools in all history, Pontchartrain, put France's municipal liberties on the auction block, suspended elections everywhere while he sold to a few citizens in each town the hereditary right to govern and administer their fellow citizens! Could a greater piece of asininity be conceived of? By comparison, feudalism was a model of justice and good sense. During the hundred and fifty years before the Revolution, the political structure of France was one of the most absurd in all history. It was not oppressive or tyrannical: it was a challenge to good sense, a challenge that can only be explained by the tendency, inherent in everything contrary to reason, to go to ridiculous extremes when under the influence of passion. Whereas, during the seventeenth and eighteenth centuries, France was expanding, and her body and soul were growing up together, royal absolutism was crystallizing into a system of expedients, of privileges, of traditions, of interests, of procedures that as time went on were becoming increasingly narrow, absurd, rigid, suspicious, slow, and irritating. From generation to generation the growing difficulties of its task and the ever-renewed fear of opposition made the monarchy more inflexible and oppressive. As the respect for aristocratic and monarchic legitimacy weakened in France, as the nation at large became better informed about the absurdities and extravagances of the court, royal authority became more jealous of its complete and uncontrolled superiority, and less capable of satisfying the exigencies of France, which were constantly being increased by its affirmation and imposition of its revolutionary superiority. It gradually became weakened, therefore, as it extended its supremacy over all the other powers: a dual instability, which increased from generation to generation, in spite of, and partly on account of, the more and more involved attempts that were made to conceal it.

We have seen that M. Cochin reproaches eighteenth-century philosophy "with having taken up its residence in the City of clouds, centered over the void." That would explain the errors of the Revolution. But, even if the reproach were justified, one could always reply that philosophy is by nature an aerial thing and therefore has a natural tendency to inhabit the clouds. What is far more serious is that in the eighteenth century not only philosophy, but also the French monarchy, which was not at all disembodied, had become centered over the void. Emboldened by the worship of the masses, secure in its almost religious legitimacy, the monarchy had increasingly abused its powers, without perceiving that the instrument it employed was wearing down as its task became greater and more complicated. The king and his Council, theoretically masters of the government, in reality were no longer capable of balancing the budget, and no longer had any authority over half their officials because the latter had bought their offices and were squeezing all they could out of them. On the surface, royal authority remained intact as long as the people continued to venerate it; but, underneath, an invisible rust was eating its way through the foundations of the government. During the half century that preceded the Revolution, the monarchic structure, still imposing and, in the eyes of the world, intact, was tottering on the brink of a precipice.

We have already stated that the nineteenth century was mistaken in its belief that the people of France revolted against the monarchy and overthrew it at the end of the eighteenth century. The people of France revolted after the monarchy had already fallen, and the monarchy fell because of a phenomenon unparalleled in history and up till now inexplicable: the six weeks that followed the capture of the Bastille, during which a national orgy of disobedience made away with the whole of the old monarchic order—laws and institutions, traditions and customs, justice, army, police, and finances. As the central pillar of the monarchic order, the authority of the king of France was one of the most majestic monuments of Western legitimacy. Before Siéyès, no one had contested that fact. How was it that the monarchic structure of Europe had collapsed in six short weeks—the six weeks that followed the Bastille—struck down by a blast of cold air, by the effect of a Parisian riot? The Old Regime was not demolished by an attack from outside; it collapsed of its own power, because suddenly, on the fated day, the people discovered that the king had not even a gendarmery, a police force, or a magistracy to enforce the most elementary laws; and therefore, in six weeks, the inevitable came to pass, a time-hallowed structure disappeared into space, thereby proving conclusively how justified the government was to be obsessed by the secret fear of a general revolt. The monarchy, by carrying the principle of its infallibility to extremes, had finally taken on a load that was too heavy for it to carry with the strength at its disposal. Too weak for its task, exhausted by two centuries of overwork, it finally collapsed under a new shock.

The consequences of that unparalleled event have made themselves felt all the way through the nineteenth century up to our time. We have seen how the fall of the French monarchy let loose all over Europe the struggle between the two invisible Genii of the City, between the aristo-monarchic principle and the democratic principle. The advance made by the democratic principle, by encouraging the spirit of criticism and by demanding the right of opposition as one of the imprescriptible rights of a man and a citizen, deprived the nineteenth century of the extreme solution for the monarchic problem that the seventeenth and eighteenth centuries had adopted in imitation of France: that is, the complete and actual recognition of the infallibility of the royal power, as understood in the Orient. Only in the Russian empire did absolutism prevail until the beginning of the twentieth century. But the nineteenth century also rejected, in almost every continental state, the other extreme solution, found by England: that of maintaining the infallibility of the royal power as a figurehead and symbol, divested of all actual powers. In nearly every continental monarchy up till 1914, the sovereign remained an active power; and a power which, just because it neither had been bestowed nor was revocable by man, was not subject to judgment. How was it possible to bring this categorical imperative of hereditary monarchy into accord with the irresistible advance of the democratic spirit, which everywhere, even in Russia, demanded the right of opposition?

From 1848 on, this problem became a sort of squaring of the circle for Europe. We have seen that France offered Europe two solutions. The first, that of Louis XVIII, proposed a division of sovereignty between the crown and the parliament. The second, that of Louis Philippe, proposed to retain the king's authority beside that of the parliament, by concealing it. The king would be free to act pretty much as and when he pleased, while his ministers would bear the brunt of the criticism his actions provoked. We have also seen that Louis XVIII's solution was adopted after 1848 by the Germanic world, but that it met with no greater success than in France in harmonizing the right of opposition with the sovereign's infallibility. In Germany it did not result in a Teutonic version of the July days, but it did cause a secret but permanent popular irritation against the sovereign, of which William II was the most illustrious victim. In accordance with her constitution, Germany had a chancellor who was responsible to the parliament and people, as though the entire policy of the empire were directed by him. Theoretically, the policy could be criticized with absolute freedom in the press and in parliament. But as the chancellor was appointed, not by the parliament but by the emperor, the opposition was really hitting the emperor when it struck at the chancellor, since the latter had been chosen and was kept in power by the emperor. This resulted in a constant seesaw movement by the political parties and public opinion, as criticisms made in all sincerity had to cease at a certain point when they came up against the invisible presence of sovereign infallibility. The king of Prussia and the German emperor were still surrounded by the respect that the crown enjoyed in the old dynasties; but the respect was accompanied by a secret irritation against the person of the monarch, as though he were the cause, not on account of the insoluble contradiction between the right of opposition and monarchic infallibility but on account of his personal faults, of the difficulties and obstacles that prevented the spirit of opposition from manifesting itself in complete freedom. That secret irritation, confined to harmless and amicable murmurings, was expressed in a weakening of the authority and prestige of the infallible sovereign—an invisible weakening that was one of the causes of the First World War.

Louis Philippe's method was taken over by the Latin countries. As we have seen, it led to the general discrediting of both monarchic institutions and democratic principles. If we now consider and co-ordinate all these ideas on the nature and history of hereditary monarchy, it will be possible to understand, at least to a certain extent, why it has almost completely disappeared from Europe during the last twenty-five years—a tremendous event that has plunged the whole world into chaos. It disappeared abruptly, at the close of the First World War, in spite of the services it had rendered and in all probability might still have rendered. It disappeared because the conditions that for so many centuries had enabled the aristo-monarchic principle of legitimacy to remain dominant had undergone too great a transformation. Above all, the number of dynasties had been too greatly reduced during the nineteenth century. After 1870, more than two thirds of continental Europe was governed by five great dynasties: the

Hapsburg, Hohenzollern, Romanov, Bourbon, and Savoy houses. The remainder—except for the two republics of France and Switzerland—was divided between about ten minor houses and thirty diminutive ones, mostly German. In the eighteenth century, the medium-sized and diminutive dynasties numbered well into the hundreds, and, together with the surviving ecclesiastical principalities and a number of aristocratic republics, covered a far larger part of Europe, each ruling over a limited extent of territory. But the smaller dynasties, like the small republics of the eighteenth century, were more firmly rooted in their circumscribed territories than the great dynasties of the nineteenth century were in their own vast lands. That subtle game of politics, involving the two conflicting qualities of omnipresence and isolation, which their prestige required, was better suited to them than to their larger neighbors; they could more easily make their presence felt everywhere and gain the love of their subjects, while they were less apt to become isolated, by losing touch with the masses, as happened only too often with the great dynasties. It was not by chance that the first kingdom to fall in Europe was the one that had first succeeded in bringing under its scepter a more extensive territory by exterminating the lesser sovereignties. On top of all the other causes of decadence that had exhausted the French monarchy, the weakness inherent in overbulkiness must be added: in spite of its splendor and might, the house of Louis XVI had less of a hold on the enormous masses of the French people than the innumerable duchies, grandduchies, principalities, electorates, and kingdoms had on the people of Germany, each house governing a more circumscribed territory and a smaller number of subjects. Thousands of small shrubs will prevent the caving in of a hillside where a gigantic oak will not.

The disappearance of a great many lesser dynasties, the concentration of vast territories in the hands of a few great dynasties, weakened the aristo-monarchic principle in

Europe during the nineteenth century. The sovereigns withdrew into the solitude of remoteness, and the peoples, without realizing it, began to ignore them. By facilitating this concentration of territory through its wars and invasions, the Revolution dealt monarchy a stronger blow than by its propaganda or its examples. The wars and revolutions that flared up in Europe after 1814; the struggle between the aristo-monarchic principle and the democratic principle that after 1848 broke out more or less violently all over Europe, except in England; the growth of quantitative civilization—great industries, urbanism, universal military conscription; the rapid progress and enrichment of new countries; the popularization of culture, comfort, and luxury; the beginning of public participation in economic and political life—all helped to bring about the moral isolation of the dynasties in a world that understood them less and less. More and more, emperors, kings, and princes retired into the depths of their immense palaces and castles, which the new generations no longer admired as had their fathers, but regarded with stupefaction and ill will. Why such gigantic buildings for a single family? What a senseless waste of the people's money! More modest or more timid sovereigns tried to adapt themselves to their age by leaving the palaces of their ancestors and going to live in those relatively modest mansions where, in great modern cities, the large industrial and banking fortunes establish themselves. A futile precaution! As the wealth of the dynasties became submerged under the tremendous flood of world riches and lost part of its relative importance because of the great wealth of the middle classes, the extravagance and avarice of the dynasties became equally hated. If they liberally spent their allowances and the income from their huge fortunes, they were accused of insulting the people's misery; if they lived modestly, they were denounced as insatiable leeches of the people because of their avarice! By getting the new generations into the habit of preferring their private comfort and personal pleasures to the Babylonian splendors of the public displays and great collective festivals of the past, the quantitative civilizations transformed one of the most powerful attractions of the aristo-monarchic regime into a cause for hostility. And to that must be added the irresistible spread of the idea of equality throughout all classes and the progressive liquefaction of all the hierarchic and ceremonial crystallizations of the Old Regime into an immense promiscuity of all classes and a growing freedom of manners. In 1840 the senate of Turin—a sort of council of state—had withheld its consent on a proposal to establish a system of public conveyances in the streets of the Sardinian kingdom's capital, on the basis that a carriage in which all classes might mingle was contrary to the principles of a monarchic state. The Turin senate, from its own point of view, was less stupid than posterity has deemed it. The principles of equality, the promiscuity of classes, the freedom of manners made it tremendously difficult for the heads of all the reigning houses to live a distinct, exceptional life, apart from the community, which was one of their most imperative duties. While the masses, instead of being dazzled, were becoming more and more irritated by these distinctions, the reigning monarchs were becoming more and more attracted by the growing freedom of manners enjoyed by all classes, and felt the ceremonial chains that bound them becoming heavier and heavier. Toward the end of the nineteenth century in Vienna, there was a sort of strike on the part of the archdukes around the old Francis Joseph. After 1848 there was a great increase in the number of matrimonial accidents throughout all the European courts. During the two decades that preceded the First World War, it became more and more common to encounter the members of reigning families in sleeping cars, in the bigger hotels, and in private houses. Little by little the masses, with which they mingled, were swallowing them up.

The complete and utter contradiction existing between the idea of sovereign infallibility and the advance of the democratic idea, which demanded the right of opposition; the failure of the two solutions put forth for an insoluble problem—that of Louis XVIII and that of Louis Philippe—after 1848 completed the deterioration of the aristo-monarchic principle that had been going on for two centuries. The institution was decaying, but no one perceived it. My generation grew up under the illusion that the great dynasties of Europe were unshakable, that the Russian, German, and Austrian masses would never allow themselves to be separated from their little father or their kaiser. The Turkish revolution in 1908, the Chinese revolution in 1911, were the first warnings. But both revolutions had broken out in Asia, and Europe scarcely noticed them. In 1917-1918 one of the greatest earthquakes in history swallowed up all the great European dynasties, just as the earthquake of 1789 had swallowed up the French monarchy. A terrible fate, which had been maturing in the obscure depths of history for a long time, was being accomplished. The roots of the institution had withered but no one was aware of it; a violent storm of discontent caused by a tremendous and unfortunate war, tore up the tree and sent it crashing to the ground. The peoples, who, unwittingly, had for a generation been free of the ancient discipline of the monarchy, had hardly realized their freedom before they threw themselves upon the other form of legitimacy—democracy—and, like France in 1792, founded republics everywhere. But it was not long before they were to see that though the aristo-monarchic legitimacy was dead it would not be easy to create legitimate democracies. The conditions for legitimate democracy are no less complicated and difficult than are those for monarchy.

XII

LEGITIMATE DEMOCRACY

For a century and a half Rousseau has been acclaimed the great founder of democracy. But we have seen that he wrote the *Contrat Social,* without even a glimmering of what nineteenth-century democracy would be like, in order to arbitrate the conflicts of the Genevan aristocracy and uphold the rights of the General Council against the encroachments and usurpation of the Council of 200 and the Little Council. The General Council, on which all the burghers and citizens of the Genevan Republic sat by hereditary right, was not a representative assembly similar to those created by nineteenth-century democracy, but the whole body of Genevan aristocracy; while the Council of 200 and the Little Council, on which sat the wealthiest members of the aristocracy, was only a small part of it. From that sprang the theory of the "general will." It was to be the unique and indivisible will of the whole social body, which aspires toward order, justice, and security when it determines subjects of common interest. In the abstract, this doctrine is obscure, transient, almost incomprehensible; it becomes clear, exact, and accessible only when it is applied to reality, to Geneva and its political quarrels, which Rousseau had in mind when he wrote. Obviously, in Geneva the general will, the source of sovereignty, could only exist in the General Council: the other two councils, therefore, had to be subordinated to it. Now this is a completely aristocratic regime, immeasurably remote from nineteenth-century democracy. The Revolution, seeking justification for its doctrine after the collapse of the monarchy, made Rousseau, who had wanted to be the physician for an aristocratic disease, the obstetrician for modern democracy. By taking advantage of the contradictory obscurities in the *Contrat Social*, it succeeded in extracting implications of which Jean Jacques had never dreamed.

Let us put aside the general will and all the contradictory obscurities of the *Contrat Social* and seek the justification for modern democracy where it really is—in the elective principle—and in its most simple, most immediate form, of most frequent and general application—the delegation of power. We see it every day: what happens when a number of people wish to pursue a common aim together—either amusement, instruction, mutual assistance, the propagation of certain ideas, or the defense of certain interests? They come together, elect a president, a secretary, or a council, and delegate to these the power to do everything necessary for the attainment of the common aim, reserving, however, the right to control their actions. Who will deny that this procedure is reasonable and altogether pertinent? Democracy is merely the principle of delegation by election, applied to society in order to solve the problems of government. The subjects of the government agree to choose a certain number of officials who will administer the common interests: public order, justice, the defense of the land. Even when the choice is a sovereign act of the most vital importance, the operation remains intrinsically the same as in infinitely more modest cases: a delegation of power by the elective process, which includes the right to supervise and to revoke the delegated power.

It is a very simple principle, completely human, exclusively practical, deprived of all transcendence, and applicable to all human affairs that are not strictly individual. But here a question rises: can it be applied to government, employed to make the most sharply defined distinction between men that exists—between those who have the right to command and those who are bound to obey? Is it possible for government to be delegated by those who are bound to obey? This has been denied since the beginning of time and will be denied till the end. Two objections have been formulated. The first maintains that democracy is contrary to the very nature of authority because it wants the latter to come from below. "Authority comes from above," proclaims M. Izoulet, the eloquent spokesman for a widespread school of thought. But the objection rises from an ambiguity. In reality, democracy today affects the young Swiss or the young American as he grows up, in the same manner that monarchy used to affect the rising generations: as a government already established by the preceding generations and placed so far above them that they are obliged to bow down before it whether they like it or not. In the democracies, the youth learn to exercise their share of sovereignty, as in the monarchies they learned to serve the king, because they are obliged to by pre-established institutions. From this point of view there is no difference between democracy and monarchy. It would be equally wrong to carry the distinction back to the source by affirming that democracy at the very beginning accepted the principle of authority from below. We have seen that no principle of legitimacy can thrust itself upon a nation solely by its own power; in the beginning every principle is imposed by an organized minority that attempts to overcome the repugnance and incomprehension of those who are bound to obey. The beginnings of monarchy and democracy are the same: in each case they are organized from above. We shall understand this better a little further on, when the question of universal suffrage is taken up.

The first objection does not stand up to criticism. The second is more serious because it bears on the difficulty of applying the principle of delegation to public affairs, which are far more complicated than the most complex private affairs. What guaranty can the sovereign people give that they will be able to choose capable delegates? The objection is reasonable, but it may be applied to every form of government. We have already seen that heredity is no better guaranty of an efficient state personnel than election, that from one age to another principles of legitimacy succeed each other, not because it can be proved that the most recent is better than its predecessor, but because it is better suited to the dominant intellectual orientation, whatever its inconveniences. The theory that those who must obey have the right to choose and control those who are to command, spread all over the West, starting in the second half of the eighteenth century, as the prestige and attraction of the monarchies and aristocracies declined for the reasons we have given. When the great monarchies collapsed in 1917 and 1918, the idea that the peoples were going to govern themselves, that idea which for fifty years had been gathering strength in European society like an explosive gas, burst into flames from one end of Europe to the other. Everywhere minorities were emboldened to take advantage of the circumstances and impose democratic republics on the peoples, who were suddenly proclaimed sovereign. As always, the initiative came from above. The masses allowed themselves to be carried along.

And so, toward 1920, all the European states attempted to find the new source of government in the principle of delegation. Republics sprang up everywhere. The objection raised by the people's incompetence was unable to halt the tremendous movement for even a moment. But then a terrible problem was raised, the same that had once confronted the founders of monarchy: the problem of legitimizing democracy by making the abstract sovereignty of the people acceptable to all the citizens, each of whom is an infinitesimal particle of it, just as the monarchies had succeeded in convincing their subjects that obedience to the king was the supreme duty and good. If, in democracies as in monarchies, the authority comes from above, in monarchies as in democracies legitimacy comes from below, since only the consent of those who must obey can create it. In every regime, therefore, the plenitude of the state is realized at the intersection of two lines —one descending, which is authority, and the other ascending, which is legitimacy. But if the process of legitimation from below is the same for monarchies and democracies, it is far more difficult for the latter. There is a fairly general opinion that nothing is easier than to persuade a people to become king. But that is an illusion. The minorities that have attempted to found democracies have run up against even greater obstacles than those faced by the founders of monarchies. We saw how persistently a large part of France—probably the majority— fled from the sovereignty with which the Revolution wanted to crown it. At the moment when the Old Regime collapsed, almost the whole of the aristocracy, nearly all the high clergy, a large part of the *bourgeoisie* and the wealthy and intellectual classes, refused to accept the direction of the state, leaving an awful abyss into which the Revolution fell and disappeared. Accustomed for centuries to venerate and obey the throne and the altar as courtiers, clerks, officials, lawyers, writers, professors, artists, too large a part of the French nobility and *bourgeoisie,* at the end of the eighteenth century, was still not a sovereign class but a subject one and glad of it—happy to bow down before royal authority as a superior power on which it depended and which did not depend on it. Subsequent generations were to see this spirit of subjection weaken, especially in the *bourgeoisie;* but it was to remain strong enough to influence the masses and keep a large part of it paralyzed in a sort of suspicious indifference toward the new principle of legitimacy. The result was, as we have seen, that even in 1848, more than fifty years after the Revolution, the French people hesitated and recoiled before the crown of sovereignty held out to it by the Second Republic. It was not until after 1870 that the democratic principle could be seriously applied in France by the Third Republic, and then only in the midst of fierce struggles. The same drama has been repeated with variations in the rest of Europe during the twenty-odd years since the collapse of the monarchies in 1917 and 1918. In none of the European countries subject to the great monarchies—in Italy, Spain, Germany, Austria, or Russia— have there ever been aristocracies, *bourgeoisies,* or wealthy and intellectual classes that were capable of governing the state. The upper and middle classes have never had the ruling spark, have never seriously considered or felt that they might demand the rights and assume the responsibilities of sovereignty; they have always preferred to remain subject to a supreme power that would assure them of order and the advantages of social superiority without the responsibilities and effort of active participation in the government of the state. From 1848 on, the contradictions and absurdities of monarchic infallibility had given rise, even in the countries where the monarchy was strongest, to subterranean currents of irritation and discontent; but a far better preparation than these vague stirrings was needed before the upper classes, accustomed to obey for so many centuries, could become capable of ruling in place of the dynasties, that had suddenly disappeared into a crevasse of history. Naturally, the masses, too, in all the monarchic countries were indifferent and passive except for the part reached by socialist propaganda.

Europe, like Asia, is still a monarchic continent. The only states in which the people desire to govern, because they have learned how to exercise the sovereignty, and in which, consequently, democratic government has been able to become legitimate, are England, Switzerland, Holland, and the Scandinavian countries. France and Belgium occupy an intermediate position: the aptitude for democratic government is widespread, but resistance is still strong. The remainder of the continent is still in the throes of preliminary fear and rejection of freedom. To legitimize democracy, that is, to make it acceptable to peoples formerly subject to monarchy, although democracy is the only government capable of becoming legitimate after the disappearance of monarchy, will be a difficult task, precisely because the conditions necessary for a democratic government, issuing from the principle of delegation, to appear legitimate, are far more difficult to fulfill than for a monarchy. We shall see why when we examine the most important of these conditions.

In order thoroughly to understand that terrible difficulty, it must never be forgotten that a principle of legitimacy cannot be a hoax and a farce. Whether just or unjust, rational or absurd, it must contain a substantial core, must be a reality, something effective and efficient. How, under what conditions, and to what extent can popular sovereignty be an effective and efficient reality? The problem would be simple and easy if there were always a unanimous, clear, and exact public opinion about the individuals, the methods, and the aims of the government. But unanimity is unfortunately a rare occurrence, while indecision is a very frequent occurrence, in collective will even more than in individual wills. It is perfectly natural that in all great questions the will of the people is divided between a majority and a minority, and that the division is laborious and painful, many people having difficulty in deciding whether to vote with the majority or the minority. Where do the majority and the minority stand in relation to the sovereign will of the people? That is the cardinal problem of every democracy that aspires toward becoming legitimate. Whatever the nature of the suffrage

by which the sovereign people express themselves—
whether more or less restricted, universal male, or universal for both sexes—it is obvious that its will cannot be
identified with either the will of the majority or with the
will of the minority; that each is a different section of the
unique sovereign will, and that the latter is to be found
in the juxtaposition of the two wills—majority and minority. It is, therefore, impossible to suppress the will of
either without mutilating the sovereign will and drying
up the source of legitimacy. The two opposite wills must
be able to manifest themselves and act together without
mutually impeding each other, that is, each in its own
particular sphere, respected by the other. What are the
two mutually inviolable and particular spheres? The government and the opposition. The majority has the right
to govern, the minority has the right to form an opposition and criticize the majority, in an attempt to become
the majority in its turn. That is why in the democracies
the opposition is an organ of popular sovereignty, as vital
as the government. To suppress the opposition is to suppress the sovereignty of the people. The Anglo-Saxon democracies recognized that essential truth by including in
the budget a salary for the head of the opposition as well
as one for the head of the government.

Majority and minority, the right to command and the
right of opposition: those are the two pillars of democratic
legitimacy. But here again a terrible complication arises,
as dangerous for democracy as the difficulty of establishing
the law of succession was for monarchy. Government and
opposition form a dualism, and every dualism tends to
model itself on that inimical pair, which, irreconcilably
and eternally at war with each other, dominate all life—
good and evil; in other words, tends to provoke conflicts
in which each force considers itself the good and regards
the opposing force as the evil. Dualism, then, leads to hate,
to scorn, to misunderstanding, to the necessity for mutual
destruction—the only result of the conflict. But a state,

whatever its nature, cannot become completely legitimate until it succeeds in winning over all its subjects by an attachment that conceals whatever is conventional and irrational in its principle. This attachment can only be created by love or by respect; and love and respect cannot exist if the application of a principle results in a conflicting dualism. In short, democracy is subject to the same essential law as monarchy: either it is a unity or it is not. That is the profound, almost esoteric, significance of Rousseau's general will. How is unity to be reconciled with the dualism of government and opposition? It is a problem that democracy has yet to solve before it can attain complete legitimacy.

In order to solve it, let us begin by establishing what is necessary to the majority and to the minority for the right to command and the right of opposition to become two effective and efficient realities. Above all, it is necessary for the majority to be, not a minority disguised as a majority through violence and fraud, but a real majority, and for the minority to be in a position to offer a serious and fruitful opposition. These two conditions are interdependent, cling to each other, can only exist together. For the minority to be able to offer a serious and fruitful opposition, it requires a firmly established system; political freedoms—press, speech, and assembly; and the guaranty of freedom of suffrage, so that the will of the people may not be falsified by coercion, intimidation, or corruption. But a false majority, which would only be a disguised minority, would always be too frightened of the opposition to allow it to make loyal use of the political freedoms it needs or to respect the freedom of suffrage sincerely. Not one of the democratic governments created by the French Revolution became legitimate because all the pretended majorities that demanded the power were nothing but camouflaged minorities, and not one of them had the courage to respect the right of opposition. Democracy can only unify the government and the opposition within the general will, and consequently become completely legitimate, through rectitude and honesty of political morals, which at the same time guarantee the freedom of suffrage and the efficaciousness of the opposition—fair play, as the English say. But, since fair play is possible only if the majority is a real majority, the majority must be real for fair play to be possible: that is the first categorical imperative to which democracy must submit. And it is also the first great obstacle that confronts monarchic countries when they attempt to become democratic, for nothing is more difficult than to create a real majority when the upper classes do not have the ruling spark and, rather than govern, prefer to submit to a superior power independent of them. Because of that, most of the parliaments that were created in Europe during the nineteenth century were nothing but abortions; they were not organs of a true majority, but camouflaged and hostile minorities. Since fair play was impossible, they often became galleries of deceit, fraud, and violence, invented in order to distort the will of the electoral bodies with the twofold aim of creating false majorities and suppressing the right of opposition. Fair play is the cardinal virtue of legitimate democracy, but a virtue that is extremely hard to understand and that must be continually watched, even in countries that are really free. "In my country, election days are horrible," my cook said to me one day, after having told me about the intrigues and maneuvers engaged in by the parties of her country. She is a citizen of a country in which democracy is an ancient institution and has attained a considerable degree of perfection. The inconveniences she mentioned were small enough compared with what has taken place in countries where the democratic evolution was slower. Nevertheless, they sufficed to produce a certain uneasiness, a feeling of repulsion in the mind of a pious and honest woman of the people, and to cool the affection that a legitimate government should inspire.

A second condition required before the right to command and the right of opposition may become two effective and efficient realities, is that the majority be not only real but recognize that it is by nature variable, and therefore give up any thoughts of using the government to perpetuate itself—in order to prevent, by means of violence and fraud, the minority from becoming a majority. Those who possess power desire to keep it, first for themselves, then for those to whom they wish to transfer it when, at the latest possible moment, they are obliged to give it up. Nothing is more repugnant to a government than to know itself in danger. A democracy can only become legitimate if the government succeeds in attaining that almost sublime state of preventive renunciation, in faithfully accepting, without mental reservation, the law of subordination to the sovereign will of the people, expressed freely and by procedures equal for all parties. Only a true majority will be capable of respecting the right of the minority to become a majority, with such admirable honesty.

A third condition for the rights of the majority and minority to be effective and efficient is that the minority must conduct the opposition in accordance with respect, not only for the letter but also for the spirit of the majority's right to command. The right to criticize can be exercised with a harshness, an injustice, and a bad faith capable of paralyzing the government and compromising its legitimacy quite as badly as the most serious electoral manipulations and frauds on the part of the majority. In a democracy, the task is easy for the opposition. The great affairs of mankind are full of uncertainty and difficulty; the most intelligent and the best-intentioned governments provoke all sorts of discontent, whether justified or not. This discontent, suppressed in regimes that do not admit the right of opposition, can be expressed in democracies. Thence the danger that liberty will degenerate into a fierce and unjust disparagement that may shake the legitimacy of the regime by making it hated or scorned, that is, by destroying the unity of the general will, on which both government and opposition must be founded even though they are in conflict. The opposition, in order that it confirm rather than weaken the legitimacy of a democracy, must be conducted, like electoral procedures, with a certain honesty and cordiality, as between adversaries and not as between enemies. Fair play again. Like the majority, the minority must be a real one, must stand for a large body of opinion and be able at any moment to become a majority within the framework of the regime, whether by compromise or through an increase in numbers. Nothing is more dangerous to a democracy than a number of small groups, moved by an irreconcilable hatred for the regime, who direct their opposition in the sole aim of bringing about the total subversion of the government. The history of the Third Republic is a decisive proof of this.

In the respect and by the respect for these reciprocal limits, the government and the opposition become the two jointly liable instruments of the unique general will and amalgamate their dualism. England and Switzerland are proof that the union of the government and the opposition within the general will through mutual respect for these rules is not a utopian dream, since it has been realized by a few superior peoples who are destined to serve as models on the day of salvation, whenever it may come. The most precious fruit of this union is the attachment of the masses to the institutions of democracy—an attachment necessary for democratic legitimacy to attain its plenitude, whose strongest bond is that of respect. A democracy cannot force itself to be loved, as a monarchy can, because it is a more abstract and impersonal form of government. A dynasty has at its head a king, a queen, princes, and princesses—living beings to which the people may attach themselves with an almost filial tenderness. All the dynasties, at least in the Christian world, attempted to inspire the people to love their sovereign as though he were a father to them and to look upon the dynasty as a sort of superfamily, to which every subject was bound by ties of affection. The European dynasties were powerful insofar as that attempt succeeded. Democracies, on the other hand, are always represented by their institutions—especially by parliaments, which make the laws, form governments, and discuss their policies. But obviously the people will never feel a filial affection for a parliament. A parliament can and should inspire respect by the quality of its members, by the loftiness of its deliberations, and by the wisdom of its decisions; it should appear as a noble academy of intelligence, of eloquence, and of civic devotion to the service of the people. We live in a quantitative civilization; we cannot crown the democracies with the diadems—the artistic glories and splendors—with which the monarchies and aristocracies of yesterday shone. Public buildings, ceremonies, festivals, assemblies, demonstrations, government acts—they have all become lusterless. The government, too, nowadays clothes itself in more sober garments. In a democracy, the prestige of the government can only spring from a reciprocal warmth—that of the people for the government, that of the government for the people. The people must be conscious and proud of their infinitesimal morsel of sovereignty; they must recognize the moral superiority of the free man over the subject in the right he possesses to be informed and consulted in all great affairs of common interest. They must want to exercise their right, whether as majority or as minority, according to circumstance. In its turn the government must seek to win the attachment of the people by respect and confidence, declaring itself to be unpretentious, humane, firm, but as far removed from evil as it can be, a government that, proceeding from the people and working for their well-being, security, and justice, does not fear them and has no need to frighten them. Democracy, when it succeeds in attaining the plenitude of its legitimacy, is that government which has the least need of frightening and, consequently, which has the least fear—less than the most legitimate of monarchies. Switzerland is the decisive proof of this.

We may now take up another problem vital to democracy—political liberty. This must not be confounded with other forms of liberty, which, while having common roots, spread out from political liberty like the branches of a single tree. Philosophical liberty, for instance. Occasionally protests are heard that the United States is not a democracy because in certain states the doctrine of Darwinism is legally proscribed. The Third Republic has often been the object of the same accusation because the Catholic Church in France possessed only a limited freedom to propagate and defend its doctrines. But behind all these accusations and protests there is a certain confusion. The liberty necessary to democratic legitimacy is political liberty. And political liberty is the sum of the conditions and powers that are indispensable for the right of opposition to become real and for popular sovereignty to be free. Obviously, if political liberty is so construed, it is not necessarily bound to philosophical liberty. In highly civilized democracies, political liberty is always combined with a large amount of philosophical and religious liberty, but the combination is not required. One may imagine a democracy that scrupulously respects the right of opposition of the minority, but at the same time makes it illegal to call in question or to affirm the inspiration of the Sacred Scriptures or the divinity of Christ.

This distinction serves to eliminate a misunderstanding which the enemies of democracy have taken advantage of: that democracy, having engaged itself to respect political liberty, is therefore bound to recognize the right of all citizens to discuss everything, including even the principles on which democratic legitimacy is based. Freedom of discussion belongs in the realm of philosophical liberty, which no democracy is bound to respect unconditionally. Democracy, like all regimes, has the right to defend, with force if necessary, the principle of legitimacy that justifies its right to command; the right to defend it against all who attack it by the pen or by the sword, by word or by deed. It has the right, not the duty. In peaceful times a democracy that is certain of its position may allow its adversaries the freedom to philosophize, even on the subject of majority and minority rights. But, if the times become difficult, no one will deny a democracy the right to disperse its enemies or constrain them to silence. "I demand freedom in the name of your principles; I deny it to you in the name of my own." The famous Catholic polemicist, M. Veuillot, has been credited with this refutation of liberalism and democracy, which to many Catholics has seemed conclusive. If M. Veuillot really formulated this objection, he has been guilty of an absurdity. In a legitimate democracy no individual, no school, no church has the right to deny citizens, in the name of its principles, the liberties that are necessary for the popular sovereignty, with its majority and minority rights, to be an effective and efficient reality. The individuals, the schools, the churches who would deny to others indispensable liberties, could be expelled from the community as though they were revolutionaries or violators of the social contract. In a democracy no one has the right to maintain either that the minority has the right to govern in place of the majority or that the majority has the right to suppress the minority and its opposition. These are political heresies, and the secular power, in case of necessity, can be legitimately employed.

But even at this point the task of a legitimate democracy is not yet completed. An extremely difficult problem remains to be solved. In order that the sovereignty of the people should not be a farce, it is obvious that the sovereign people must be a living entity, possessing a real will, and that it must have a body and a soul. Where do we find the body and soul of the sovereign people? This is a decisive question for democracy; if the people are sovereign, we must know who is and where is the sovereign. To answer this question, we must remember that, since a principle of legitimacy cannot be a hoax or a farce, insofar as it is rational, it must remain consistent through all the developments that logic is capable of inferring from it. Now, if it is first acknowledged that the people are sovereign and then the question is asked as to where they must be sought, the final conclusion to which logic leads us is a very simple one: if the people who pay taxes, who serve in the army, who make war, are the sum of the citizens, what justification is there for the people to be reduced to a minority when powers are to be delegated, that is, when authorities are to be chosen who will assess taxes, and decide on war and peace? Only the irresistible strength of this reasoning, together with the requirement for every serious principle of legitimacy to be consistent, can explain why, in every Western state that, after the French Revolution, accepted even in part the democratic principle of delegation and control by the people, one can perceive a slow but irresistible movement toward universal suffrage. In those countries where the mingling of sexes is most complete, the sovereign people has been identified with the sum of the men and women who have reached a certain age. But it would be a mistake to attribute this movement to pressure on the part of the masses ambitious to dominate the state. When the authoritative history of universal suffrage is written, it will be ascertained that in none of the monarchies of Europe, not even in France, where the struggle between the two principles of legitimacy was most violent, did the masses take any action to conquer their sovereignty, which they hardly understood. Universal suffrage was everywhere thrust upon the masses by a minority recruited from the upper classes and applied by small popular groups; it came from above, exactly like monarchic power. And it descended from above because the government, after having admitted that the will of the people was alone or in part the source of legitimate authority, was unable to stop in mid-stride for very long before arbitrary distinctions that restricted sovereign rights to a part of the nation. The people means everyone—a simple and inescapable solution.

But this movement was for a long time slowed up and temporarily checked by an unyielding opposition. Ever since the French Revolution, the West has been dominated by an intangible horror and terror of universal suffrage, which is logically the necessary climax of democracy. The French Revolution was the first to be afraid of it. We saw how Rousseau constantly mentioned the sovereign people all through his *Contrat Social* but never defined them. A strange omission, which permitted the Revolution to hail Rousseau as the great founder of nineteenth-century democracy. If Rousseau had admitted that the people whom he had in mind were the Genevan aristocracy, everyone would have understood that the solution of the political problems raised in France by the collapse of the monarchy was not to be found in the *Contrat Social*. Not finding a definition of the people in Rousseau, the Revolution took advantage of the omission and, following Siéyès, replaced the "people" with the "nation." On June 17 and 18, 1789, in the hall of the third estate at Versailles, Siéyès and Mirabeau were already having long discussions as to whether the third estate should declare itself the representative of the French "people" or "nation." Article 3 of the Declaration of the Rights of Man is conceived as follows:

The principle of every sovereignty resides fundamentally in the nation. No body and no individual that does not emanate expressly therefrom may exercise authority.

The "people" gives way to the "nation." Why? What is the difference? The "people" is and can be only the sum of all citizens without discrimination; the "nation" is the people organized and arranged in classes and professions. The Revolution substituted the "nation" for the "people" so as not to identify the sovereign people with the sum of all citizens, which would have obliged it to grant universal suffrage as the only legitimate expression of popular sovereignty. Moreover, the Convention was the only assembly of the Revolution to be elected by universal suffrage; and among the constitutions of the Revolution only one, that of June 24, 1793, acknowledged universal suffrage as the instrument of popular sovereignty. But it was never applied. All the other constitutions were qualified constitutions with dual elections. Similarly, all the constitutions that were drawn up in Europe, from the Revolution until 1848, with the aim of rendering certain states more or less democratic, attempted to identify the sovereign people with a wealthy and cultured minority, excluding the masses, that is, the majority of the people, from the sovereignty. As we have seen, it was the Revolution of '48 that gave France universal suffrage, although the people had not seriously claimed it; in fact everyone feared it, simply because the Revolution had to be consistent with itself and neither wanted nor could contradict itself. But we saw the frightful result of its attempt to be consistent: the people, proclaimed sovereign, hesitated to accept the crown; the parties of the extreme left, champions of popular sovereignty, rose in armed revolt during the June Days against universal suffrage, because it was too conservative; the upper classes, crazed with fear, flung themselves into the wild adventure of the Second Empire. Napoleon's nephew entered the scene to shackle the new sovereign.

From 1848 on, Europe was torn by a grim underground struggle between the logic of the democratic principle, which impelled all states toward universal suffrage, and the deep-seated, obscure, and tenacious resistance offered by fear and tradition. This conflict was added to the secret conflict between the right of opposition and the principle of monarchic infallibility, thereby further aggravating Europe's restlessness. It took the World War of 1914 and the collapse of the dynasties in 1917 and 1918 to dispel all the open and secret resistances and to make universal suffrage really universal. But then, from one day to another, all Europe found itself confronted by the greatest obstacle to democracy. For democracy to become legitimate, the sovereignty of the people must be a living reality, and for it to be a living reality the group in which it is incarnate must be aware of its task and active in proportion to its means and its possibilities. When democracy results in universal suffrage, it is the whole people that must accept and learn to exercise the sovereignty, insofar as it is necessary so that popular sovereignty is no longer a farce. But the difficulty of educating a people to exercise its sovereignty increases with the numbers involved. Human masses become more passive, lie more heavily upon themselves, as their bulk increases; and the more numerous the sovereign people the more difficult it is for the minority that originally gave them the power to stir them out of their passivity and turn them into an active sovereign, and the greater the need for intermediaries that will divide the masses up between them in order to organize, mobilize, and enlighten them. That is the task of the parties, which in their turn become necessary instruments of popular sovereignty. But with the sovereign masses being mobilized and the multiplication of parties, there is also an increase in the possibility of discord, in the difficulty of extricating a clear, exact, and distinct majority will, a source of swift and resolute action. The great democracies, based on universal suffrage, are slow of action and lacking in foresight.

Democracy, therefore, is a more difficult form of government than monarchy. While monarchy is easily adaptable to barbarous ages and indigent peoples, democracy requires economic comfort and culture to be universal. That is the reason for another major difference between monarchies and democracies. We have seen that in order to become legitimate a monarchy must instill in the indigent masses the admiration for the privileges of the aristo-monarchic government—wealth, luxury, and culture. Democracy, on the contrary, only becomes legitimate through the growth of equalitarianism. Democracy rejects the great inequalities of wealth, culture, luxury, and comfort that built up the prestige of the monarchies and aristocracies to such an extent. As the minister of an absolute king, Richelieu was able to write that the people should not be too well off because they became harder to govern as they became wealthier. The minister of a democracy who dared to utter such an aphorism would be in danger of being cut to pieces. There is an irreconcilable antagonism between democracy and great fortunes, between democracy and the Babylonian splendors of the Old Regime. That may be seen in the United States, where the millionaires are forced to make excuses for their wealth by giving tremendous presents to the sovereign people and by living in relative simplicity. American luxury is a myth; Europeans who have seen the houses of millionaires know that in Europe, thirty years ago, they would have been taken for modest dwellings.

We may now easily understand why the peoples who had been subject to monarchies for centuries and who, in 1917 and 1918, tried to improvise so many parliamentary republics, were unable either to get beyond the phase of prelegitimacy or to remain in it long enough to obtain sufficient democratic apprenticeship. They had too little training. Although the aristo-monarchic principle of legitimacy had been weakening for the last century all over Europe, it was still strong enough to offer a great many obstacles to the principle that should have replaced it. The terrible disorder caused by the First World War, the frightful mistakes in the peace treaties and the policy of the victors, helped to aggravate the situation. The greater part of Europe found itself hanging in mid-air between monarchy, which was no longer possible, and democracy, which was not yet possible. And in desperation it turned toward revolutionary governments—a new adventure, which we are going to study in the light of the first experiment, made almost a century and a half ago.

XIII

REVOLUTIONARY
GOVERNMENT

We have already taken up legitimate and prelegitimate governments. We must now turn our attention to illegitimate governments and make a study of their origin, the shapes they assume, and their nature.

Let us return once more to the principal question: What is a legitimate government? We have seen that it is a government in which the power is established and exercised according to rules long predetermined, recognized and accepted by everyone, interpreted and applied without vacillation or hesitancy but with unanimous agreement, in accordance with the letter and the spirit of the laws, re-enforced by traditions. England and Switzerland, for instance. Illegitimate government is the antithesis of legitimate government: a government in which the power is bestowed and exercised according to principles and rules imposed by force over too short a period of time and not accepted by a large majority. But this definition, if exact, is yet insufficient, for it may also be applied to prelegitimate government. It must be completed by adding to it the differentiation between revolutionary government and prelegitimate government. We may make the following distinction: Prelegitimate government desires and is able to respect the principle of legitimacy that the majority still opposes; it even counts upon this example it gives to instill the same respect in the people. On the other hand, illegitimate government neither desires nor is able to respect the principle of legitimacy by which it pretends to justify the power it imposes on a reluctant people.

Prelegitimate government, therefore, is a government in which the power is bestowed and exercised according to rules and principles not yet accepted by the people but observed by the government; while illegitimate government is a government in which the power is bestowed and exercised according to rules and principles that the people do not accept and that the government proclaims but neither desires nor is able to respect, that it transforms into a fraud.

Once this distinction has been established, a preliminary fact becomes established. Theoretically an illegitimate monarchy may be conceived of in the person of a usurper who takes the place of the legitimate heir by pretending to be the latter. But no example of this type of usurpation exists, at least not in the West. A new dynasty, wherever it may originate, belongs more in the category of prelegitimate government than illegitimate government. Take the Napoleonic empire, for instance. It was not recognized by a considerable body of public opinion in France and in the rest of Europe. It could not claim ancestral legitimacy. But, if it had lasted, time and the prescription of which Talleyrand speaks might have legitimized it. It is possible to imagine the second or third generation acknowledging Napoleon IV or V as the legitimate sovereign of France.

That is not true of democracy. During the last century and a half the most serious cases of illegitimacy, at least in the Occident, have been caused by distorted or perverted applications of the democratic principle. The governments that we call revolutionary or totalitarian are nothing else but democracies which are not fulfilling the conditions of their legitimacy—the right of opposition and freedom of suffrage. In fact, revolutionary government, which is evoking so much comment today, made its first appearance in the West with the French Revolution and the failure of the first attempt at democracy, made in France from 1789 to 1799. Let us then go back and reexamine the French Revolution from this viewpoint, let us try to find in democratic illegitimacy, at odds with itself, in the insoluble contradiction between the principles of the Revolution being declared as an almost religious absolute and their being constantly violated or perverted in practice, the origin of revolutionary government and its growth, up to the maturity it attained with the Constitution of the Year VIII and the Consulate.

We saw that the Constitution of 1791 was too great a novelty in France's history for it to be understood and accepted at once by a majority of the people. The Legislative Assembly should have been the first prelegitimate government of the new regime, entrusted by history with the task of beginning to accustom France to representative institutions. In order to accomplish that task, the Assembly should have set an example by respecting and putting into practice the principles of the new order. Instead, what did it do? It is well known that the abstentions in the elections of 1791 were extremely numerous. The masses, still attached to the Old Regime, had forfeited their sovereignty by their indifference. Dismayed by the general revolt and anarchy that had followed the fall of the Bastille, appalled by the revolution and the great panic, angered by the civil constitution of the clergy and the persecution of the Church, the upper classes had taken advantage of the 1791 elections to try to asphyxiate the new regime by plunging it into a vacuum. Because of this general abstention on the part of the lower and upper classes, the Assembly was a middle-class assembly, consisting of lawyers, doctors, journalists, intellectuals, most of them very young, who had had a short democratic apprenticeship in the municipal and departmental assemblies that had been in existence since 1790. The nobility and the high clergy were almost completely lacking.

Having been elected by a minority in elections that were not very sincere, because of inexperience and ill-will, composed of elements in their turn drawn from a minority that was homogeneous but spiritless and lacking in prestige, the Legislative Assembly could hardly feel itself to be the expression and the instrument of the will of the French nation. Weakness number one: As we have seen, for a democracy to be legitimate, the sovereign will of the nation or of the people must not be a constitutional fiction but a living, acting reality. Weakness number two: The new representative state had neither a police force, nor a judiciary, nor an administration capable of ensuring order. Scarcely had it convened when the Assembly was seized with fear: the fear of its own inexperience, the fear of its unrecognized or hardly recognized legitimacy, the fear of its incompetence; and it allowed itself to become dominated by violent minorities, either within its own halls or without: by popular demonstrations, press campaigns, and systematic intimidation. Democracy is government by majority: as soon as the Assembly allowed the minority to dominate it, it was no longer either a prelegitimate or a legitimate democracy: it had unconsciously and involuntarily become a revolutionary government. Thus, the first appearance of a revolutionary government was unconscious, groping, stumbling. But it was enough to unleash a general war that lasted for twenty-two years.

From its very inception the Convention could be neither a legitimate government nor a prelegitimate government; it had to be a revolutionary government because it appeared in violating the two cardinal principles of legitimate democracy—the right of the majority and freedom of suffrage. The Convention was elected by a suffrage that in theory was universal but that in practice was distorted and enchained by a minority which justified its action by the state of danger France was in. The justification was serious, so serious that it not only prevented the Convention from applying the principles of '89 but obliged it to suppress them all. The Convention was afraid of France, whose revolt seemed not only possible but momentarily imminent; it was afraid of Europe, of the great and small courts with which the Revolution was at war; was even afraid of itself, divided as it was into groups that hated and feared each other because they were fighting for the power, to which none of them had a clear and indisputable right because none had a majority. Under the impact of these multiple fears, revolutionary government appeared abruptly within a few months in all its terrible plenitude. Overthrowing the democratic principle of legitimacy, it established upon the ruins its own fear-driven conception of Public Safety: a sanguinary idol, an insatiable Moloch, to which it sacrificed majority rule, the rights of man, the principle of opposition, and thousands of victims, guillotined, drowned, and shot.

It spilled so much blood that at last the Convention itself revolted and made an attempt to restore harmony between Constitution and government. Thermidor 9 and the Constitution of the Year III restored the right of opposition with all the implicit freedoms; the Directory made an attempt to become a prelegitimate government capable of setting an example by showing respect for the new rules and principles that the people had not yet accepted. But it, too, met with failure because its fear both in internal and external affairs was too great. After the *coup d'état* of September 5, 1797, it became a prey to revolutionary fevers, intermittent and irregular fevers with sharp attacks and remissions. By 1799 it was obvious that the Revolution of '89 had failed. The French people had not been given the time necessary for apprenticeship; the general anarchy that had followed the capture of the

Bastille had swept everything away. The governments that had succeeded each other since 1791 had not had the strength to face the test of prelegitimacy; driven by fear, they had all more or less revolted against the principles that alone could have justified them and enabled them to last, but not one had remained very long in existence after its revolt; one after another, they had eliminated and replaced each other, accusing each other of being too revolutionary or not revolutionary enough. In other words, a series of spectacular suicides. Toward 1798 and 1799 the Directory appeared to be heading for the same fate; everyone felt that it could not last much longer, for its supply of *coups d'état* had been exhausted; but what was to replace it? Since both democracy and monarchy were impossible, what was to be done? How was France to be governed?

In 1799, as we saw, there was one man who thought he had discovered a new constitution that, without drawing inspiration from any model, would be capable of accomplishing in the domain of politics what amounted to a squaring of the circle: that is, of applying in all seriousness the doctrine of the sovereignty of the nation, in a nation where the majority refused to be sovereign, either through indifference or through repugnance. That man—the *abbé* Siéyès—was the most skillful political architect of his age, the most intrepid wrecker and builder of constitutional structures: we saw him at work in '89. We have already studied his Constitution of '99 in detail; we are going to recall the broad outlines of this Constitution, now that, in the light of our definitions of legitimate government and revolutionary government, we are able to study the profound historical significance of the Revolution which produced it, understand it at its primary source, and, by understanding it, justify to some extent its obvious absurdity. Starting from the principle that authority should come from above and trust from below, Siéyès had conceived of a large assembly, independent of popular suffrage and invested with an august authority, which would choose the members of the legislative and administrative assemblies from among an elite chosen and elected by popular suffrage on a wide scale. By having the supreme assembly composed of men deeply attached to the new principle of legitimacy proclaimed by the Revolution, by taking all necessary precautions so that the Assembly would be unable to deteriorate in the future, Siéyès hoped to give France a representative government that would be able to govern with respect for its own principles: the right of opposition, the contest between majority and minority, and all their implicit freedoms. The sovereignty of the nation would become a reality, almost in spite of the nation, in a wise and stable government that would ensure order and prosperity by respecting the rights of man.

There is no question but that in 1799 the skillful architect did not want to tear down but to rebuild on more solid foundations the structure he had erected in 1789; to save the principles of the Revolution by means of the ingenious contrivances of his rather fantastic Constitution. And he might have succeeded if the group charged with the application of the constitution had had the courage to respect it, if, after the 18 Brumaire, the Revolution had finally decided to face the dangerous and decisive test of prelegitimacy with the Constitution of the Year VIII. But the whole group was immediately seized with the fear that all France would revolt against so fantastic a constitution. We have seen how Bonaparte was afraid; placed at the head of the group charged with applying the Constitution, he was the first to be frightened; and in less than three months, with a few strokes of his pen, he had suppressed freedom of press, parliamentary liberty, the right of opposition, and all the decentralization carried out by the Revolution. Neither the suppression of the right of opposition nor unlimited centralization by the departmental dictatorship of the prefects was to be found in the

Constitution of the Year VIII; Bonaparte introduced them one after the other within three months, because he did not feel strong enough to resist a somewhat vigorous opposition. As we saw, he confessed that himself: "If I should give the press a free hand, I would not remain in power for three months." Moreover, it seems obvious that he would not have stifled the opposition with such violence from the very beginning if he had felt strong enough to resist it. France was complaining of the Directory because it was a revolutionary government that was violating all the principles of the Revolution and had suppressed all political liberties and constitutional guaranties. Siéyès and his friends had conceived the 18 Brumaire to give France a government that would no longer be revolutionary, that would try to become legitimate, and that would free itself from fear by the attempt.

The Senate should have been opposed to it. Siéyès had conceived and the Constitution of the Year VIII had created it to be the guardian of the principles of the Revolution, the custodian of the laws in the new regime. Why, then, did it help Bonaparte to pervert the letter and the spirit of the new Constitution? Was it because it did not know how to resist the miraculous fascination of the First Consul, as so many historians claim? Not at all: it was because, like Bonaparte, it was frightened, and for the same reason. The Senate created by the Constitution of the Year VIII was not elective; it had been made up by Siéyès himself, by Roger Ducos, by the second and third consuls, who had filled it with their friends, and new members were elected by co-optation. It represented nothing, therefore, save the desire of Siéyès and his friends to remain in power by satisfying, if possible, certain justifiable aspirations of France. Not representing anything, it was supported only by the organized strength of the state, which in turn was supported only by the Constitution of the Year VIII. But that Constitution was unsatisfactory to everyone, and failed to meet the requirements of either one or the other of the two conflicting principles of legitimacy. The masses did not understand it, the republicans distrusted it, the royalists hated it. From 1800 to 1804, with the help of London, they launched an implacable guerrilla warfare against the Consulate—outrages and conspiracies of every kind. Under such conditions it is easy to understand why the Senate had no more courage than the First Consul, and why the Senate and the First Consul came to a speedy agreement to suppress the opposition.

But by suppressing the opposition they completely perverted the Constitution of the Year VIII and from it evolved the most complete revolutionary government, the best co-ordinated, and at the same time the most absurd and impossible—the most contrary to the fundamental nature of government and, consequently, the most incapable of functioning regularly. This point must be thoroughly understood, for it is a vital one. Let me recall once again what Siéyès' system consisted in. Six million Frenchmen selected 600,000; these chose 60,000, who in turn chose 6,000. From these, all taken from the upper classes, the Senate selected the members of the legislative assemblies, which were the instruments of the national sovereignty. This organization of the national sovereignty was complex and extremely artificial; nevertheless, it might have prepared France to govern herself by means of a legitimate representative regime if the national sovereignty had remained a living reality within the artificial bounds by which the Constitution had surrounded it. We have emphasized that as the condition for a democracy to become legitimate. But, in order that the national sovereignty should not become a fiction in the Constitution of the Year VIII, it was at least necessary that the successive steps by which six million Frenchmen recognized themselves in the six thousand chosen in the last drawing, should be free. In order that they should be free, it was necessary that freedom of speech and press, the right of opposition, and freedom of suffrage should be respected.

Once the opposition was suppressed, the national will became nothing but a fiction, a farce, and a fraud. The legislative assemblies were appointed by the Senate, that is, by the government; they were not the instruments of the national will but the expression of the government's will. The formula of national sovereignty was completely reversed and misconstrued: instead of creating the government, the national will was created by the government; the government, which claimed to be legitimized by the national will, was really legitimizing itself, for it was able to manufacture the national will as it pleased.

It was by means of this inversion of the democratic formula that revolutionary government for the first time attained its maturity with the Constitution of the Year VIII. This maturity included the claim that it was a definitive regime, under ordinary circumstances. The Legislative Assembly, the Convention, the Directory had all been revolutionary governments, but by exception, for they had all announced or implied that their illegitimacy was justified by the public welfare and would last only as long as the danger. Neither Bonaparte, when he distorted the Constitution of the Year VIII in applying it, nor the Senate and the other constitutional organs who helped to distort it, thought that they were creating a transitory and exceptional regime. They considered it from first to last as the ultimate climax of the Revolution, and it was not their fault if it lasted only fourteen years.

The Consulate, therefore, is the first example of a revolutionary government, which attempts to legalize the systematic violation of democratic legitimacy, the suppression of the right of opposition and freedom of suffrage, by distorting and inverting the principle of national sovereignty. An example that every revolutionary government had modeled itself on for almost a century and a half. The essence of every revolutionary government in the Western world is that inversion of the democratic formula, applied for the first time by Bonaparte to France under the Consulate, after a trial attempt in the Cisalpine Republic: the national will, shackled and directed by the government that should emanate from it, proclaimed sovereign and deprived of the instruments essential to sovereignty—the right of opposition and freedom of suffrage. But the operation is contradictory, and, as a principle of legitimacy—this can never be repeated too often—cannot be a fraud, it has failed and will always fail. In its plenitude, revolutionary government—today called totalitarian—remains more than ever an illegitimate government; instead of overcoming its fear, it becomes more and more the victim of it as it tries to overcome it. Revolutionary government is the regime of fear *par excellence;* its terrible fate is that the more it seeks to protect itself the more it becomes frightened by real and imaginary dangers that threaten it. If it suppresses the lawful opposition of the press, does it rest in peace for that? Far from it: it is more frightened than ever of the latent opposition in people's minds. It knows that the people are grumbling, but since it has broken the barometer of popular discontent, it can no longer measure it, constantly thinks about it, becomes obsessed with it, and ends by thinking it greater than it is. It detects, glimpses, and thinks to discover signs of hostility everywhere: between lines of newspapers submitted to censorship; in discussions held in cafés; in private conversations, within the intimacy of every family. The slightest whisper of popular grumbling takes on the shape of an unfailing prelude to general revolt. It would like to be a gigantic ear to eavesdrop on everything said in every hovel and palace; it would like to read every letter, look into every mind, know every secret—those of the confessional as well as those of the parlor. It multiplies its spies and its censors, it increases its surveillance; it establishes a huge police force to watch everyone, rich and poor, wise and ignorant, humble and mighty; it creates a superpolice to watch the police. It trusts no one or nothing. The censorship, at first confined to the opposition press, little by little spreads to include all manifestations of thought. The mischief may be hiding anywhere—in literature, in art, in philosophy, in mathematics, in the schools, in the universities, in the churches, in banks, in farms, and in factories. And to defend itself, it sees but one solution: increase its powers, increase them further, increase them ever more. Even full powers do not satisfy it; it must have still more. At first it obtains a monopoly over every branch of the government; after a while it must extend its control over industry, over agriculture, over commerce. But even then it is not satisfied but needs to direct the family, manners, social life, hygiene, cooking, artistic tastes; as a crowning instance, it wishes to determine what is beautiful and what is ugly, to dominate every step in intellectual life from school to the French Academy. It becomes totalitarian. Totalitarianism is merely the most complete outward form of the fear that gnaws revolutionary government.

Such is the engrossing story of the Consulate from 1800 to 1804. In 1799, Bonaparte had been elected First Consul for ten years. Why two years later, in 1802, did he have himself appointed Consul for life? Boundless ambition? No, anxiety to consolidate his power against the real and imaginary oppositions that surrounded it. He knew that France had not accepted his decennial government; he was far from quiet, he had misgivings about the future, he was afraid that he would not last ten years, and he thought he could strengthen his power by prolonging it. But, if the majority of Frenchmen were far from pleased with a decennial power, they regarded a life power as even more unjustified, whether from the point of view of monarchic legitimacy or from the point of view of democratic legitimacy—the only two that Frenchmen were in a position to judge. Thus prolonged to reassure the uneasy leader, the government became even more illegitimate and made the unfortunate man in power even more afraid. And in fact he did not remain quiet very long but soon proclaimed a new and even more dangerous amplification—

hereditary power. At the same time he had himself granted the right to appoint the members of the Senate; as the Senate appointed the legislative assemblies, the latter would be his creatures, and he, the hereditary emperor, would at the same time also be the whole sovereign nation, all by himself. The national sovereignty became a power, and the imperial crown would only aggravate it by adding to its deception. An emperor without ancestors, the European monarchies at the beginning of the nineteenth century would never take him seriously.

That is the fate of all revolutionary governments; the more they extend their power and approach totalitarian absolutism, the more anxious they become about the opposition they feel hidden underneath public opinion. It explains the strange disease that appeared for the first time in the Consulate and that one finds in every revolutionary government—a mania for self-advertisement. The nineteenth century honored Napoleon as the author of the Civil Code, which was the work of the Constituent Assembly, the Legislative Assembly, and the Directory; as the founder of an empire, which never existed because it was nothing but a precarious juxtaposition of ungovernable lands; as the inventor of real or absolute war—when he had only perfected to the point of absurdity and catastrophe a new form of war, less rational and more spectacular and violent than the wars of the Old Regime, which had been invented and put into practice by the Revolution. The nineteenth century missed the really original achievements of Napoleon, the most effective of which was the invention of propaganda in all its forms, beginning with a fraudulent press. It was during the French Revolution that newspapers began to acquire a political power in war and peace. Of all the revolutionary leaders, none understood better nor utilized to a greater extent the new instrument than Napoleon. "Newspapers are worth an army of three hundred thousand to Napoleon, for the latter would not supervise the interior any better and would frighten other countries less than half a dozen pamphleteers in his pay," wrote Metternich to his master on June 23, 1808, from Paris, where he was minister. It was Napoleon who first conducted the entire press like an orchestra and made it into a gigantic gramophone that every day played the same record for his subjects and his enemies: that he was infallible and invincible. It was Napoleon who first transformed the administration into a machine able to manufacture enthusiasm: speeches, demonstrations, processions, triumphant arches, orders of the day, illustrated vindicatory pamphlets, gifts of city keys, torrents of flowers, public receptions. It was Napoleon who first organized mass movements into a state monopoly, taking them away from the parties.

A legitimate government has no need of propaganda. We have seen that legitimacy implies a reasonable conviction on the part of the people that the government is capable of conducting public affairs in a satisfactory manner. That conviction is enough for a legitimate government not to become alarmed by the criticisms or grumbling of the people whether justified or not. Revolutionary government is not permitted to enjoy any such peace. It knows that its power does not appear to be sufficiently justified to a part of the population, and it is not content to stifle all complaints and criticisms but hires more and more numerous and varied groups of minstrels to go and sing its praises at every crossroads. The head of the government is a genius, a hero, a great man, a superman, a demigod, and all his ministers, friends, collaborators, and agents partake of his almost divine nature so long as they serve him, only to change into monsters when they have quarreled with him; the people, under his rule, are overwhelmed with every advantage: with prosperity, for instance, even though they may be dying of hunger. "As false as a bulletin," was a popular saying during the first empire. No falsehood is beyond the capacity of a revolutionary government.

This frantic attempt to win over public opinion against
its will came to a climax in the policy followed with respect to crimes against the government. Bonaparte was
also the great forerunner of this diabolical scheme. Toward the end of 1800, the consular government had put
forward a bill on special tribunals that was anathema to
the people because it reshaped justice into a new instrument of political oppression. But the secret rumble of
public discontent had once again frightened Bonaparte
and his government. They hesitated. Then suddenly, on
the night of December 24, the royalists exploded a bomb
in the Rue Saint-Nicaise at the moment when the carriage
of the First Consul was passing on its way to the opera.
Bonaparte was not hurt, but about sixty people were
killed or wounded. The attempt—the first of its kind—
resulted in a frightful panic. The fear was mutual: if Bonaparte's government was afraid of France, France was afraid
of Bonaparte's government, of his police, of his courts, of
his treacherous and irresponsible policy. All who were hostile to the regime and to its head were afraid of being suspected or accused of being in sympathy with the attempt;
in particular, those who regretted that the bomb had
missed its intended victim, were most indignant about it
in public. The bill on special tribunals was almost forgotten in the general uproar. Bonaparte took advantage
of this to have it passed, and drew a lesson from this revealing episode: an abortive attempt to assassinate the
head of the government resulted in a sort of temporary
vacuum in public opinion, across which the most despised
laws might furtively be passed like contraband under the
noses of sleeping customs officers. For several weeks the
national consciousness went to sleep. How nice it would
be if a similar attempt should come at the right moment
to perform this service every time the revolutionary government needed it! This was too powerful a temptation
to resist. What if, instead of waiting for chance to provide
the opportunities, they should be made to order? It ap-

pears that the sinister butcher of Lyons, Fouché, was the first teacher to acquaint the revolutionary police with the new and treacherous art of domestic assassination attempts that fail at the desired moment and terrify the people. The conspiracy of Cadoudal, the arrest of General Pichegru and General Moreau, the abduction and trial of the duc d'Enghien are the most sensational episodes in a long government drama directed from behind the scenes and intended to make France accept the empire by frightening her.

Yet all these frantic efforts came to naught; instead of convincing the public, they only succeeded in bewildering it. Why did they fail? No one has studied or explained this disturbing phenomenon more profoundly than Benjamin Constant, in a book he published in 1814, after the fall of Napoleon: *De l'esprit de conquête et de l'usurpation, dans leurs rapports avec la civilisation européenne.* Having witnessed the formation, development, and suicide of the first revolutionary government in Western history, Benjamin Constant wanted to point out its dangers to posterity. How many tragedies would have been avoided if subsequent generations, instead of neglecting it, had read and reflected upon this marvelous little book! I have extracted several illuminating pages, with the warning to the reader that by despotism Constant means legitimate absolutism, and by usurpation the government we have called revolutionary.

I am far from being an advocate of despotism; but if it came to a choice between usurpation and a consolidated despotism, I do not know whether the latter would not seem the better to me.

Despotism does away with all forms of liberty; usurpation, in order to bring about the overthrow of what it seeks to replace, has need of these forms, but in securing them it profanes them. The existence of public sentiment being dangerous to it, and the appearance of public sentiment being necessary to it, it strikes the people with one hand to stifle any real sentiment, and it strikes them again with the other to compel them to the simulacrum of a pretended sentiment.

When a great Sovereign sends one of his ministers in disgrace to the scaffold, the executioner, like the victim, does his part in silence. When a usurper condemns innocence, he orders calumny so that, repeated, it will appear to be the judgment of the nation. The despot forbids discussion and exacts only obedience: the usurper decrees a ridiculous investigation as the prelude to approval. This counterfeit liberty combines all the evils of anarchy and slavery. There is no end to tyranny which wants to drag forth tokens of consent. Peaceable men are persecuted for indifference, energetic men for being dangerous. The bondage is without rest, agitation without remuneration. This agitation resembles the moral life in the same way that those hideous convulsions that an art more frightening than useful imparts to cadavers without reanimating them, resemble physical life.

It is usurpation that has invented that pretended sanction of the people, those speeches of adherence, a monotonous tribute that in every age the same men lavish on the most contradictory causes. Fear comes to ape all the appearances of courage, to congratulate itself on dishonor and give thanks for unhappiness. A strange sort of artifice, of which no one is the dupe! A conventional farce that meets with no respect and should have succumbed long ago to the attacks of ridicule! But ridicule attacks everything and destroys nothing. Each person imagines that through mockery he has reconquered the honor of independence, and, satisfied with having disavowed his actions by his words, feels at ease to give the lie to his words by his actions.

Who does not feel that the more a government is oppressive the more quickly the terrified citizens will hasten to pay it homage in their enthusiasm for command! Do you not see, beside the registers that each signs with a trembling hand, the informers and soldiers? Do you not hear the proclamations declaring those whose voting would be negative, seditious or rebellious? What is this questioning of a people, surrounded by dungeons and under the sway of the arbitrary, but an effort to obtain a list from the adversaries of the government so as to recognize and strike them at leisure?

Nevertheless the usurper records his acclamations and harangues. Posterity will judge him by these monuments erected by himself. Where the people were so vile—it will be said—the government must have been tyrannical. Rome did not prostrate herself before Marcus Aurelius but before Tiberius and Caracalla.

Despotism stifles freedom of press; usurpation parodies it. Now, when the freedom of press is altogether suppressed, public opinion may slumber, but nothing leads it astray. On the other hand, when bribed writers take possession of it, they argue, as though it were a question of convincing, they fly into a passion, as though there were an opposition, they become insulting, as though there were any chance of replying. Their absurd defamations presage savage condemnations; their fierce jestings announce illegal condemnations. Their exhibitions would have us believe that their victims are resisting, just as, upon seeing from afar the frenzied dances of savages around the captives they are torturing, one might conclude that they were combating the wretches whom they are going to devour.

In a word, despotism reigns by silence and allows man the right to remain still. Usurpation condemns him to speak; it pursues him into the intimate sanctuary of his thoughts, and, by forcing him to lie to his conscience, deprives him of the only consolation that remains to the oppressed.

When a people have only been enslaved without having also been degraded, there is still a possibility that they may attain a better state of things. If some happy circumstance should reveal it, they show themselves worthy of it. Despotism leaves mankind that chance. The yoke of Philip II and the scaffolds of the Duke of Alba did not degrade the noble Dutch. But usurpation debases a people at the same time that it oppresses them: it accustoms them to trample underfoot what they once respected, to court what they once scorned, to scorn themselves; and, regardless of how long it endures, it renders, even after its downfall, all liberty, all betterment impossible. Commodus is overthrown, but the praetorians put the empire up for auction and the people obey the highest bidder.[1]

[1] Benjamin Constant de Rebecque, *De l'esprit de conquête et de l'usurpation—dans leur rapports avec la civilisation européenne* (Paris, 1814).

It would be impossible to describe the hopeless incoherence to which revolutionary government is condemned by the contradiction that is its *raison d'être*: the justification of absolute and incontrollable power by means of the democratic principle. "Consolidated despotism," that is, legitimacy acquired through the sincere consent of the subjects, can show itself as it really is and act in accord with its principles. Revolutionary government, desiring to pass itself off as the expression of the free and sincere will of the people, must camouflage its despotism by a parody of freedom which renders its despotism ever more intolerable and against which the human intellect, in every age and clime, will always revolt. Continual revolt—that is the decisive factor that obliges us to classify revolutionary government with the monstrosities, the unhealthy freaks, the teratological specimens of the political fauna. An absolute government may become legitimate—"consolidate itself" as Benjamin Constant says—but on one condition: that it have the courage to declare that it is accountable to no one because it is either a sorcerer, the vicar of God, or even God Himself—the representative, in short, of a power superior to a wretched humanity that has need of its enlightenment and its commands. It may then be acknowledged and become legitimate, if and in the extent to which it succeeds in convincing those who must obey it. Beginning with Bonaparte, all the founders of revolutionary government for the last century and a half have been afraid to show themselves to the people in this semidivine light, because they knew that they would have met with a tremendous burst of laughter. They were obliged to seek justification in the democratic formula applied in reverse, to present themselves to the people as the interpreters of the latter's will, which they claimed to know better than the people, because they forced upon the people, in their name and as though they desired them, actions, deeds, and sacrifices that the people loathed. They sought justification for their power in a permanent, irresolvable, and therefore perpetually fluctuating contradiction. As the government continually pretends to be the opposite of what it is and always remains the opposite of what it wants to appear, the people can attach themselves neither to the substance of the government, which is oppression and which it hates, nor to the disguises that it assumes, because they continually change and are fallacious. Sometimes they seem to be dazzled by one or another of these disguises, but the fascination does not last very long, the contradiction soon appears to destroy it with grim reality. Revolutionary government can never become legitimate, whatever it may do, even if it last for a hundred years; it is welded to illegitimacy, from birth to death. A principle of legitimacy must be consistent with itself; it may not be a permanent contradiction that systematically varies its premises in their application.

That is why the history of every revolutionary government is a continual spasm: the search for an imaginary stabilization that is never found. That is why every revolutionary government is even more alarmed and uneasy when public opinion is quiet than when it is stirred by deep emotion—sorrow for an injustice committed, terror of a great danger threatening—by war, or by revolution. Bonaparte did not have the opportunity to pass himself off on France as the redressor of the wrongs she had been subjected to. In 1800, France already occupied a preponderant position in Europe; she neither had been invaded nor was in danger of invasion, and she had no wrongs for which to demand reparation. But Bonaparte was able to make excellent and skillful use of three fears, which were not completely imaginary: the fear of the Old Regime's being restored, with all the attendant reprisals; the fear of a return of the Jacobin terror, which would again erect the permanent guillotine, as in '93; and the fear of England. As the creation of a national bogy, anti-British propaganda launched after the rupture of the Treaty of Amiens, is a model; all revolutionary governments were to imitate it with profit.

> Tremble, o modern Tyre! A new Alexander
> On the wave thou once ruled will scatter thy ashes:
> Thy name is dead already.

The revolutionary state and war: there we touch upon the decisive point. Distrust is the natural state of international relations. Political states, whether legitimate or not, are suspicious neighbors who permanently distrust each other. But legitimate states, feeling sure of their power, are capable of mastering their distrust. Revolutionary governments, which are afraid of everything because they are sure of nothing, are the miserable victims of it. Just as they are always imagining their subjects on the threshold of revolt, they very easily impute aggressive plans to the states with which they are in contact, and are far more afraid of the possibilities of war. A defeat, a failure, a disaster is always far more difficult for a revolutionary government to support than for a legitimate government. Revolutionary governments are thus a great deal more impressionable, more defeatist, more cowardly than legitimate governments when they are in conflict with a state which they consider stronger. The adversary has only to frown, and the revolutionary state precipitately retires. But what happens when the revolutionary state is and knows itself to be militarily the stronger? It will see an equal danger in the weaker states, which become potential enemies, to be feared, if not in the present in the future, if not alone then in an ever-possible coalition. But instead of giving way and capitulating it will attack them. An aggressive fear, the essence of Napoleonic policy. We have seen that Napoleon never aspired after either a world empire or the hegemony of Europe, that the plans attributed to him are imaginary, that his wars were precautionary wars to provide in anticipation against possible future wars.

But for him precautionary defense was a never-ending affair because no sooner had it been averted by a victory than it rose again from its ashes. No sooner had he beaten Austria at Austerlitz than Napoleon became frightened of Prussia; when he had beaten Prussia at Jena, he became frightened of Spain; after he had occupied Spain and made an alliance with Russia, he was again frightened of Prussia and Austria combined, of a possible alliance between them; no sooner had he beaten Austria for the second time at Wagram than he became frightened of Russia. He saw himself surrounded by monsters, half real, half imaginary, that were waiting to devour him; he struggled indefatigably against them, but the more he slew the more there were. No sooner had he defeated the monster before him than he was obliged to turn around to meet another. If he cleared his left flank, he immediately saw himself attacked on his right. He was in a veritable inferno from which there was no escape. But what was the mysterious power that kept this frightful chain of precautionary defenses in perpetual motion? Now we can furnish the answer: it was the illegitimacy of his power, the revolutionary character of his government. Distrust, which is inherent in all relations between states, becomes aggravated to a real mania of persecution when a revolutionary state succeeds in defeating all its rivals: it knows itself to be feared and hated; it sees hidden enemies, revolts, and coalitions in embryo everywhere; and, since it knows that a defeat may be fatal to its existence, it does not resist the temptation to use its strength in order to stifle the danger while it is still in embryo. But its fear is never dissipated because it originates in its own mind and in nowhere else. The government's immense power, instead of calming its anxieties, aggravates them—a tragic inversion, the replica in foreign relations and the result of another inversion, the one that the revolutionary government accomplished with the principle of democratic legitimacy.

A revolutionary state may make war and make it very

well, but when it makes war successfully it cannot make peace. Talleyrand was the first to make this fearful and decisive discovery after Campo Formio, a startling proof of his superiority over his contemporaries. That is why the formation of a revolutionary government gifted with a preponderant military power is a very serious event, especially in Europe. Europe, because of her variety, has always been and always will be a rich collection of different states of every size. She has never been and never will be able to live except held in balance by a system of states of which the strongest are strong enough so that they are not afraid of the weaker and do not abuse their superiority. Only by means of this equipoise will the minimum of confidence required by all to live be established between the European states, if in the midst of so many states which can so easily do each other harm, a revolutionary state arises, fated by its own illegitimacy to see enemies everywhere; if this revolutionary state is the stronger, it will try to subject and disarm all the others. It will destroy any balance of powers, even a relative one, and will only be able to replace it with the terror of its own hegemony, because it is by nature fitted to be preoccupied only with its own interests, especially with its security, which it constantly and everywhere pursues and which it never and nowhere attains. Napoleon was the first incarnation of this powerless omnipotence. Revolution begets war; peace can only exist and endure between legitimate states.

Such was the origin and growth of the first revolutionary or totalitarian state of the West. The great mistake of the generations born in the dazzling parenthesis of peace and order, that 1815 opened and 1914 closed, was to have believed that it had been a brilliant exception, a unique epic that would not be repeated. It had been too great, God had forever destroyed the mold. And yet the Second Empire had been a discreet warning that the revolutionary state could reappear under certain conditions. Which one's? Today we may define them, by comparing the first great experiment with the subsequent ones. Revolutionary or totalitarian government is merely the death pangs of monarchy. It appears in the countries where monarchy has governed for centuries and trained the nobility, the *bourgeoisie*, the intellectual classes, and the people to obey it. And it appears when the monarchy falls or has reached the point where it no longer has the strength to hold the rudder. The former Genius of the City must then be replaced by a new one, the aristo-monarchic principle of legitimacy must be replaced by the democratic principle. But that is a difficult task, especially when the monarchy disappears abruptly. The idea of servitude, inherent in the nobility, in the *bourgeoisie*, in the wealthy and intellectual classes, and in the people, is the chief obstacle. There is no longer a sovereign power capable of replacing the dynasty and the court; not feeling capable of ruling, the upper classes become discouraged and frightened lest the masses try to take advantage of their weakness and their fear, and they throw themselves into the adventure of revolutionary government, behind the first leader who comes forward.

Napoleon, then, looms up in the history of the West on the morrow of the fall of the French monarchy, as the creator of the first revolutionary government. He was the first to make the attempt to fill the void between the disappearance of the monarchy and the yet impossible appearance of the republic. His task was far more difficult than that of his numerous imitators in the twentieth century, for he had no model or precedent to go by. At his own risk, he advanced into the unknown, the first to confront the unexplored dangers of a new adventure that was a challenge to reason, to history, to the nature of government: no less than that of enslaving the two invisible Genii which alone could rule the Western world with their sovereign power. Without realizing it, he attempted a monstrous revolution, compared with which that of '89 was mere child's play; he attempted nothing less than to overthrow the world order, as it is imposed by the very structure of man's intellect, and to rebuild it contrary to human nature, with the roof for foundation, that is, to become the sovereign himself, above the aristo-monarchic principle of legitimacy and the democratic principle of legitimacy. The 18 Brumaire, the Constitution of the Year VIII, and its consequences are not developments of the Revolution that had begun in 1789 but its antitheses. The French Revolution is not a single, integrated event but a conflicting and irreconcilable dualism. There are two French revolutions, each the negation of the other: the first and the second, the great and the small, the revolution of '89 and the revolution of '99: the revolution of the rights of man and the revolution of the Constitution of the Year VIII, the liberal revolution of a representative regime and the dictatorial revolution of the totalitarian state, the revolution that is the daughter of the eighteenth century and the revolution that was spawned by the great panic after the storming of the Bastille. As long as this dualism is not understood, the history of the West will remain an incomprehensible enigma. The French Revolution did not upset the world, as men have repeated for a century and a half, by the subversive force of its principles and ideas. Both ideas and principles were excellent and were in no respect forces of subversion: wherever they were applied with common sense, good faith, and courage—in Switzerland, for example—they created the most humane, the most coherent, the most solidary, and the least imperfect order in history. It is the struggle between these two hostile revolutions, the fearful reappearance of the dualism between Good and Evil, between Ormazd and Ahriman, let loose across history, that for the last century or more has been devastating the West. After 140 years of terrible combats, France was annihilated in 1940 by a supreme encounter between two hostile revolutions that she had given birth to within ten years of each other. Today everyone is up in arms, fighting for one or the other of the two French revolutions, the Anglo-Saxons for the first, continental Europe for the second.

It is a saint, one of the greatest saints and doctors of the Church, who has given the best definition of the *étaïra,* of the courtesan, of the geisha, or, if you prefer a more sophisticated word, of the cocotte. It is a definition with an almost sublime penetration: "Those women who live as though they could be loved." *("Tamquam si amari possint.")* I am tempted to borrow that definition from the Confessions of Saint Augustine, and apply it to revolutionary government: "Those governments which rule as though they could be obeyed."

XIV

QUASI LEGITIMACY

On July 29, 1830, the army left Paris. After three days of fighting the Revolution had gained possession of the capital. Charles X, who for three days had refused to make any concession, decided to yield. During the night of the twenty-ninth he annuled the ordinances that had provoked the colossal uprising; replaced the prince de Polignac by the duc de Mortemart as premier; appointed General Gerard Minister of War and Casimir Perier Minister of Finances; convoked the parliament for August 3. The new premier, who had entered Paris in disguise, wandered around the city all day on the thirtieth looking for his ministers and for the leaders of the Revolution, but without being able to find either Casimir Perier, or General Gerard, or the presidents of the two Chambers, or even a printing press to print the night's ordinances. Lafayette, who since the day before had been installed in the Hôtel de Ville, did not know what to do; he escaped from the importunities of the Revolution, protesting that the hour to proclaim the republic had not yet struck. Finally, on the thirtieth, he attended a small meeting of parliamentarians—about thirty peers and two hundred deputies—

convoked without any particular aim, privately, in the vague hope that—who knows what? Perhaps, in all this confusion, somebody would have a plan. A king without ministers, without a capital, imprisoned in the château de Saint-Cloud; a premier wandering around Paris carrying in his pocket the decrees that recognized the triumph of the Revolution, but unable to find a single person to read them to; a former revolutionary leader of sixty who was as frightened by the triumphant Revolution as the king; two fragments of parliament assembled and deliberating without authority—that is what remained of the Revolution and the Restoration on July 30, 1830, after three days of the Paris uprising.

But there was one man in Paris who knew what he wanted, and who, to remake the government as he wanted it, was prepared either to bribe or to betray either the Revolution or the Old Regime. This was M. Laffitte, a well-known banker on the Rue de Provence. This banker, this moneylender, persuaded the peers and deputies who had privately assembled on June 30 that in order to re-constitute the government it was necessary to convoke parliament, but that Charles X could not do it as he had spilled too much of the people's blood. He suggested that the duc d'Orléans, the head of the younger branch, be invited to replace the king, accepting the position of lieu-tenant-general of the kingdom. The suggestion was ap-proved, but where was the duc d'Orléans? He, too, had disappeared. All day they looked for him; at last, very late in the evening, they found him. He had returned secretly to Paris alone and on foot after sundown. At first he refused: thirty peers and two hundred deputies hap-hazardly assembled possessed neither the authority nor the constitutional power to dispossess the king and appoint a lieutenant-general. The financier insisted; the prince, who in his youth had been a Jacobin, was not very strict on the question of legitimacy, and in the end allowed himself to be convinced. On the morning of the thirty-first it was announced that the duc d'Orléans had accepted the position of lieutenant-general of the kingdom. But no sooner had this revolutionary usurpation been accomplished than the duc d'Orléans tried to have it legitimized by Charles X and by the people. The same day, the thirty-first, he told the duc de Mortemart to say to Charles X that he had accepted the lieutenancy in order to prevent the proclamation of a republic and, in accordance with the king, to serve the interests of the monarchy; and he proceeded to the Hôtel de Ville to show himself to the people with Lafayette on the balcony waving a tricolored flag. Reassured by the duke's *démarche*, becoming more and more intimidated by his unpopularity, Charles X decided to sacrifice himself in order to save the principle of monarchy, the Genius of the Old Regime; on August 1 he appointed the duc d'Orléans lieutenant-general of the kingdom, and on the second he abdicated in favor of the duc de Bordeaux, posthumous son of the duc de Berry, entrusting the regency of Henry V to his loyal cousin.

The July 31 usurpation was legitimate. The king, at the moment of abdication, appointed the duc d'Orléans the regent of his grandson. Henry V was one day to be the legitimate successor of Charles X, of Louis XVIII, of Louis XVI, and of Louis XV. But M. Laffitte, the banker from the Rue de Provence, did not see it that way. He began by scaring Charles X, sending revolutionary bands to threaten an attack on the château de Rambouillet, where the king had taken refuge. The government having declared that it was not in a position to guarantee the safety of the king, Charles X left for England on August 4, and on the sixth the two hundred and fifty peers and deputies who had usurped the role and the authority of the Chamber, assembled once more. Led by Laffitte, they stated that the senior branch had left France, declared the throne vacant, approved several modifications of the Charter, and, by 219 votes out of 252, proclaimed the duc d'Orléans king of the French, with the name of Louis Philippe.

Within four days France had fallen into the toils of another usurpation. The Old Regime Monarchy in France fell not during the July uprising but on August 6. On August 6 there was a definitive break with the principle, an irrevocable revolutionary act: because an illegal assembly without mandate or power had pretended to create a king, Louis Philippe's monarchy is not a monarchy of the Old Regime but a usurpation. Was it a usurpation to the extent that Napoleon's monarchy had been, and for the same reasons? There is a difference between the First Empire and the July Monarchy. A legitimate king of the Old Regime had to be led to the throne by an interminable procession of ancestors, which dwindled off across the centuries to lose itself in the dim past. The Empire would only have become legitimate if it had succeeded in lasting uninterruptedly until the reign of Napoleon VII or VIII. Louis Philippe belonged to the royal family and might have become the legitimate king of France if the senior branch had petered out or had voluntarily given up its rights. Because he was a usurper of good family, as Wellington said, the scandal of usurpation was allayed. A Bourbon of the junior branch seated on the throne of the Bourbons was less offensive to the aristo-monarchic legitimacy than the son of an Ajaccio lawyer.

The democratic legitimation of the July Monarchy was also more serious. The plebiscites and legislative assemblies of the Empire had been nothing but farces; their operation, directed beforehand by the government they were supposed to legitimize, was not actuated by any spontaneity or sincerity. Under Louis Philippe the right of opposition, limited but effective, was a reality and not a comedy. It could annoy, and did annoy, the government. Finally, Louis Philippe did not possess himself of the power by means of a new 18 Brumaire. The July Days had not been his work, even though he had benefited thereby. He, too, had been overcome by fear and had fled from Paris; he had been pursued, caught, and brought back, and he had been entreated to accept the crown. Why? Because he had been needed. The July Monarchy was going to be the bridge between the senior branch of the Bourbons, hated by one part, and the republic, hated by another part of France, expeditiously built but necessary to clear the gap between monarchy and republic. This necessity still further extenuated the original usurpation by obliging everyone to be satisfied with a dubious king for fear of worse.

The July Monarchy was neither the legitimate monarchy of Louis XV or Louis XVIII nor the illegitimate monarchy of Napoleon. What was it then? It was a quasi-legitimate monarchy. The definition is contemporaneous with the period. It has been attributed to M. Guizot, who denied it. Whoever coined it, the phrase is in any event a happy and ingenious one. There are not only legitimate governments and illegitimate governments: in between, there are governments, which, without being legitimate, are able to count on a large enough acceptance so as not to be obliged, like illegitimate governments, to make use of corruption, deception, and violence alone. They are assured of this consent, partly by the elements of legitimacy they contain, partly because they are necessary to prevent anarchy.

We have now discovered the fundamental nature of the government that we called "Philippist"; of the political system by which Louis Philippe attempted to bring into collaboration the two invisible Genii of the City, the two conflicting principles of legitimacy. His attempt resulted in the creation of a quasi-legitimate government, which differed from a revolutionary government because it could count on more support, did not have as great a need to use violence, and consequently was less afraid. That is why under Louis Philippe, France was able to enjoy a greater degree of freedom.

The July Monarchy was far from being the only quasi-legitimate government in history. The kingdom of Italy, for instance, from its foundation in 1861 up to the fascist *coup d'état* in 1922, was also a quasi-legitimate government, and it lasted for sixty years. Though legitimate in the former kingdom of Sardinia, the house of Savoy did not carry its legitimacy with it when it annexed the lands of the other Italian dynasties by a unilateral act, without cession by the preceding sovereigns. In Parma, in Modena, in Florence, in Naples it was a usurper to the faithful subjects of the preceding dynasties, while to the liberals and adherents to the principles of the Revolution, because it was a dynasty, it was no better than the local dynasties. That is why the house of Savoy, outside of Piedmont, offered itself as a liberator and unifier, bearing representative institutions and unity as the gifts of a happy accession. By giving satisfaction in some measure to liberal and nationalistic aspirations, it took the place of monarchic legitimacy, which was lacking outside of Piedmont; it managed to win approval and build up interests that were rapidly crystallized by necessity. By combining two legitimacies, each insufficient by itself, with necessity—that is, the impossibility of another government taking its place— the constitutional and liberal monarchy acquired a quasi legitimacy, thanks to which Italy, too, was able to enjoy a certain amount of freedom until 1922.

But the most celebrated of quasi-legitimate states was the Roman empire. The nineteenth century completely falsified the history of Rome by introducing the struggle between the monarchic principle of legitimacy and the democratic principle of legitimacy, which has ravaged Europe since the end of the eighteenth century. This struggle assumes the existence of ancient monarchic institutions, deeply rooted in history, which never did exist in Rome. Nineteenth-century historians made Rome start as a monarchy because during the early centuries they discovered a "rex" at the head of the republic. But the Roman "rex" was neither an oriental king of antiquity nor an occidental king of modern history. Like the *serenissimo doge* of Venice, he was the elective president of an aristo-cratic republic. We do not know how or by whom he was elected, though it was probably by the people, but we do know that he did not inherit his power and that he was elected for life. The events that abolished the "reges" from Roman history were not, like August 10 or like '48 in France, a revolution that overcame a monarchy and re-placed it by a republic. They were a constitutional reform of the aristocratic republic that did not transform the re-gime, a reform that replaced the single, lifetime president by two annual presidents. The meaning of the reform is clear: it weakened the executive power to the advantage of the senate and the comitia—of parliamentary power and democracy. S. P. Q. R.—those were the initials of the power that conquered, organized, and long administered the em-pire. *Senatus populusque romanus*—the two sovereign powers, an assembly of nobles and an elective body of citizens.

Similarly, it was only through a tremendous misunder-standing that they were able to transform Julius Caesar into a nineteenth-century revolutionary, the precursor and model for Napoleon and the modern dictators. There is nothing in common between Julius Caesar and the latter, between the turbulences of the Roman republic in his time and the European revolutions of the nineteenth and twentieth centuries. Napoleon rose upon the ruins of an ancient monarchy at a time when the forces that over-threw it were still powerful enough to prevent its restora-tion but were incapable of expediting the parliamentary and democratic republic that they attempted to put in its place. In order to find a substitute for both of them, he in-vented and created, as we saw, the first example of a to-talitarian government, which was copied by the modern dictators. Nothing like this took place in Rome, in the time of Caesar. In the old republic there was not an earlier principle of legitimacy that was growing old and a new principle of legitimacy that wanted to replace it. The invisible Genius that protected the City against fear was alone, without any competitor or rival; there was only one principle of legitimacy, accepted and respected by everyone and symbolized by the glorious initials, S. P. Q. R. The senate and the people were the two indisputable sovereigns, with the multiple magistrates as their instruments. The agonizing problem of the republic was another—the legions. *Qui gladio ferit, gladio perit:* I cannot help but see in this sentence from the Gospel an esoteric prophecy on the fate of the Roman empire. The legions had created it and were maintaining it, but were they not going to destroy it? A formidable instrument of power, the legions had faithfully served Rome and the empire, so long as they had obeyed the legitimate authorities of the republic. But after the Gracchi, Roman aristocracy became divided into two great cliques or coteries rather than into two parties, and these ended up by making use of the legions to settle their quarrels by force of arms. The two leaders of the two groups of legions fighting each other were no longer, as the generals of the republic, the right arm of the sovereign senate and people; they had become temporary sovereigns themselves, at war with each other, disposing of the legions as they desired in the interests of the clique that supported them. Nothing in these wars reminds us of the French Revolution and the struggle of equalitarian and liberal democracy against the absolutism and aristocracy of the Old Regime. Although the two coteries attempted to secure the sympathy of the middle and lower classes by means of promises and gifts, they were both headed by members of the aristocracy, equally resolved to hold on to their privileges. Neither one nor the other for a moment believed that birth, as a claim to power, could be replaced by real or assumed ability, by culture and wealth. Furthermore, the middle and lower classes demanded no sacrifice to an equalitarian Moloch. The aristocracy was not torn by opposing doctrines but by ambitions, rivalries, and fears, caused by the too rapid growth of the power and wealth of the empire. The former economic, political, and moral stability of the city was shattered; certain families of the aristocracy had become too rich and powerful, others had lost their wealth and prestige; some people clung to tradition, while others, dazzled by Greece and Asia, wished to change everything; both sides became restless, quarreled, hated each other, accused each other of wishing to bring about the downfall of Rome. The discord, the hatred the distrust became aggravated and in the end led to open fighting. Hatred and fear: nothing else.

The civil war between Marius and Sulla was the first. And it was frightful. In order to understand what a civil war must have been like between Roman legions who had conquered so many armies and enemies in Europe, Africa, and Asia, we must realize the nature of war in ancient times, before the great humanization and demilitarization of the West that Christianity accomplished. At that time war was a means of extermination. In battle the object was to break up and put to flight the enemy formations. If this succeeded, the fugitives were pursued, and those that were caught were either killed outright or made prisoners; those prisoners who could not be sold as slaves were almost always massacred. In the third century, under Aurelian, children were taught to sing on holidays, when they played at soldiers and imitated their dances, songs like the following in honor of the emperor:

> *Mille mille mille decollavimus*
> *Unus homo! Mille decollavimus*
> *Mille bibat qui mille occidit*
> *Tantum vini nemo habet, quantum fudit sanguinis.*

"We, the emperor, we, a single man, we have decapitated a thousand, thousand, thousand enemies. Let whoever has killed a thousand, drink a thousand times. No one has as much wine as our emperor has spilled blood."

Or else: *"Mille Sarmatas, mille Francos semel et semel occidimus, mille Persas querimus."* "At one blow we (it is the emperor talking) have killed, once a thousand Sarmatians, once a thousand Franks, and now we must kill a thousand Persians."

These sanguinary songs, invented for the education of the youth, exaggerated: Aurelian never caused so many heads to fall. But the abject adulation of the third century personified and glorified in the emperor the implacable ferocity of a military tradition that stretched back to the golden age of the republic. Mass executions of prisoners by the soldiers often followed wars, especially in less civilized countries which had revolted. After the battle, the soldier was transformed into executioner, the general-in-chief, besides being strategian, tactician, diplomat, and administrator, was also hangman of the republic, charged with a bloody vengeance against the rebels. The enemies of Rome, when they could, returned the courtesy: how many legions were massacred, how many aristocrats left Rome with an army, never to return! Those who did return, leaving so many bodies behind, had in the end, after centuries, made up a sanguinary, hard, implacable aristocracy, convinced of its divinity, an aristocracy that wanted to rule over everything and could conceive of only one punishment for disobedience and revolt—extermination.

But even this aristocracy of warrior-executioners, which had created them and made use of them to destroy so many peoples, was alarmed when it saw its gigantic machines of extermination, the legions, hurl themselves upon each other in the furious conflicts of civil war. It had come out of the first civil war—that of Marius and Sulla—already a prey to the obsession of ever-possible revolt on the part of the legions, and it had kept an implacable rancor against the minority of aristocratic families that had fought under Marius. Unfortunately for it, however, the family of Julius Caesar was one of these: his aunt had been the wife of Marius. It is because of this that his career never had anything in common with that of Bonaparte and the contemporary dictators. The latter enjoyed all the opportunities that, at a time of revolutionary chaos, were offered to their ambition by a civilization which had been humanized to the very marrow by fourteen centuries of Christianity, by the spirit of liberalism that began to make itself felt in the fourteenth century, by the spread of wealth, abundance, and knowledge, and by the elimination of a great many imaginary terrors that victimized mankind until three centuries ago. They all conquered the power, not by the sword but by speeches, pamphlets, more or less carnivalesque masquerades, and a few scuffles. Bonaparte became First Consul at the age of thirty-one, with two disasters as great as those of Campo Formio and Egypt for claims to the title, and emperor at thirty-five, after having broken, by a policy of fear, the Treaty of Amiens, which had made France the strongest power in the world!

At thirty-five, when Napoleon had already become emperor with such disconcerting ease, Julius Caesar was just beginning his political career, which was to be slow, difficult, and full of dangers. The story was related that Sulla had said he was equal to several Mariuses. It is probably a legend, but it was enough to fill his path with obstacles provided by an implacable opposition that forgave him less for his great qualities than for his undeniable faults. A very powerful party always saw in him the potential leader of a new revolt by the legions, and tirelessly watched his progress as he climbed to power, ready to cut him down at the first opportunity. The moments when the high Roman nobility sincerely admired him were very few and far between; for a long time it submitted to him without ever accepting him. Julius Caesar did not love it, but it is impossible that he could ever have dreamed of ousting it. The Roman aristocracy of his time was not the revolutionary oligarchy of 1799, improvised five years before, that the argument of Lucien Bonaparte and a few companies of grenadiers sufficed to disperse. Firmly entrenched in power for seven centuries, sovereign over a vast empire that it had conquered by wars of extermination, it would have required something else than a petty affair like the 18 Brumaire to dispossess it: a gigantic war in which the empire might collapse. Caesar, who was not a petty revolutionary of the nineteenth or twentieth centuries, was aware of that.

That is why he never contrived or carried out any reform or revolution of the state that would have destroyed the power of the aristocracy. Not one of the schemes of this kind that were attributed to him by nineteenth-century historians ever existed; I defy any historian or archeologist to find the slightest documentary or conjectural evidence of this. The cause of the civil war was a simpler one. The coterie of his implacable enemies wanted to make him return to private life by trying and condemning him to exile, while he wanted to retain the position he had acquired in the republic. Neither more nor less than that; and that is the explanation for the desperate efforts Caesar made to avoid war. He would have been the maddest of scoundrels or the most scoundrelly of madmen if, as his nineteenth-century admirers claim, he had contrived, prepared, and unleashed a civil war for so petty a quarrel. But the petty quarrel had broken out in the midst of an oligarchy of sovereign, implacable, and sanguinary demigods, already hardened by a permanent war of extermination. They could not admit that Caesar would not yield; and, as Caesar did not yield, they provoked a tremendous civil war that had not the slightest resemblance to the wordy and bureaucratic revolutions with which, after 1789, France set the fashion in the Western world.

For the second time the armies of the republic split into two groups, sought out and massacred each other everywhere, in Italy, in Greece, in Egypt, in Africa, in Spain. This was the second civil war in Rome, which bore no resemblance to modern revolution. Few speeches and no literary deception: the great machine that the West invented to manufacture revolutions—the press—was not yet in existence; in its place there were only engines of destruction: armies that massacred each other in a merciless struggle between sovereigns who did not compromise their sovereign rights one jot. Caesar won the war, but his victories, instead of resolving, complicated the inextricable difficulties of the republic by a new and more serious problem: that of the legions. One after another, his adversaries fell on the field of battle, committed suicide, or took refuge in a distant province in order to recruit new armies and begin the struggle anew. After each victory Caesar's army acquired part of the defeated legions; but the number of nobles on which he could count to keep them in line diminished. At the same time his authority as supreme commander became more and more uncertain. The senate and the comitia rarely came together and held their deliberations in an atmosphere of terror and constraint, without discussing anything. The two sources of legitimacy for every government—*senatus populusque*—were dried up; all authority was tottering.

It took the stultification of a bookish civilization to conceive of Caesar, toward 45 B.C., during the course of the fourth year of civil warfare, as being engaged in fabricating for the benefit of the Roman people the illusion of a new era that was beginning, with the help of one of those politico-literary deceptions that every Western revolution during the last century and a half has made use of. After four years of civil war, there was only one problem for him and for Rome: how was he going to feed, pay, occupy, and keep disciplined the tremendous armed force that the civil war had produced? How was he to prevent it, after it had revolted against the senate on Caesar's orders, from revolting against Caesar and destroying the empire? We know that when Caesar was assassinated he was getting ready to leave for a great campaign against the Parthians. The Parthians were not threatening Rome; if Caesar was taking the initiative in an aggressive war that would mean a three-year absence, it was because he was more concerned with keeping his army occupied than with reforming the republic. It was the price he had to pay for his victory; he could not abandon the power because he alone could hope, yet without too great assurance, to exact the obedience of the legions. Since he was unable to abandon it, he was forced more and more to protract and extend his power. Perpetual dictatorship meant the supreme command of the armies for an indeterminable period of time— a revolutionary expedient, imposed by civil war.

But the perpetual dictator was the unique, lifelong president, the "rex" of the first centuries of the republic; the Roman aristocracy would have none of it. Two weeks later Caesar was stabbed to death in the senate. It is easy to understand why, having nothing in common with modern dictators, he had not been afraid of assassination. But, since he was dead, the legions again split into two groups— the enemies and the friends of Caesar; the civil war and the massacres began anew. The friends of Caesar defeated and exterminated the enemies, and then turned to exterminate each other. Before the eyes of the world it had conquered, the Roman aristocracy committed suicide: *"Altera iam teritur bellis civilibus aetas."* The framework that had governed it having practically vanished, the empire fell apart; what was to be done with all these soldiers who for more than twenty years had lived only for mutual extermination? The last victor and only survivor of the frightful conflict that had lasted seventeen years, the adopted son of Caesar, a young man of thirty-six, had become their leader, with dubious authority and uncertain funds with which to pay them. What if they revolted against this shadow of power after having revolted against the senate and people? What would then become of Rome and the empire? *"Qui gladio ferit, gladio perit."*

Fate determined that Caesar's son should be a builder. He belonged to that small elite of men, the most recent of whom were Talleyrand, Alexander I, and Louis XVIII. He understood that the world needed a new order, but that for it to become possible the old order would first have to be reconstructed as it had been devastated by civil wars. The republic and the army were in need of a "rex," a single leader who would have power for a longer period than the consuls and proconsuls, and would possess the authority and the means necessary to assure the republic of the discipline of the legions. He was the only one who could assume this duty; even if he had desired to relinquish the power—and it appears that he gave it serious consideration—he would not have been able to. After seventeen years of civil warfare the soldiers acknowledged no one but him as their leader and were not accustomed to obeying anyone but him. Moreover, he had become fabulously wealthy during the war, whereas a great many aristocratic families had been impoverished. Either he put this immense wealth at the disposal of the empire by governing it or he foundered with all his treasure, together with Rome, in the inevitable revolt of the legions. But it was also necessary to make the idea of a single head of the government with long-lived power acceptable to the aristocracy. In order to make it acceptable, he reconstituted the ancient republican order—traditions, spirit, institutions: senate, comitia, magistracies—and at the heart of the republican order he resuscitated the "rex" without a word to anyone and almost without the world's knowledge. He secured the extended powers he needed to direct the army and the state by cumulating various republican magistracies—primarily the *potestas tribunicia* and the *imperium proconsulare*. He did not mention the word "rex"; he denied any intention of creating a new magistracy; realizing how repugnant the idea of a lifelong authority was to the nobility, he only accepted temporary renewals of all his powers, for periods of five or ten years. In theory, and in all probability fundamentally his intention, his authority was to be transitory: as soon as the situation had become normal, the republican constitution would be completely re-established, which permitted only collegiate magistracies with short durations. But this hope was never realized. He was enslaved all his life by his victory, as by a lifelong punishment.

Essentially, then, the supreme authority that ruled the empire during the first three centuries of its existence was a provisional state that became permanent. That is why imperial authority never succeeded in going beyond the intermediate stage of quasi legitimacy. Its imperfections as a quasi-legitimate power explain all that was vague, ephemeral, and vacillating in this strange and tremendous power, with which the fate of a large part of mankind was bound up for so many centuries. So tremendous was it that it never had a name: neither of "rex," which would have been the correct one, nor of any other. Our term, emperor, is an anachronism; in the classical world "imperator" was not the name of a ruling power but an honorary title peculiar to the military. Sometimes the head of the empire, especially on inscriptions, was called "Augustus" or "Tebartos"; here again these were adjectives that indicated, not a state government, but human qualities. Tacitus often makes use of the word "princeps," but we would lose the meaning if we translated it as "prince." In Latin "princeps" means the first, the president: we are in the presence of a republic. When did the office first become a life office? We do not know. We can date all the quinquennial and decennial renewals of Augustus' powers; beginning with Tiberius there is no more mention of renewals; history seems to imply that the power is conferred for life. But it seems impossible that a change of such significance should have taken place without legislative acts of the highest importance. Why should they have been lost to history? How and by whom was the emperor invested with supreme power? On this point, too, information does not agree. The history of Augustus' family, as told by Suetonius and Tacitus, would have us believe that the emperor had to be chosen and invested by the senate. The jurists of the second century say that a law transferred all the powers of the people to the emperor and that this law was called "lex regia." [1] What was the meaning of "lex regia"? The law that creates a "rex." "Rex" in the Latin sense of the word, a "princeps" or president for life? These passages, then, prove that contemporaries, even if they did not dare say it, recognized the head of the empire to be the "rex" resuscitated from ancient times. But when was the imperial power first conferred by the "lex regia"? We can find no trace of this law for the emperors belonging to the Julian-Claudian family, from Augustus to Nero. We have an important fragment of the "lex" that conferred the power on Vespasian. Might this "lex" that concerns Vespasian be the first application of the "lex regia"? We cannot tell. As we are unable to determine what the juridical foundations and limitations of the imperial authority were in the various spheres, Mommsen's attempt to supply a juridical system of the imperial authority met with failure.

It could not succeed because the imperial power contained certain elements of legitimacy drawn from the republican tradition; but it had never been accepted as a definitive, sanctioned, and systematized modification of the constitution. It was a transitory and fluctuating expedient, necessary to ensure the loyalty of the legions and the unity of the empire, and some day the republic would get rid of it—the old Romans kept telling each other. In reality, this power, which in Rome had no name and operated outside any constitutional system, had become a sort of divinity to all the provinces where the constitutional subtleties of Rome were little known, and the heir and continuer of the monarchic power before the conquest to the Asiatic provinces. Thus, the imperial power was neither legitimate nor illegitimate but quasi-legitimate, like the monarchy of Louis Philippe.

[1] Dig. I, 4, 1; Cod. Just. I, 17, 1, 7.

XV

THE CATASTROPHIC EFFECTS
OF QUASI LEGITIMACY
(France, 1848—Italy, 1915)

———————————✦✦✦✦———————————

"Louis Philippe is one of the great mysteries in French history. That he was a great man, no one can deny. And he had given France what she really wanted and not only what she said she wanted: a democratic monarchy, a conciliation between the Old Regime and the Revolution, freedom and order, peace and prosperity; peace and prosperity crowned with a certain amount of military prestige, but without too much danger. France asked for nothing better. Why should this government have fallen suddenly from one day to the next, for no serious reason, following an artificially produced agitation for universal suffrage, which had no interest for anyone? Whoever can answer that will do Europe a great service."

"But why don't you make up your mind for once to read Metternich's comment on Louis Philippe, *König der Franzosen,* which is in the fifth volume of his *Nachegelassene Papiere?* I have already pointed it out to you several times, and you promised me to read it. The problem that worries you is cleared up in this comment that anticipates future events."

The above dialogue recapitulates and schematizes a discussion that I have had several times with an old French friend of mine, with whom I always took pleasure in discussing the great problems of history. Here is Metternich's note to which I alluded:

The monarchy of August 9 ascended the throne in place of the one that had fallen. Is its condition a healthy one? Certainly not. On the one hand it lacks the authority of popular elections, which supported every form of government that existed between 1792 and 1801; on the other hand it does not have the all-powerful support of the historic law upon which rested the restored monarchy; of the Republic, it lacks popular power, however brutal that power may be; of the Empire, it lacks the military glory, the genius and the might of Napoleon; of the Bourbons, it lacks the support of the principle of legitimacy.

The result is a situation bearing the stamp of these faults, exactly as Napoleon's reign was characterized by conquest, and that of the Bourbons by birthright. The monarchy of 1830 is a hybrid; the future will show up its weakness.

Every time the King of France attempts to turn toward the Right, the latter closes its ranks to him; he cannot turn toward the Left without ruining himself. In this manner, condemned to hover between two realities, Monarchy and Republic, Louis Philippe is in a vacuum, for a lie is a vacuum.

An insuperable difficulty for the King results from his having condemned himself to a living death.

The Charter of 1814 had its faults; but the power from which it emanated rested on solid foundations.

The Charter of 1830 added new faults to the old ones, while the restricted authority of the Government, charged with seeing to the execution of the laws, lacks foundation and stability. It originates neither in hereditary right nor in the nation's choice. In defiance of every right, seditious assemblies proclaimed Louis Philippe King. He took possession of the throne and the government of the nation. No right results from these facts. Louis Philippe is King *de facto*.

A mere fact, to perpetuate itself, needs more than one solid support. As it does not possess within itself the strength necessary to subsist, it must borrow from external conditions, moral as well as material. Power does not reside in a second-hand throne: the Charter merely gives the King conditional power. It reduces him to procuring the authority he needs by methods that condemn themselves. The only real power that the King of the French commands is in the general feeling about the need for public order, and, consequently, the need for a Government that will prevent the immediate onslaught of anarchy. The power that proceeds from this feeling is negative and shares the fate of all negations. The mere appearance of a power that subsists by itself is sufficient to destroy the other. A barrier erected against disorder loses its value as soon as order is re-established; its importance is wiped out with the feeling of the need for security. If that is true in every case, it will be especially so in a country where the people are bewildered, where for a long time already, even in the least prejudiced individuals, the feeling of the need for order has not relied upon the voice of conscience pointing out the real means of establishing it.

Since the Government of King Louis Philippe has merely the value of factuality, one may as well assign it a day's existence as an indefinite continuance.

It is impossible to base any estimate on such an existence, for it depends on a concatenation of fortuitous circumstances.

It is from usage alone that, in the course of time, the July Monarchy will be able to draw its strength. But, in the case of peoples, habit comes only from a state of prosperity. Surrounded as it is by republican institutions, will the monarchy attain that aim?

The matter is at least open to question.[2]

Metternich, unlike Talleyrand, was not a philosopher. He was an artist, gifted with an extraordinary intuition, which sometimes stood him in good stead, sometimes misguided him. He completely failed to understand the case of Napoleon. "If his passions had not completely blinded his intellect, his reign would only have come to an end with his life," he wrote in the first part, not quoted, of the

[2] *Mémoires—documents et écrits divers laissés par le prince de Metternich* (Paris: Plon, 1882), Vol. V, pp. 83-85.

same memorandum. He assumes that passions can befog the intelligence of a great man; and he does not even suspect that a man whose intelligence is blinded by his passions cannot be a great statesman. That time his intuition miscarried. It served him better in the case of Louis Philippe, but why? Because he judged the case of Louis Philippe by applying the doctrine of quasi legitimacy, although he had never heard of it; and he was able to apply a doctrine he had never heard of because his intuition, coming across it, succeeded in seizing on the wing this fragment of truth from the immense tornado of lies and illusions that is the history of the nineteenth century.

. . . On the one hand it lacks the authority of popular elections . . . on the other hand it does not have the all-powerful support of historic law . . . of the Republic, it lacks popular power . . . of the Bourbons, it lacks the support of the principle of legitimacy . . . it originates neither in hereditary right nor in the nation's choice. In defiance of every right, seditious assemblies proclaimed Louis Philippe King.

This time, thanks to his intuition, Metternich could have taught even Talleyrand a lesson. With one jump he had grasped the essential point of Louis Philippe's position in history. The new king of the French attempted to justify his power by both principles of legitimacy; but without success because he applied neither the one nor the other with the sincerity and the coherence that a principle of legitimacy needs before it can take effect. The consequence is that:

. . . condemned to hover between two realities, Monarchy and Republic, Louis Philippe is in a vacuum, for a lie is a vacuum.

But in that case what is the July Monarchy founded upon? Here Metternich, in a few definitive lines, discovers and determines the essence of quasi-legitimate government:

. . . No right results from these facts. Louis Philippe is King *de facto*.

A mere fact, to perpetuate itself, needs more than one solid support. As it does not possess within itself the strength necessary to subsist, it must borrow from external conditions, moral as well as material. . . . The only real power that the King of the French commands is in the general feeling about the need for public order, and, consequently, the need for a Government that will prevent the immediate onslaught of anarchy. The power that proceeds from this feeling is negative and shares the fate of all negations. The mere appearance of a power that subsists by itself is sufficient to destroy the other. A barrier erected against disorder loses its value as soon as order is re-established. . . .

That explains why quasi-legitimate governments are precariously situated. They have an advantage over revolutionary governments of being less subject to fear and having less need to resort to force, thanks to their inferior legitimacy. But, unlike revolutionary governments, which depend only upon force, they cannot defend themselves by force to the very end. If the consciousness of its necessity weakens, if the contradictory principles of legitimacy to which it clings come into conflict, a quasi-legitimate government may disappear in a few days, with practically no resistance. Metternich had divined it and had cast an amazingly correct horoscope of the July Monarchy, then in its cradle.

Since the Government of King Louis Philippe has merely the value of factuality, one may as well assign it a day's existence as an indefinite continuance.

It is impossible to base any estimate on such an existence, for it depends on a concatenation of fortuitous circumstances.

Metternich, who had not believed it possible either to overthrow Napoleon or to restore the throne of the Bourbons, had for once been a prophet: he foresaw from the very beginning of the regime the catastrophe of '48. Why does my friend still torment himself about this historical enigma, which has been solved for a century? He has one of the greatest minds of our age; a philosopher and a historian, he knows mankind and its history through books and experience, he has made a thorough study of nineteenth-century history from documents and has taken part in various ways in the political life of his own country. But principles of legitimacy have no place in his vast and profound knowledge and experience of mankind. He has never discovered them, has never suspected their invisible effect; and I have never been able to convince him that they bear the same significance to the history of man as roots do to a tree: they are not visible but it is they that uphold and condition everything. In the great drama of history he sees only psychological forces—interests, emotions, ideas, doctrines, prejudices, traditions—that the statesman actuates, combines, and exploits; and he is convinced that the result is primarily dependent upon the intelligence, the daring, and the luck with which the statesman actuates, combines, and exploits them, to the exclusion of any other, invisible influence. A great admirer of Napoleon's, he manages to explain his downfall; he sees the errors he committed and explains them, like Metternich, by the unsettling influence of passions. If the emperor had only been more prudent! But he is unable to explain the catastrophe of '48. Louis Philippe was the most intelligent head of government that France had had since the Revolution, he had not committed Napoleon's faults, he had been prudent; why, then, did his prudence avail him nothing and, like the senseless imprudence of the other, lead to catastrophe?

My friend has never explained and never will explain the downfall of the July Monarchy because it is inexplicable from the point of view of pure statecraft, which he refuses to abandon. Metternich explained it because for once he envisaged the problem from the only point of view that enables it to be solved—the invisible effect of the principles of legitimacy. But my friend's case is far from being a personal mishap: it is almost the application of a universal law. Of all governments, quasi-legitimate ones are the hardest to understand. Because they seek justification in two conflicting principles of legitimacy, they live under an inadmissible contradiction; because they live under an inadmissible contradiction, they are in constant danger of insulting the common sense and morality of their subjects; as a result, they must strive to conceal their real nature. They may enjoy the advantages of quasi legitimacy only insofar as they succeed in disguising themselves. Whole generations may obey a government of this kind without ever suspecting its real nature, or even believing that it is the opposite of what it is: a terrible misunderstanding and a mysterious and incurable agony, which may result in the most dangerous individual and collective follies. I am a living proof of that. My life has been a network of different tragedies centering around one major tragedy, resulting from the quasi-legitimate government to which I was subjected: that I was obliged to live until I was fifty under a regime which I knew was not what it ought to have been, without being able to discover what it really was or in what the imperfection consisted which was tormenting and afflicting me. I intend to tell the story of that tragedy; perhaps it will serve to enlighten those who have passed through the same experience, and there must be many of them in Europe.

In Pisa and in Turin, I had had two teachers who had instructed me in the classic constitutional law of England. They had taught it to me as a system of inviolable and imperative rules, establishing rights and duties: rights and duties of the people, rights and duties of Parliament, rights and duties of parties, rights and duties of the Crown. To my juvenile way of thinking and feeling that system of rules had seemed the supreme code of the elite of mankind, of the high aristocracy of the peoples, which had won its freedom and to which Italy belonged. Did not the official demagogues repeat every day that, thanks to the *Risorgimento,* Italy was one of the freest nations in the world? And so I had studied with a sort of religious exaltation the law of freedom, which, as my teachers taught it, seemed to me to be sublime. Consequently, I was greatly astonished when, on going out into the world, I began to ascertain that the sacred code of freedom, as applied outside, bore very little resemblance to the one taught in the universities. The parties—there were only two of any importance, the Right and the Left—did not have a large following in the country. The elections were neither free nor honest, which deeply injured my sense of justice. The people, with the exception of a few small minorities, were passive, indifferent, fearful, and in certain social strata easily corruptible. Their participation in the government was fictitious. Furthermore, it was only too obvious that the parties and the government were not dissatisfied with this situation and had no desire to have to deal with a more exacting people. In Rome, the governments seemed to be what my teachers had taught me in the university: the emanation of parliament and the parties. But it was also obvious that they attempted to restrict as far as possible the actions and the influence of the parliament, from which they pretended to be the emanation; to shut it out from the more important affairs, to deprive it of its rights, and to discredit it. At the same time they did their best to destroy, either in the country or in the parliament, the strength and the influence of the two strongest parties. The Left had come into power in 1876 and had been governing for ten years when I began to take interest in what was going on in Rome. One of the leaders of the Left, Signor Depretis, had for several years been firmly installed in the presidency of the council, and, as head of the government, made it his principal task to exterminate his own party, both in the country and in parliament, by amalgamating with the Right. He and his friends wanted—it was said—completely to transform the two great historical parties that under the preceding reign had brought about the union, and this policy had even been baptized with the uncouth term of "transformism"; in reality, under pretext of transforming them, they wanted to annihilate them in order to stifle the opposition. And this "transformism" was only too successful: the two parties meekly submitted to amalgamation at the hands of the government, except for two small groups, which, from the Right and Left, kept up the opposition, splitting it up into two parties with different points of view. The little group on the Left was reinforced by two even smaller groups—the Radicals and the Republicans—two extreme leftist parties, which were still very weak in the country but which managed to elect a few deputies—about twenty in all. The small leftist opposition, reinforced by the two tiny groups on the extreme Left, defended the principles of English classic parliamentarianism with a certain amount of vehemence against the dissembled but numerous violations of Signor Depretis. All my sympathies were with them.

Signor Depretis died in 1887, and Signor Crispi replaced him. Signor Crispi was the noisiest leader of the small leftist opposition: for a while I hoped that he was going to reinstate the constitution as it had originally been conceived. What he did was to continue the policy of his predecessor on a larger scale. One day when a deputy reminded him of his opposition speeches, he replied, "From the top of the pyramid one sees things in a different light than from the base." After more than half a century, I have never forgotten the terrible impression that this sentence made on me. The opposition, then, was not a chivalrous tournament involving high convictions and eloquence but a battle of swindling and deception. Signor Crispi remained in power four years, from 1887 to 1891, and he did not waste his time: he embroiled Italy with France, he ruined the old liberal economy, based on agriculture, by precipitating it into the hazards of industrial protectionism, he launched Italy into the grand policy of vast armaments, continual alarms, ubiquitous claims. During the course of those four years I began to see that the constitution, the workings of which had been explained to me at the university, instead of an instrument of state, was a screen behind which something was going on. But what exactly? I did not succeed in finding out. Obviously, Signor Crispi had no intention of governing in the name and to the advantage of the country, as the leader of a party, in honest concurrence with other parties. Like his predecessor, he intended to stay in power indefinitely and to exercise it all by himself, suppressing all opposition. And it was also obvious that Signor Crispi was assisted, either by invisible and very powerful supporters or by the indifference of the greater part of the nation.

I was young and knew little of men or of history; everything I was taught I took seriously. The mysterious disguise behind which the government had concealed itself, and which left so many Italians indifferent, tormented me, angered me, put me in a spirit of rebellion. My teachers were making a fool of me when they tried to make me believe that I belonged to a free people! Among all the rules of parliamentary government, there was at least one at that time being followed in Rome: the minister had to have a majority in the Chamber. One day Signor Crispi, angered by something a rightist deputy had said, lost control of himself and insulted the whole party; the Chamber, which had always supported him, found a new energy and gave him a minority. The king called upon a Conservative, the marquis Rudini, who made up a ministry composed mostly of what remained of the former Conservative party, and attempted to govern according to the classic rules, as if the parliament were really what it claimed. It lasted only a little more than a year, because this strange parliament seemed to prefer governments that ignored it to those that wanted to make a sovereign power out of it. In 1892 it received a minority after a debate in which the Chamber had seemed to split up for the last time into Right and Left. The king appointed a Liberal ministry, but, for premier, he did not choose the patriarch of the party, Signor Zanardelli, an oldster who considered himself and was considered to be the foremost by right of seniority. Instead he chose a much younger man, Signor Giolitti— he was only fifty—who had only been a member of the Chamber for ten years. But the unexpected selection of Signor Giolitti resulted in a final violent conflict between what remained of the two parties. Signor Giolitti's government now found itself between two fires: the Right was against it because it belonged to the Left; a part of the Left would have none of it because it was headed by an intruder who by a surprise move had cheated the senior members of the party out of their rights. Besides, the times were tempestuous anyway. The ruin of the national wealth caused by the protective system, the world-wide agricultural depression, the imprudencies and mistakes of Signor Depretis' rather reckless finance had all contributed to the impoverishment of the country. Every class was suffering, everyone was discontented, and for the first time the people woke out of their traditional apathy to protest. For the first time, a general murmur rose from all over the country—from the people, the middle classes, the upper classes—and penetrated to the ears of the government and the throne. For one section of the grumblers had begun to ask if perhaps it was not the king who was behind a great many things that seemed difficult to explain—among others, so many unexpected denouements of ministerial crises. At the same time a handful of the youth, almost all from the lower middle classes, discovered Marxism, which was organizing political parties all over Europe and piercing through the veil of the peoples' misery to bear its message to every town and countryside. It proclaimed a new revolution to the people, a revolution that would be accomplished by the proletariat and would complete the work of the French Revolution by regenerating the entire world. Nothing less! But the hour was opportune. The missionaries found open ears and minds almost everywhere: peasants, workers, clerks and shopkeepers, until then passive or indifferent, at last seemed to rouse themselves.

Signor Giolitti did not have an easy task. He did not neglect to smile cordially at the socialist movement, which brought forth the accusation from the Conservatives that he was carrying on a flirtation with the revolution. The failure of a few large banks, the dismay that this produced, the real and imaginary compromises of which the members of parliament were accused or suspected made his burden still heavier. In order to secure a stable majority, he held a general election, and, leftist, man of the people, and liberal though he vaunted himself, he fixed the ballots with a shamelessness remarkable even for the times. I was horrified! Here was the government violating its own laws in order to falsify the national will, of which it declared itself to be the faithful servant! I could not bear to live under such an abomination. Signor Giolitti managed to obtain a large majority, but with little advantage to himself. Battered by the wave of popular discontent that swept over it, his ministry gradually disintegrated and finally, toward December, 1893, was forced to resign. The Liberal opposition tried to force the appointment of a Zanardelli ministry. The king, who was utterly against this, got rid of him by means of a stratagem: he charged Signor Zanardelli to make up a ministry and secretly did all he could to prevent him from doing it. Having accomplished his purpose, the king recalled Signor Crispi. But this time the king's secret had come out; the public had fathomed the maneuver.

Once again Signor Crispi was in power, from November, 1893, to March, 1896, until the battle of Aduwa. During the entire period of the new ministry—almost two and a half years—I lived abroad, in England, Germany, and France. I left in November 1893, just as the Giolitti ministry was collapsing. He had disgusted me as much as his predecessors, and I went abroad unhappy and worried about my country, in search of a remedy for the evils that racked it. In England I was present at the passing of the Victorian age; in Germany, at twilight of the Bismarckian era; in France, during the lull that preceded the storm of the Dreyfus affair. But my visits to these three countries still further aggravated the unhappiness and anxiety that preyed upon me. In France and in England, I began to understand that a true regime of freedom was a very different thing from what was commonly thought in my country; in Germany, what struck me most of all was the power and perfection of organization. It was evident that Italy, as a modern nation, was still only a beginner, but this fact tormented me, by adding, in the midst of so many other preoccupations, the mental burden of causes and remedies. Why had Italy been outstripped, and how could it make up for lost time? While I was asking myself these questions in a foreign land, Signor Crispi in Italy was experimenting with a new method of government, one that I had never seen used anywhere: that of keeping himself in power by exploiting the fear of revolution and the prestige of conquest—both of them imaginary. Taking advantage of a few small riots that had broken out in Sicily and central Italy when he had returned to power, he declared that the socialist revolution was at hand and hastily set up a system of repression modeled after a well-known pattern: martial law, state of siege, muzzling of the press, dispersal and persecution of socialists, real and manufactured *attentats,* regulative administration, government deportations. At the same time Signor Crispi made believe that he was going to conquer Abyssinia, upon which he had already attempted, in his previous ministry, to inflict a protectorate. This policy, conducted with insufficient strength and the most colossal blunders, came to a head in the battle of Aduwa: an insignificant battle from the point of view of numbers of soldiers and victims, but one of the most tragic episodes in the military history of the nineteenth century from the point of view of what took place in the mind of the people. The Crispi ministry collapsed.

I returned to Italy a few months after the battle of Aduwa. Signor Rudini, recalled by the king, was at the head of the government. After this last disaster, I returned with the conviction that King Humbert wanted to go back on the liberal concessions of his father and grandfather, shackle the parliament and people, and re-establish absolute power; and that to frustrate this plan it would be necessary to modernize the country, industrialize it, organize it, democratize it, awaken a civic spirit in the middle and lower classes, fill them with a new inspiration, strong, bold, and sovereign, give them a real parliamentary government, in which well-organized parties would strive for the power—even a republic if the monarchy should be opposed. On returning, I found the country in the throes of a general restlessness and a lively anger, not only against Crispi and his coterie, but also against the king. In private conversations he was being accused as the one primarily responsible for the woes of the country; it was he who had wanted Africa, reactionism, vast armaments, it was he who had ruined the country by his senseless ambition to make the dynasty more powerful. It was in that atmosphere of general restlessness and anger that I began to make myself known by my writings and speeches. In 1897 I became a regular collaborator on the staff of the *Secolo* of Milan, in which I could develop and defend the ideas that I had elaborated during my stay abroad. The *Secolo* was at that time the organ of the radical party. The party was small; it had only about twenty deputies in the Chamber and some membership and organization in a few provinces of Italy, especially in Lombardy and Venetia. But it was backed by the paper that then had the largest circulation in Italy, and by its policy. In order to become a free country modeled on the countries I had admired, Italy needed a party that would establish a firm liaison between the socialists and the monarchy, between the poor and the rich. The radical party was the right party for this task.

From 1897 to 1900, I served my apprenticeship as a political polemist and propagandist on the *Secolo*. Two years of almost uninterrupted tempests. After Aduwa, Marquis Rudini had attempted to calm the people's discontent with a liberal regime. But the economic crisis became worse, the restlessness of the people increased, and the socialist party made rapid progress. In 1898 a rise in the price of bread provoked a number of riots. A frightful panic swept through the court, official circles, and the upper classes. This time it was honestly believed that the revolution had arrived. A state of siege was set up in a number of provinces; the Rudini ministry was replaced by that of General Pelloux, a Savoyard and a personal friend of the king's. The general was implacable against the small parties of the extreme opposition: socialists, republicans, radicals, and Catholics. Societies were dissolved, newspapers suppressed, leaders imprisoned, pursued, condemned; the *Secolo* was also suspended for several months. Finally bills were submitted to parliament that would have suppressed all political freedom and to all intents and purposes established an absolute government. Out of five hundred deputies, only about forty—radicals, republicans, and socialists—had the courage to oppose these bills. Driven by despair, they attempted to prevent their approval by means of obstruction. A period of general upheaval began. Public opinion was against the ministry and its laws and persecutions, and it was rising more and more against the king, as the cause of all the evils: Aduwa, the national crisis, the chaotic state of finances, the military tribunals, the reactionism that was filling the prisons, the "liberticidal" bills, as they were called. The conflict between the king and public opinion seemed irreconcilable. And then all at once a thunderbolt put an end to it. On the evening of July 29, 1900, King Humbert was attending a gymnastic festival held in the park at Monza, adjacent to the superb castle where he spent his summers. A young anarchist who had come from America a few days before, was able to get close to the royal carriage in the midst of the joyful crowd, and fired three shots at point-blank range. The king's death was instantaneous.

There, in broad outline, is the story of the drama in which, from the age of twenty to thirty, I participated. But I participated to the meager extent of my powers, without having the least understanding of what was going on, any more than my compatriots, beginning with the ministers and the king, who lost his life. Like everyone else, I thought that I had courageously fought to repel a distasteful reversion to absolutism and the Old Regime from the liberties of the French Revolution. It was not till much later that I learned what had really taken place: that I had been present at an obscure tragedy of quasi legitimacy, in which King Humbert had been the sacrifice of the two struggling invisible Genii of the City. His youth had been lulled by the clamor of the applause and adulation that had greeted the foundation of the kingdom. He had heard the destiny, the success, the star, and the past, present, and future grandeur of the house of Savoy glorified by poets and historians, by pamphleteers and statesmen, by parliamentarians and state officials. If he had been a young fool, in 1878, when he succeeded his father as the second king of Italy, he might have taken all that adulation, both the sincere and the interested, as the expression of a historic truth. But, if he was no genius, neither was he a fool. During the first part of his reign, when he used to shut the huge windows of the Quirinal on the acclamations of the forum, in order to envisage the situation from within, the second king of Italy saw around him only too many reasons for perplexity and alarm. We have already mentioned that the Savoy dynasty was legitimate only in the former kingdom of Sardinia, and that in the rest of Italy it would have been considered nothing less than a usurpation if it had not appeared as a liberating and unifying power, and not brought with it the representative institutions and the unity demanded by an influential and powerful minority. But, though its policy had brought many advantages, there had been a heavy price to pay: it had been obliged to break with the Church, which did not forgive, and ally itself with the revolution, which it, too, like every other dynasty, feared. The second king of Italy, like the first, was king by the grace of God and the will of the nation; but would he have the strength and the authority to bring about a peaceful collaboration between the two invisible Genii of the City, which never ceased quarreling, wherever they encountered each other? The formula was contradictory: supposing one day the "will of the nation" were to come into conflict with the "grace of God"? The conquered kingdom was large, but to transform it into a great modern state everything still had to be done. It was necessary to create an army, a navy, and the industrial system needed to maintain the army and navy; highways and harbors had to be built, railroads and schools constructed, culture spread in every sphere and every direction; finally, the country had to be enriched by perfecting its agriculture, by developing its commerce and industry, and by multiplying its resources. An immense, difficult, and complex task! It could be accomplished only by fighting against the Church and all the remnants of the Old Regime grouped around the Church; by vanquishing the passivity, the misoneism, and the inconsistency of the majority, which willingly welcomed the advantages of the new regime but rejected the sacrifices and duties; by dominating the inevitable discords of the minority, which, accepting both the advantages and sacrifices of the new regime, did not agree on the respective doses. Where could the dynasty find the strength to overcome all these active and passive resistances? Not in itself alone: it was the supreme legitimate government only in Sardinia. The dynasty could not govern and modernize the kingdom without the collaboration of the parliament and the two parties—the Right and the Left—that dominated it. But at the accession of King Humbert the parliament and the two parties represented only a small minority of the upper classes, from which the Catholics were excluded: the small minority that had demanded unity and parliamentary institutions. The electoral body was strictly qualified and very restricted: in certain electoral districts 150 votes were enough to confer the right to represent the nation and its will. The vast majority of the nation was indifferent or hostile, while the two parties that claimed to represent the nation were two brilliant general staffs at the head of a few scattered troops with a wealth of generals who continually quarreled. From 1860 to 1870, so long as it was necessary to fight against Austria, against the pope, against all Europe in order to unify the kingdom, the fictitious parliament, elected by fewer than two hundred thousand voters, had been able to pass for a real parliament, for the instrument of national sovereignty. The contradiction had begun to make itself felt after 1870, in the last years of the reign of Victor Emmanuel II. It became patent under the new king. No, the parliament was not the instrument of the national will, as the university professors taught: it was nothing but a myth.

The two invisible Genii of the City were both powerless; neither the dynasty nor the parliament could alone assume the entire responsibility of the government: the dynasty because it was not legitimate enough outside the kingdom of Sardinia; the parliament because it was not yet a real parliament. I see that clearly today; but I did not see it then; and I demanded parliamentary government along English lines, without realizing that certain conditions essential to authentic parliamentarianism were not yet in existence. The new regime, moreover, had indirectly recognized this by widening the suffrage: in the first great reform of Humbert's reign, two million new voters—the middle classes and a small advance guard from the lower classes—had been added to the meager ranks of the electoral body in the first reign. The sovereign people began to spread out somewhat, even if they did lose something of their intelligence. This was inevitable: it was impossible, without flying in the face of reason, to identify the nation—a nation having thirty million inhabitants —with 200,000 electors; a certain consistency had to be given the constitutional formula of the national will. But now I see the new complication that was caused by this inevitable reform: by giving a certain consistency to the formula of the national will, the problem of knowing what the nation wanted was raised. It was a terrible problem to shift from the small liberal minority that, from 1848 to 1870, had supported the unification policy of the dynasty, to the middle and lower classes! Today I understand all that, having witnessed how this "national will" has manifested itself for the last half century! When Bonaparte invaded her in 1796, Italy still had the medieval spirit of a religious zealot and an eternally credulous pupil. The three primary passions of the Old Regime— religion, authority, the splendors of art and wealth—unified her in the pursuit of a few common aims, that were superior to daily contingencies. Her Catholicism was a little too superstitious, a little too accommodating, and almost overpowering in its excessive crystallization; but at least it still retained the sincerity of a habit. The authorities to which she submitted were all spiritual and temporal powers of the Old Regime: the pope, the prelates, the aristocracies, the monarchies; but she submitted willingly, sometimes even with an almost mystical sincerity, force of tradition making coercion unnecessary, even for the most lukewarm. And with what passion she became intoxicated on the art and luxury that were the sumptuous garments of authority in the Old Regime! The revolutionary invasion had defiled, stolen, broken, and scattered all the hallowed objects of those three passions.

Deprived of its age-old nourishment, the old spirit had rapidly expired, leaving behind it a vacuum, an immense vacuum, a frightful disease from which Italy has suffered since 1815. What efforts have not been made to fill this vacuum with something, to rekindle the fragments of the old spirit, to kindle a new spirit! Into it have been thrown all the mysticisms and all the philosophies of every age and every country, authoritarian and liberal, bourgeois and socialist, religious and atheistic, Catholic and anti-Christian, nationalistic and humanistic, Guelf and Ghibelline, materialistic and idealistic, immanent and transcendent. Everything slid into this immense vacuum and disappeared, swallowed up by nothingness. Only two passions succeeded in illuminating this bottomless vacuum, two elementary passions, easy to kindle but hard to satisfy: wealth and power. Overpopulated, exploited for centuries, possessing meager resources, with no subsoil, Italy, even after 1848, and in the immense prosperity that marked the second half of the nineteenth century, could look forward only to a relatively modest share of wealth. The exalted desires of the country did not take into account that unity had been achieved in a few years with no great difficulty, but that unity did not yet ensure power even if it made it possible. It was necessary to create, assert, and make other states recognize the power of the new kingdom—a complex undertaking that required time and patience. National feeling, however, always wanted to push forward with all haste, was constantly impatient with the inevitable inferiorities of the youthful state, never accepted either the long delays in a necessary period of preparation or the momentary checks. The country was always ready to obey no matter what government that satisfied her aspirations; the terrible thing was that there was always an element of unreality in these aspirations.

For thirty years I lived in this dreadful situation, like the rest of my fellow countrymen without the least suspicion of it. Looking back, I can now see it with all its awful implications, and I have penetrated the secret of King Humbert, which at the time had tormented me because I could not understand it: the secret of why he attempted to govern Italy after Louis Philippe's system, whether he took his inspiration from the July Monarchy or whether circumstances required similar solutions to twin problems. Concealed, like Louis Philippe, behind an apparent inertia, he set himself officially to respect the constitutional freedoms, but actually to exert control from behind the scenes: by amalgamating the two parties, he would create a government strong enough to control the instruments of national sovereignty—that is, the parliament and the electorate—and to prevent them, while appearing to be led by one or the other, from going too far to the right or left. No explanation was given nor could any be given. Theoretically, Italy continued to be governed by English parliamentarianism, as the universities taught us. The system existed by means of a twofold lie— royal inertia and parliamentary pre-eminence: to explain it would have necessitated the revelation of the lie. The system would have collapsed. But Metternich had observed a long time ago that "a lie is a vacuum." Humbert's reign, like that of Louis Philippe, rested over an invisible vacuum that no one was aware of: a novel and frightful situation, which, combined with the king's character, explains the tragedy of his reign. An extremely intelligent person, who knew and served him, said of King Humbert that he "knew men" and that he "knew how to make decisions." For the head of a state that is already something. It seems certain to me that he had understood the difficulties and dangers of the situation into which his father's successes had placed him, which would indicate a certain depth of vision. But it was this depth of vision that harmed him still further, taken in combination with his weaknesses and his character. Melancholy and hesitant, having little confidence in his talents and doubtful of his destiny, hindered by his lack of culture and tormented by his insufficiencies, all his life he was appalled by the difficulties of his task, which he realized more fully than his immediate circle. He had devoted friends, both men and women, but I am under the impression that he never found the friend, man or woman, whom he needed: the farsighted friend who would have understood how justified were his fears and known how to inspire him with the confidence and the courage which he lacked. His friends, in spite of their sincere devotion, were of little use to him because they attributed the king's fears on the dangers of the situation to an overimaginative mentality. Thus he was always alone, discouraged, a prey to an unhappy pessimism; and he never found a man he could rely upon in the political personnel around him, such as Louis Philippe had found, after ten years of more or less happy experiences, in Guizot. King Humbert at first seemed to be more fortunate, for he discovered Signor Depretis at the beginning of his reign. The latter was a shrewd, cunning, clever, skeptical oldster, a leader of the old guard who, knowing his party well, hated it. Signor Depretis had understood and applied the king's policy with cunning and success. But he had died in 1887; and the men to which the king turned after him—Crispi, Rudini, Pelloux—were failures, at least to his point of view. He had discovered Signor Giolitti, who was to become the Guizot of the next reign, but he had quickly become discouraged at the first hardships.

What a price was paid for the astounding good luck that blessed the first reign! The most horrible thing about the whole affair is that all the actors, without exception, were completely unconscious of the tragedy they were acting out. I am the first who has understood and reconstructed it piece by piece, in the far-off solitude of exile, after fifty years of reflection and unhappiness, which finally revealed the key to the history of the nineteenth century. And I am the first to conjure it up, after fifty years, in the hope that it may serve as an atonement. We understood nothing, we who were both victims and executioners in the middle of the tragedy; we were all inexorable. We all demanded from the king what he was unable to give us, and, furious with our deception, we persecuted him pitilessly; we frightened him, bewildered him, pushed him to right and left; by the vehemence of our discontent we multiplied his perplexity and uncertainty; at one and the same time we surrounded and isolated him with our malice; and, finally, with our clamor we drove him to the muzzle of a revolver, which put an end to his misery within half a minute. Peace on thy shade, oh unfortunate sovereign! But was there anything else we could have done but misunderstand and rage? The Philippist policy was justifiable because of the incapacity of parliament and the political ignorance of the people; but it perpetuated the two maladies and made them incurable. The people must learn to govern just as a child must learn to walk: by trying when it does not yet know how, at the risk of falling. The king did not want to leave the instruments of government in the hands of the people and their pretended representatives because they did not know how to make use of them: from his own point of view he was quite right. But we were also right to protest because that way the people would never learn to govern and the government would end up as a permanent deception. "A lie is a vacuum," Metternich had said. As in France in the time of Louis Philippe, the king and the people were shut within a vicious circle; and every effort they made to get out resulted only in drawing the circle tighter. In Italy as in France there was no escape from the situation; which meant that it could only be resolved by a catastrophe. That is the fate of every situation without an escape.

The regicide on July 29 was only the beginning of the catastrophe immanent in every quasi-legitimate government, a catastrophe that for Italy was to stretch out over

half a century. It destroyed the first experiment of Philippism, but only to clear the way for another attempt, a
more determined one. The third king immediately turned
to the Left, and called Signor Zanardelli to the power, the
old party leader whom King Humbert had ignored. Signor
Zanardelli took Signor Giolitti with him, giving him the
Ministry of the Interior. The new reign, therefore, opened
with a Zanardelli-Giolitti ministry. Zanardelli was old;
after having made a number of fine speeches, it was not
long before he left his position to Signor Giolitti and
died. Left victorious on the field of battle, Signor Giolitti
became the Guizot of triumphant Philippism. He began
by giving a free hand to the press of every party and to
social agitation. Strikes were permitted and grew to be a
veritable epidemic; every trade and profession, and even
government employees, were allowed to organize, agitate,
draw up and present their lists of claims. The three small
parties of the extreme Left—radical, republican, and socialist—became the objects of a kind of benevolent friend-
liness on the part of the government. They had only to
ask favors for themselves and for their electors: the government, formerly so suspicious and surly, did everything
possible to satisfy them. The people became the fashion;
in salons and taverns, at the court and in parliament,
everyone was supposed to have confidence in the people, go to them, enlighten them, flatter them; everyone
was agreed that in this lay the secret of welfare. It seemed
that liberty had triumphed for once and for all. As a
matter of fact, two years after Signor Giolitti had become
premier, the opposition had completely disappeared, having been reduced to a very small cluster of deputies from
the extreme Right, among whom Signor Sonnino and
Signor Salandra were the two shepherds practically without a flock, and to a few republican and socialist deputies
who had not followed their parties in the general con-
version to the government. All the remainder—Right,
Left, extreme Left—had become partisans of Giolitti, had

either ceased to carry on an opposition or were merely playing to the gallery, taking great care not to cause the government any serious annoyance. It was a tame opposition, carried on with the consent of the government. With liberty, indulgence, smiles, good grace, compliments, favors, and a policy of satisfying interests, Signor Giolitti had pursued the same end that Signor Crispi and General Pelloux had pursued with martial law, persecutions, the gags and muzzles of reactionism: that of disarming the opposition. The only difference was that mildness and liberty had succeeded where violence and reactionism had failed. As soon as the right of opposition had been recognized, the opposition had renounced the use of it. In two years Signor Giolitti had worked himself into the position of virtual dictator of the state, using a more perfected method than that of Guizot: controlling the parliament through the king and the king through the parliament.

The Chamber consisted of 500 deputies; of the 500 electorates who selected them, there were a hundred with which the government could do nothing because they were controlled either by firmly held personal positions or by one or other of the three small parties from the extreme Left. In the other 400 electorates, the seats were always contested by ambitious individuals or interested groups, without political standing, almost always in competition with the radical, republican, and—most often of all—socialist candidates. In all these electorates the support of the government was the decisive factor of success. By a skillful management of the electorates, with the help of a body of prefects carefully trained for that task, Signor Giolitti had managed to obtain a majority of 350 deputies in the Chamber, on which he could count with absolute assurance, by means of a secret and complex system, about which the deputies spoke to each other only in lowered voices. At that time the dissolution of the Chamber was a royal prerogative. What every deputy, after Signor Giolitti's advent to power, whispered to every other was that the king would give the decree of dissolution to no one but Signor Giolitti and that all general elections would be carried out under his supervision. Where this belief had come from, how it had taken hold of people, would be hard to say; but it had been widespread from the very beginning and subsequent events had only confirmed it. From the accession of Victor Emmanuel III until 1919, every general election was directed by Signor Giolitti. Signor Giolitti could count on the loyalty of 350 deputies because the latter knew that all the elections would be directed by him and that they would be in danger of losing their seats if they revolted between two elections. That was how he controlled the parliament through the king. But the king, seeing that the elections directed by Signor Giolitti produced submissive and pliable parliaments, could only remain confirmed in the idea of giving the decree of dissolution to no one but him. And that was how Signor Giolitti controlled the king through the parliament.

The game was a simple one, and success seemed certain to last forever. But this game, too, like every game, had a weakness: later on we shall see what it was. So there was Signor Giolitti ensconced in power for all time. But Signor Giolitti, who in 1902 was sixty years old, had begun to think about the necessity for conserving his strength. Besides, any interruption to his rule would have broken to some extent the totalitarian excesses of a permanent personal government. He thought up a refinement that M. Guizot had never dreamed of: he ordered a general election and installed his loyal majority; then, a few months later, he found a pretext to resign, handed over his power and his loyal majority to one of his lieutenants, and retired to his estate, Rocca di Cavour. Naturally, after a year, everyone in Rome was sick of the lieutenant and his provisional government and appealed to the chief to return to the capital. Finally a ministerial crisis was fabricated, Signor Giolitti returned to Rome amid ovations, formed a new ministry, and governed until the next general election. He went through this maneuver after the elections of 1904, 1909, and 1913. Little by little his power became consolidated into a real dictatorship, which replaced and wiped out every other power. The throne, the parliament, and the parties no longer had any authority; everything depended upon, everything was determined, put into motion, arrested by Signor Giolitti's will. But he was not a revolutionary dictator like those who swarmed upon the scene after 1917; he was a quasi-legitimate dictator, and he was less afraid than his future revolutionary colleagues. He might be encountered taking a walk all alone during the evening, without a police guard, in the neighborhood of the Via Cavour, where he lived. He was a good-natured, paternal dictator, who allowed himself to be insulted by the press, who, not being afraid, did not feel the need of terrorizing his real or fancied enemies: he preferred to disarm them by smiles or favors. Two circumstances had favored his policy. In 1900 the Age of Gold began, the period with the most marvelous universal abundance. Italy, too, had benefited; the privations of the lean years had been replaced, even for the people and middle classes, by a more ample existence and more abundant gains; for the state an age of treasury surpluses had succeeded the former age of chronic deficits. The state was able to spend more every year without increasing the taxes. Signor Giolitti knew how to take advantage of this condition skillfully and wisely, and to make the general prosperity his accomplice. The abstention of the Catholics from elections was another factor in his favor. At that time the Catholics already possessed a stronger and more wide-spread organization than that of any other party. If they had participated in politics, as they were to do in another twenty years, Signor Giolitti would not have been able to disperse and paralyze their party as easily as he had those of the conservatives, the liberals, the radicals, the republicans, and the socialists. Be that as it may, Signor Giolitti and his benevolent dictatorship had in a few years succeeded in appeasing the lower and middle classes, in rallying to his side the upper classes, and in making the country forget the storms of Humbert's reign. After having handed over the keys of the government to Signor Giolitti and helped him to establish himself in power, the third king had shut himself up in the Quirinal, playing the part of a strictly constitutional king in the English sense. He had yielded to the wishes of Signor Giolitti and his majority, as an English king yields to the wishes of the majority party, pretending to recognize in the premier and his majority the mandataries and executors of the national will, of which a constitutional king is the foremost servant. The professors who had taught me constitutional law at the university had not lied to me! But it was still a fable and a lie; for it was the king and not the people who had put Signor Giolitti at the head of the state and had given him the means to fabricate his faithful majority. The latter was not the mandatary of the national will but the tool of Signor Giolitti.

I understand all that now because I am familiar with "Philippism" and the nature of quasi-legitimate government. Then I understood nothing. I was repelled by that artificial, ambiguous, and, in spite of its universal benevolence, insincere government. But I did not persist in fighting it. I had tried to renew my campaign in the *Secolo* for the formation of a radical party, but Signor Giolitti, instead of wanting a large radical party, was on the point of annihilating the little one already in existence. There was only one outstanding man in this party—Felice Cavallotti. In 1898 he was killed in a duel. The other leaders were old and mediocre men who were weary of opposition; with a few honors and favors, Signor Giolitti was able to buy every one of them. Moreover, I had begun to publish my history of Rome. I resigned from the *Secolo,* and abandoned politics for history and for my second series of travels, which was to lead me, by way of a long sojourn in France, to the two Americas. I must confess that I, too, had begun to accustom myself to this rather weird system of governing, without understanding it. Since the country in general accepted it and, if not overenthusiastic, was not dissatisfied with it, why struggle! But in spite of my attempts to separate myself from her affairs and occupy myself with ancient history, with the evolution of mankind and the destiny of man, I was constantly drawn back to my country. Yes, the country was becoming wealthy and all the classes were benefiting, public spirit was awaking, was becoming conscious of its strength, the government was beginning to relax its harshness and fall into a tolerant liberalism. But the opposition had disappeared. Everyone bowed to the power of Signor Giolitti, everyone obeyed, in accordance with his positive or negative interests, but without conviction or good will, in a frame of mind that was becoming more and more contemptuous or insolent. The prestige of the monarchy, of the government, of the ministers, of parliament, of the administration, of the nobility, of the wealthy classes, and of the Church rapidly declined. Everywhere the lower classes, if they still obeyed, had less and less respect for the upper classes, and no longer respected them for the simple reason that they were the upper classes. The traditional inertia of the people suddenly turned into a spirit of revolt, up till that time unknown in our history, as insolent as it was cautious, a spirit of revolt that knew when to stop, as soon as there was any danger of a reaction, but that held nothing in respect whenever it had no fear of punishment. The most significant manifestation of this spirit of revolt was the swarm of small newspapers or periodicals, in which juvenile groups took advantage of the liberty of the regime to bring chaos into everything, including literature, philosophy, and politics. They ransacked every country in Europe in search of new ideas, or ideas that seemed new to their

rather abridged education. As long as they were extreme,
unusual, paradoxical, revolutionary, subversive of tradition, of morality, of common sense, of every sensible, humane, lawful way of life, they proclaimed it as the latest
conquest of the mind and propagandized it by attacking
everything that up to then had seemed most worthy of
respect: the glories of the past as well as the authorities
of the present and future, beginning with Signor Giolitti.

Among the political groups, the most ·violently revolutionary were the nationalists on the Right, the ultrarevolutionary socialists and the syndicalists on the Left.
On the extreme Right the nationalists attempted to
popularize a mixture of French nationalism and Pan-
Germanism, to convince Italy that she should arm, acquire
colonies, found an empire, find new energy in a bath of
blood. War was the tonic of mankind; Italy should seek
health and vigor in war. The ultrarevolutionary socialists
and the syndicalists attacked everyone and everything—
the king, Signor Giolitti, his government, his finance,
parliament, the army, the banks, industry, landed property
—as a secret conspiracy on the part of the bourgeois forces
to stifle freedom and equality and to enslave, despoil, and
impoverish the masses. They were particularly violent in
attacking the official socialist party and the deputies who
represented it in parliament. They denounced them as
sham socialists in the pay of Signor Giolitti and the
bourgeoisie; they did all they could to arouse a general
and systematic spirit of revolt in the masses and did not
hesitate to provoke riots whenever they could without
danger. One of their idols was Georges Sorel. Signor
Giolitti allowed the young revolutionaries on the Right
and Left to agitate, speak, write, preach war and revolution to their hearts' content; this scurrilous opposition,
crammed with German philosophy and French literature,
and the tiny exclusive and hostile coteries that made it
left him indifferent. He was concerned only with the opposition in parliament and in the electorate. There he

had succeeded in completely disarming it, which he considered the important thing. By giving free rein to this giddy youth, the government secured a reputation for liberalism without running any risk. At any rate Signor Giolitti thought so.

None of these political, philosophical, or æsthetic movements was either profound or sincere. Hastily improvised by youths who had little education, a great deal of ambition, and no experience, even when sincere they could be considered ephemeral and of no great danger. And so they would have been in a society strongly organized and governed by a stable legitimate government. Italy, on the contrary was an atrociously divided country and, what was even more serious, governed by a quasi-legitimate government. But I was not to understand this danger until much later; for the moment what worried me still more was to see this spiritual disorder spreading in the midst of the intellectual and moral deterioration, which is inherent in the quantitative civilizations of the nineteenth century. Everyone was trying to earn money, taking advantage of the general prosperity and of the opportunities that the "Philippist" system offered in Italy, as it had offered in France. Wealth was the great passion that, combined with nationalism, had set the nation on fire after the end of the Old Regime: the time had come in which it could be satisfied with relative ease. There was a precipitous rush. Everyone was in business, including the socialists, after their fashion, with a system of co-operatives that became the matrix of a small Marxist *bourgeoisie*. With the increase of salaries and receipts, comfort and luxury spread through all classes; nearly everyone wanted to earn more and be able to live better and was proud of earning more and being able to live better. At the same time education was spreading; literature, art, even philosophy and science, which up till then had been the privilege of a restricted elite, began to interest a public that was far more numerous, more heterogeneous, and less prepared. But, by becoming general simultaneously, wealth and education deteriorated in a vulgarization and increasing instability of every qualitative standard of value, especially moral and æsthetic standards. A kind of general mediocrity, self-satisfied, vain, convinced that it had nothing more to learn and that it was perfection itself, became the rule. The expression of this mediocrity was public opinion, of which the great papers with huge circulations became the servants and exploiters: an opinion that was fickle, impulsive, superficial, versatile, cautious to the point of meanness with the mighty, with Signor Giolitti for instance, hard and pitiless with the weak, easily mistaken, intractable in its errors and obstinacies, more and more incapable of understanding the greatness, truth, or the real interests of the people.

During my travels to America, I had come across that quantitative lowering of every standard, which has dominated Western history since the first half of the nineteenth century. I could not be very surprised at what was taking place around me, which more or less resembled what was taking place all over the world. But my discovery did not fully satisfy me. Though I was convinced that I was witnessing a new chapter in the eternal struggle between quantity and quality, I suspected the action of other mysterious forces whose nature escaped me. A series of strange events took place which increased my uneasiness. Toward 1908 and 1909 the electorate was still that of Humbert's reign: from two to three million voters, for a country whose population was approaching the forty-million mark. Practically the whole of the peasantry and a considerable part of the workers were excluded from the sovereign nation. Nevertheless, they did not complain about it; as in France between 1840 and 1848, the vast majority bore their exclusion with indifference. Since every party and every power were hostile, the question of suffrage should never have come up. On the contrary, as in France at the time of Louis Philippe, it was not long before it had to be

considered. The socialists had begun to raise it toward
1907 and 1908, not very convincingly, however, and in the
midst of general indifference, in order to give the impression that they were protecting the people's sacred rights.
In 1909 a general election took place. Signor Giolitti had
obtained his customary majority, and a few months later,
at the beginning of 1910, he had resigned in favor of
Signor Luzzatti and retired to Rocca di Cavour for a rest.
Signor Luzzatti, who clung firmly to his reputation as a
man with liberal and daring ideas, thought to please the
socialists by proposing to increase the electorate. The
proposal, which was extremely complex and rather artful
led to a great deal of discussion and resistance. Moreover,
Signor Luzzatti, who had made a good Minister of Finance,
had much less success as premier. At the beginning of 1911
his ministry was overthrown; Signor Giolitti returned as
usual to power, and included universal suffrage in his program. He took over Signor Luzzatti's idea, simplifying it
and making it more coherent. Signor Giolitti was no less
adverse to universal suffrage than Signor Luzzatti and all
the other party leaders, whether Right or Left. From
where, then, came the mysterious impulse that forced them
to do everything which they considered dangerous and
which no one asked them to do? The contradictions and
lies that were inherent in the system in Italy, as they had
been under Louis Philippe. Signor Giolitti's system functioned extremely well, but it gave rise to a obscure and
deep-seated discontent because it was based on a lie. "A
lie is a vacuum," Metternich had said. Senators and deputies were not instruments of the national sovereignty but
extras in a farce, at which everyone willingly laughed up
his sleeve but which ended up by wearying and dissatisfy-
ing everyone. It wearied and dissatisfied even those who
benefited from the regime, so it may be imagined how
those who, rightly or wrongly, complained of being the
victims of it, felt! The opposition was very diminished,
but it still existed, either in parliament or in the nation.

But in Signor Giolitti's system the opposition had no chance at all of ever getting into power, which incensed it. This irritation was muffled but very strong, especially in the extremely conservative circles, in the small opposition parties of which Signor Salandra and Signor Sonnino were the leaders and the *Giornale d'Italia* the organ. These circles openly complained that the king was distorting the operation of the parliamentary system to Signor Giolitti's advantage by making him the sole recipient of the decree for the dissolution of the Chamber. The beneficiaries and victims felt themselves shut up in this false and artificial system, as in a sealed room; and, if the majority were resigned to stay there indefinitely, the more energetic minorities were asking themselves, as the minorities under Louis Philippe had asked themselves, whether there were not some way of renewing the air. Toward 1908 universal suffrage began to appear in Italy, as in France toward 1845, as a means of opening the windows, if not breaking the panes. That was why, if the question failed to arouse the interest of the masses, it interested parliamentary and political circles. The logic of the principle tended, as under Louis Philippe, to favor reform. As we have already seen, when once the people have been acknowledged to be the source of sovereignty, it becomes difficult to stop halfway: logic impels that the people be identified at least with all the men, if not with all the men and women.

That is why Signor Luzzatti, in order to court both the active and latent opposition, had somewhat thoughtlessly launched his proposal for a widening of the suffrage, and why Signor Giolitti, so as not to seem less progressive and advanced than Signor Luzzatti, had put forth the proposal for universal suffrage. It was the spring of 1911. I was in Rome during May, and one Monday morning about eleven I was going down the Corso Vittorio Emanuele in the direction of the Tiber when I encountered an old friend coming in the opposite direction. My friend held a position of trust close to Signor Giolitti, whom he saw nearly every morning. I gathered that he was coming from the Palazzo Braschi, where at that time the Ministry of the Interior was located, and I asked him jokingly what the "old man" had said to him.

"He is furious with the nationalists," my friend replied.

The nationalist party had for some time been conducting a campaign for Italy to seize Tripoli, and it was this campaign that irritated Signor Giolitti. In a few sentences my friend summed up the attitude of the premier on this campaign: the sentences were so clear and lucid that thirty years later they still remain photographed on my mind. I quote them exactly.

"Do the nationalists imagine that Tripoli belongs to an insignificant black kinglet, whom a European state can dispossess at will? But Tripoli is a province of the Ottoman Empire, and the Ottoman Empire is still a great European power. The integrity of what remains of the Ottoman Empire is one of the principles on which the stability and peace of Europe are founded. In order to acquire Tripoli, I would have to make war on the Ottoman Empire, and to make war on a great European power, I would need at least a pretext if not a reason. I cannot justify a war with the Ottoman Empire by telling Europe that the nationalist party covets Tripoli. And furthermore the integrity of the Ottoman Empire is a condition of the stability and peace of Europe. Stability and peace are two structures that are beginning to decay. Is it in Italy's interest to shatter tomorrow one of the cornerstones of the decaying structure? What if, after we have attacked Turkey, the Balkans should rise? And what if a Balkan war should lead to a collision between the two groups of powers and a general European war? Can we take upon ourselves the responsibility of touching off the explosion?"

Signor Giolitti was no ordinary man. "In his own sphere he was at the very top," I was told one day in 1910 by one of the most intelligent of the ambassadors accredited to Rome. After Cavour he was the most gifted statesman of

Italy. He had indisputable qualities of leadership: clarity of thought, co-ordination of intellect, self-control, a certain amount of humanity, and culture. He was not entirely detached from the splendid generation that had produced the Congress of Vienna. The reasoning he had given my friend was worthy of Talleyrand. It proves that he knew Europe and the limits within which the great powers had to confine themselves if they did not want to commit mass suicide. At that period in Italy there were not many people in the high bureaucracy and in the upper classes who would have been able to see the problem with such clarity and precision. In short he was superior to the intellectual level of the ruling classes of his country. And yet this man who in May saw so clearly, so logically, so penetratingly, four months later in September, declared war on the Ottoman Empire "without reason or pretext," and hurled Italy and Europe into an adventure that three years later was to result in a European war. Why? What was the reason for this frightful recantation? Upon learning that France, after coming to an agreement with Germany, was going to take Morocco, a storm of feeling such as had never been seen in Italy, swept the whole country. For the first time since the French Revolution the country was in complete agreement: rich and poor, peasants and workers, literate and illiterate, Catholics and free thinkers, leftist parties and rightist parties, were all agreed upon a single clear, concise, and irresistible thought. There was no *casus belli?* The attack on the Ottoman Empire without cause or pretext was an outrage from the standpoint of international law? The repercussions in Europe might be frightful? Reasoning had no effect: public opinion was oblivious to everything, made no allowances. France was going to take Morocco, Italy should not always be the Cinderella of Europe, Italy should seize Tripoli. To the devil with international law, with the Ottoman Empire, with Europe, with the whole world! A confused but profound feeling—the anguish of an entire people who felt shut up in a land that was too confining and too poor for their numbers and needs—suddenly exploded in a tremendous burst of flame, like a subterranean oil lake roused from quiescence by the descending drill; and the column of fire threatened to set everything about it on fire, even the power of Signor Giolitti. The latent and active oppositions to the Philippist government of Signor Giolitti realized that an extraordinary opportunity lay before them, that if Signor Giolitti did not satisfy their demands, the people's fury would break the powerful hold he had established and still maintained, by snatching from his grasp either the king, or the parliament, or both. The opposition parties did everything they could to inflame public sentiment even further, in the belief that Signor Giolitti would never dare to throw Italy into so dangerous an adventure. Signor Giolitti realized that his system was in danger, and to save it he declared war. He snuffed out the tremendous pillar of fire that was threatening to set Italy and his own power ablaze with the sands of the Lybian desert.

It must be admitted that he waged war like a statesman of the old school: by softening insofar as he could both the collisions between Italy and the Ottoman Empire and the European repercussions of his Mediterranean and African enterprise. Compared with the folly in which all the other African adventures of the kingdom were conducted, the campaign of 1911 was a masterpiece. The great diplomats and warriors of the seventeenth and eighteenth centuries would have appreciated it. D'Annunzio, the Tyrtaeus of the *Corriere della Sera,* directed a stream of rhymed insults at Signor Giolitti—inferior literature in the service of a people gone wild, who wanted an empire without having the slightest idea of what had to be done to build one. But, in spite of all the violent follies for which public opinion was clamoring, Signor Giolitti managed to secure the approval of the law on universal suffrage, to conquer Lybia, and to control the general election of 1913 with an electorate of seven millions. The first experiment in universal suffrage seems uncertain: though the enlarged electorate appeared difficult to handle, though the socialists made fairly important gains, Signor Giolitti once more obtained his usual majority. His system did not appear to have been overthrown. But the moral impact produced by the conquest of Tripoli, the anxiety and alarm that universal suffrage had evoked in the upper classes, a state of excitement that seemed to have seized hold of the masses, even of the peasants in the fields, as a result of all those events, were now added to the subtle, mysterious, indefinable uneasiness that Signor Giolitti's artificial, complex, esoteric system was causing. Everyone felt that serious difficulties lay ahead. That Signor Giolitti was also convinced of this is proved by an idea which came to him and which he put into practice, a wise and patriotic idea which does him honor but which was to end disastrously. After the general election, as usual, he wanted to retire to Rocca di Cavour for a year's rest. But this time, instead of choosing one of his lieutenants to replace him, he came to an agreement with the most outstanding leader of the small rightist opposition, Signor Salandra, who accepted the leadership of the transition government. Thus, there was now a Salandra ministry, which had the consent of Signor Giolitti and the support of the latter's faithful majority. Signor Giolitti was making peace with the constitutional opposition—an act of conciliation that the grant of universal suffrage, the awakening of the masses, and perhaps also the general situation in Europe seemed to demand. This took place at the beginning of 1914. In July the Great War broke out with Signor Salandra as interim premier and Signor Giolitti, the real head of the government, on vacation. He was taking the waters at Vichy.

What then took place in Rome is a mystery. I have an idea that the Rome government was aware of the German plans and was inclined to fulfill the terms of the alliance. If the information I have is correct, military agreements regarding the approaching war were concluded between

Rome, Vienna, and Berlin during the winter of 1913 and spring of 1914. Why did Italy suddenly declare herself neutral at the end of July? All the agreements had been concluded from the standpoint of a war between the *Dreibund* and the Dual Entente—France and Russia. It was calculated that the Italian and Austrian navies, together with a contribution from the German navy, would be able to cope with the French navy in the Mediterranean. As soon as the intervention of England appeared certain, Rome became frightened of a naval war in the Mediterranean against France and England, and declared Italy's neutrality. The government skillfully took advantage of the general opinion, which was against the war; instead of stifling it, as it would have done if it had decided to take part in the war, it encouraged it and was able to declare its neutrality in the midst of general satisfaction. By intervening in 1914, England perhaps saved France from the gravest danger she had yet faced. Without England's intervention, Italy would also have attacked France in August 1914, and it is not impossible that the catastrophe of 1940 would have been anticipated by twenty-six years.

But neutrality put Italy in a difficult position, for reasons that everyone is familiar with. It was not long before the question of intervention was raised. The nationalists, who had conducted the campaign for the conquest of Tripoli with brilliant success and who, in July 1914, had declared that France must be attacked, now began to agitate in favor of a new war, this time against Germany and Austria. But the fire of 1911 had been extinguished by the sands of the Lybian desert; by far the greater part of public opinion would have nothing more to do with war, either with or against Germany and Austria. The king and minister hesitated. To attack the central European empires, allies for thirty-two years, with public opinion as intractably hostile as it was, would be to take a terrible risk. But what would neutral Italy's position be at the end of the war, no matter who came out ahead? The king and his government were between Scylla and Charybdis. With the encouragement of the government a war party was organized in the country. All the oppositions to the Philippist system were at its head, which indicated that the party consisted of extremely varied elements: ultrarevolutionary socialists and syndicalists, Mazzini republicans, sincere radicals and liberals rubbed shoulders with nationalists and conservatives from the extreme right. It was a tower of Babel in which everyone spoke only his own language and did not understand his neighbor's: some wanted war because they hoped that it would restore authority to Europe, others hoped it would bring the benefits of liberty to the peoples, and still others that it would lead to universal social revolution. With great adroitness Signor Salandra let them all do and say what they wanted, with the intention of guiding the opinion and consulting it.

During this period, what were the relations between Signor Giolitti and Signor Salandra, between the real head and the provisional head of the government? No one knows. Signor Giolitti's friends accused Signor Salandra of having deceived Signor Giolitti, of having engaged Italy in a war without the latter's knowledge, in the sole aim of stealing his position. Signor Salandra's friends accused Signor Giolitti of having allowed Signor Salandra to take all the gravest responsibilities, without once compromising himself, in order to put him out when there would be nothing left to do but to gather in the fruits of his predecessor's labors. Probably there is truth in both accusations. In any event, at the beginning of the spring of 1915 the king and his ministry determined on war, in the midst of feverish excitement and the most violent arguments between neutralists and interventionists. In April, Signor Sonnino signed the London Treaty with France, England, and Russia; during the first part of May the actions and speeches of the ministers and their spokesmen removed all further doubt: the decision was about to be taken. The neutralists then turned to Signor Giolitti, who in his villa

Rocca di Cavour was surveying the course of events. Signor Giolitti had not yet definitely announced his stand on the question of peace and war, but it was argued that he would not want an immediate rupture, because of the violently neutralist attitude of a number of friends and well-known spokesmen. Toward the middle of May it was announced that he would go to Rome. Everyone understood what this trip meant: Signor Giolitti was going to Rome to overthrow the Salandra ministry, take over the government, and put off Italy's entry into the war. In due time he arrived in Rome, and during the day two thirds of the deputies went to leave their calling cards on him. It was a way of saying, extraparliamentary if you like, but clear, that Signor Giolitti was the leader of the majority and had the right to govern. Signor Salandra immediately handed in his resignation. Several days went by, during which the king held the prescribed consultations to resolve the crisis. The interventionists took advantage of the delay to organize in Rome, in Milan, in Turin, in every city of importance, violent demonstrations against Signor Giolitti, in favor of Signor Salandra and war. The government secretly encouraged these demonstrations as far as it could. Finally, after several days and in the midst of all this rather artificial agitation, the king made his decision: he refused to accept Signor Salandra's resignation. That was the signal: the king was abandoning Signor Giolitti, rejecting the policy of neutrality, and declaring in favor of war. Feeling that it could no longer count on the king, the majority of the parliament in its turn became frightened and abandoned Signor Giolitti. A few days later Signor Giolitti was obliged almost to flee from Rome, where he was no longer safe, and take refuge in the country. In twenty-four hours, his power, which for ten years had seemed *aere perennius*, had been broken.

No one understood either the fundamental cause nor the historical significance of the event; each person judged it good or bad, according to whether he considered it favorable or unfavorable to his views, his hopes, and his interests. My own personal reaction had been a more sinister one: this strange civil war on the threshold of a titanic war appalled me. But in spite this vague uneasiness I was no more clairvoyant than the others. Only now do I understand that during those May days of 1915 I witnessed one of the most mysterious and terrible events of history: the downfall of a quasi-legitimate government, as abrupt and unforeseeable as that of Louis Philippe had been in 1848, and for the same reason that Metternich had already set forth in these extraordinary lines.

Since the Government of King Louis Philippe has merely the value of factuality, one may as well assign it a day's existence as an indefinite continuance.

It is impossible to base any estimate on such an existence, for it depends on a concatenation of fortuitous circumstances.

Signor Giolitti and his power succumbed to that law. Signor Giolitti was neither Richelieu nor Mazarin, the minister of an absolute king and the instrument of his uncontrollable power. And nor was he the leader of one of the two English parties, whose right to govern is established by the majority that his party has obtained in the elections. His power could be justified neither by monarchic legitimacy nor by democratic legitimacy. Why had his power remained so strong and stable for ten years? Because he had managed to hold a secure intermediate position between king and parliament, in which he had controlled the king through the parliament and the parliament through the king. But that intermediate position was not a principle of law but a *de facto* condition created by a concatenation of circumstances, "fortuitous circumstances," as Metternich put it. In that concatenation of circumstances there was nothing stable, permanent, definitive, organic; brought into being by circumstances and by the skill of one man, it was destroyed by other circumstances, by the errors of the man who had created it, and by the skill of his rivals. And this power crumbled away within twenty-four hours.

And I also understand today what neither the king, nor Signor Salandra, nor I, nor anyone understood at the time: what a frightful catastrophe this sudden collapse of Signor Giolitti's power on the threshold of war really was. Once Signor Giolitti's power had been destroyed, the direction of the state ought to have been taken either by the king or by the parliament. The king was unable to on account of the same weakness that had already paralyzed King Humbert; the monarchy did not possess a national legitimacy strong enough or widely enough recognized to enable him to assume the supreme responsibility of the national policy. But neither did the parliament have either the desire or the strength to take the reins; it did not represent the national will, which anyway did not yet exist, and it was a strange hybrid, belonging to fiction rather than to reality, a demi-parliament. Created by Signor Giolitti, it was actuated only by his will; its creator eliminated, it became a nonentity. In 1915, Signor Giolitti was the only ruling power because he alone could co-ordinate the acts of the Crown with those of the parliament, each of them being insufficient by itself. In his place the Salandra ministry had no solid foundation either in parliament or in the country; it was supported by the war party but this represented, both in parliament and in the country, only a minority divided into several groups with conflicting programs. The appalling result of this catastrophe was that Italy entered the Great War without any government or directing power. The war had to support the government instead of being directed by it. The civil and military administration did what it could; but, being naturally an executive organ, it could not take the place of the government in conducting the major policies of the war. The causes and aims of the latter remained indecisive, confused, and fluctuating, for the country as for the government. Italy fought for more than three years, spilled oceans of her blood, spent her entire fortune without knowing exactly what she was fighting for. That explains the tremendous chaos that broke out in Italy right after the armistice, and the great national and international catastrophe in which the Italian intervention resulted. Among the causes that explain the devastation of Europe today, we must not forget the revolutionary government that was formed in Italy after her intervention in the Great War. The intervention led to revolution because in 1915, on the threshold of the war, the only instrument of government that Italy possessed was destroyed.

I understand all that now, and I see Signor Giolitti's error, the king's error, and also, alas! my own error. Signor Giolitti's error lay in having based his power completely on the king and parliament, neglecting to base it on the nation as well. Instead of destroying the small radical party by corrupting its timid leaders, he should have modernized it, developed it, reorganized it, and given it the strength to play the same role in Italy that the radical party played in Switzerland after 1840 and in France after 1870. He had, after 1900, the authority and the power needed to initiate this great enterprise, and what a service he would have rendered his country and himself if he had succeeded! Instead of miring Italy in the dangerous quicksands of quasi legitimacy, he would have started her on the road to the firm order provided by a legitimate democratic government. And in May 1915 he would have been able to face the storm, retain the dual support of Crown and parliament, and prevent their defection, if he had had a powerful party behind him in the country. Let that terrible experience serve as a warning to those who some day will give Italy a regular government that will allow her to live. Without a strongly organized radical party in the middle classes, conscious of its role and determined to play it, Italy will never have a legitimate government, that is, one as exempt from fear as a government can be.

The king's error lay in not having understood that he could only engage Italy in a war with the concurrence of Signor Giolitti and with the latter in power. If in 1915, Signor Giolitti was the only man who could have governed the state with a minimum of intelligence and coherence, if the political factory could produce no one else, it was also in part the work of the king, the result of his policy. Whatever the inconveniences of the situation, certainly the least favorable time to attempt to alter it and create a new government was when Italy was about to engage in the most terrible of all wars. It is not at all certain that Signor Giolitti would have directed the war better than Signor Salandra or Signor Orlando, and there is a strong possibility that he, too, would have been overwhelmed, bewildered, and paralyzed by the enormity of the undertaking. But it cannot be doubted that the chances of a satisfactory outcome were greater for him than for any of the others because he had the strongest position in the state. Because this state of affairs was not taken into consideration, a really extraordinary situation resulted: Italy was governed by a single power as long as peace lasted, that is, as long as rivalries would not have been dangerous, or would even have offered advantages; but she was governed by rival groups as soon as she engaged in war, from the moment that unity of command became obligatory. What a frightful contradiction! Signor Giolitti's power broken, every attempt to reconstitute a new power, which might at least have the advantages of quasi legitimacy, met with failure. At the end of the war, anarchy broke out all over the country; Signor Giolitti himself, recalled in 1920, was no longer capable of repairing the instrument that had been broken in his hands in 1915. When in 1922 the king, in despair, decided to entrust the government to fascism, he still hoped to re-establish the pseudoparliamentarian and quasi-legitimate system of Signor Giolitti by rejuvenating it and decorating it with the trophies of war. Signor Mussolini's aspirations did not go any further than that. But fascism had only come into power, which enabled it in 1922 to intrigue for the succession to Signor Giolitti, by committing a number of more or less serious violations of the law. The final act by which it seized the government, the pretended march on Rome, was but a final violation of the law, of little danger to the authors. Having seized the government by a violation of the law, Signor Mussolini experienced what Bonaparte experienced in 1800 and what every usurper experiences: he was overcome by fear and was unable to form even a quasi-legitimate government; he was obliged to form a revolutionary government. As the head of a revolutionary government he was fated from the very start to end in catastrophe, together with his country and the rest of Europe.

And finally my own error. It was a twofold one. I made my first mistake in 1914, when the whole world revolted against Germany, who had violated Belgium's neutrality. I thought that this noble explosion of anger was the beginning of a new era, one that would be more just, freer, more averse to abuses of force. On the contrary—I understood this later—it was only the last convulsion in the death pangs of a great era that had been born in Vienna in 1815, and of which Talleyrand, Louis XVIII, and Alexander I had been the parents. That first mistake engendered a second. In 1915, when the question of intervention or neutrality was raised, I was for intervention. I had never favored the *Dreibund,* and I considered the monarchic regime that governed Austria and Germany according to Louis XVIII's system, inapplicable to Italy. Coming from the middle classes, grown up in a liberal milieu, without being a republican, I desired my country to have a regime similar to that which governed Switzerland, France, and England. Believing that a more equitable and freer era had begun with the general reaction to the invasion of Belgium, I was sincerely convinced that the victory of France and England would regenerate the whole of Europe. If I had imagined that victorious Italy,

France, and England would not be capable of doing anything to reconstruct the European order on the principle of liberty, and that the quasi-legitimate government of Signor Giolitti, instead of being replaced by a legitimate government, would be replaced by a revolutionary government, modeled on that of the 18 Brumaire, I would never have advised my country to take part in the Great War.

But, since I had been wrong, I did not want to escape from the responsibilities of my error. I had promised my country that the price of the war would be liberty, and at least I did not want it said that my promise had been made lightly and without seriousness. With all my strength I opposed the revolutionary government that discredited the war in my eyes and transformed it into a hideous joke. The revolutionary government in turn did a great deal of harm to me, to my family, and to my sons. But at least it did me one service, which I acknowledge in all sincerity: it showed me what revolution is. Before 1919 I had had no idea, in spite of all the books on the French Revolution that I had read. When, in 1930, I was obliged to take the path of exile, I had discovered the fundamental meaning of that word, "revolution," which our age had so abused, and I carried away with me the key to the gigantic revolutionary hoax of which the Western world has been the victim for 150 years. It is that key which for the last ten years has enabled me to understand. I am only a writer and a professor without power, but I have one advantage over all the mighty ones of the earth—both usurpers and legitimate rulers—who, often with enormous powers, have been ruling for ten years and are ruling today: they have been accomplishing and are accomplishing the destruction of the world, without knowing what they were and are about, whereas I do understand. I know why they are destroying the world in the belief that they are ruling it.

XVI

GOVERNMENT

(Past, Present, and Future)

━━━━━━━━━━━━━━❖❖❖❖━━━━━━━━━━━━━━

Principles of legitimacy are not to be found in philosophy, in religion, in history, in law, or in any of the intellectual culture of the West. I have already told how it was not until I was forty-seven that I even suspected their existence, although they never ceased either helping me or tormenting me. My ignorance, moreover, was only a drop in the sea of universal ignorance. The seven pages from Talleyrand's *Mémoires*, to which I alluded at the start of this book, are as far as I know, with a few *pensées* taken from Pascal, the entire literature on legitimacy in the West. Men have never written about principles of legitimacy because they have always been unaware of their existence. Their actions, their vital cycles, their struggles, which nevertheless decide the fate of men, as we have seen, are invisible, esoteric, mysterious. They are hidden in the depths of history.

"Might not legitimacy be a forbidden subject, one of those deep mysteries that men are not permitted to touch? Had I any right to meddle with it?" I often asked myself these questions while writing this book, which for the

277

first time propounds the problem of the legitimacy of government. But I finally convinced myself that the ignorance of so many generations was not desired and had another explanation. Ancient civilization—both Mediterranean and Asiatic—hardly knew really legitimate government, save for one exception—Rome. The Roman republic, during its great period and for at least five centuries, was a completely legitimate government; the authority of the senate and the comitia was understood and admitted without discussion by all the citizens, the constituents of the city. This legitimacy of the government was probably the secret behind the strength of the Roman republic in its innumerable conflicts, a secret that was all the more effective in that it was the rarest of exceptions. Perhaps China, too, at certain periods created and acknowledged principles of legitimacy, but her case is less clear, at least to me. Every other government in the history of antiquity was either completely illegitimate or barely prelegitimate and quasi-legitimate, in forms that were still very confused and precarious. This fact easily explains why the philosophy, religion, and law of antiquity have nothing to say about legitimacy. It was impossible to know and to theorize about something that did not exist or existed only in vague and summary prefigurations.

Legitimacy of government became a historic reality only in the West and in the bosom of Christianity. Beginning in the sixteenth century, Europe produced monarchies and aristocracies that are truly legitimate governments, that is, they were actively or passively, but sincerely, recognized by the people who had to obey them. This explains why during the last few centuries of Western history mankind has begun to breathe a little more freely, to despair of life not quite so completely, to make dreams for the future. We have seen that instruments of force inspire fear both in those who submit to them and in those who make use of them. We have seen that the fear of government rises to a frenzy, through the reciprocal effect and countereffect on government and subjects; that it engenders hatred and the spirit of revolt; that, terrified by the ever-present danger of a general revolt, the government attempts still further to terrorize its subjects. But, if the fear of the latter increases, hatred and the spirit of revolt are also increased; on the other hand, the more fear the government inspires, the more fearful it becomes; the more fearful it is, the more it needs to inspire fear.

This inevitable sequence may lead to unimaginable horrors. Among all the evils from which mankind has suffered, this reciprocal fear on the part of a government and its subjects has been the most terrible. As we have seen, principles of legitimacy are merely an attempt by the mind to free mankind from this frightful torment. But in that case how are we to explain the fact that so many great civilizations were not conscious of them? Were they resigned to their misfortunes? No, they sought to free themselves by other means—by ultramystical philosophies and religions, for instance. The longer I reflect upon man and the nature of man the more evident it seems to me that in every age mysticism has been the chief desperate protection against the fear of death and the fears of life, among which the reciprocal fear of government and its subjects is the most oppressive. The great Hindu philosophy and Buddhism, in which it culminated and which popularized it, are striking examples of this. The fundamental tenet of this philosophy and of the religion it engendered is a veritable challenge to common sense: the physical world has no real existence; time and space, life and death are only present in the mind. The sorrows of life are born of that illusion of the mind, which binds us to things which are perishable, because unreal, and the loss of which, inevitable because of their nonreality, afflicts us, even though it be only imaginary. There is only one method to put an end to the incurable sorrows of life: to free ourselves of the illusion; tear away the veil of maya, which deceives us by making us believe in the existence of particular objects, which disappoint us; lose ourselves in the changeless unity of the Absolute, which is the sole reality, the supreme peace, the ultimate haven of unalterable calm. By freeing ourselves from the illusion, we free ourselves forever from sorrow and death.

By far the greater part of mankind has nearly always believed in the reality of the world it lives in, even that part which has never read the first chapters of Genesis, in which God creates first the world, then man, and places him in the world, in his kingdom as it were. How is one to explain the fact that a philosophy so contrary to common sense and the instinct of life was able, through Buddhism, to convince part of mankind? I can see only one adequate reason for this tremendous reversal of thought: the insupportable and irremediable atrocities of government, aggravated by fear. Even government, with the fears it caused and the horrible cruelties that its own fear led it to commit, disappeared with the world and was reabsorbed by the supreme peace of the Absolute; when there was no other remedy or defense, the annihilation of the universe through thought might console mankind to some extent and render life less intolerable. I believe, too, that one must see in the mystic tendencies of Christianity, which at certain periods in history have become so powerful, a reaction against the horrors of ancient government, also driven only too often by fear to acts of folly. But the West has never done more than to sample this solution, has never gone into it very deeply. Until the seventeenth century it was too firmly attached to common sense not to believe in the real existence of the world; it considered space and time as the supreme realities and, being unable to reduce everything to nothingness, discovered a solution to the problem that was more practical, more human, less radical than the theoretical annihilation of the world, but at the same time more difficult—that of principles of legitimacy. It has been emphasized that legitimacy consists of a tacit and implied agreement between government and its subjects upon certain rules and principles that determine the conferment and limits of its power. Now obviously, if a reasonable agreement can be reached on this point—conferment and limitations—an agreement that will satisfy both the government and its subjects, the former will be freed from the fear of ever-present revolt in the enforced obedience of its subjects, and will no longer be obliged to maltreat them. Since they are being treated better, the subjects will no longer be afraid or distrustful of the government; life will become easier for everyone.

Thus, it has only been during the last few centuries that a part of mankind—the West—has enjoyed a period of legitimate government: a tremendous novelty, a tremendous conquest, and a tremendous progress. But it entered upon this period hesitantly, almost without wanting to know the fundamental nature of the new solution it strove to give to the most terrible problem of life—the fear of the ruling power; without ever daring to ask itself what these principles of legitimacy were, upon which it was now basing the small measure of happiness that man is capable of achieving in life. Why this attitude? There we have one of the deepest mysteries in the history of mankind. The first principle of legitimacy that the West created, and the only one it recognized until the American Revolution and the French Revolution, was the hereditary, aristocratic, and monarchic principle. But we have already brought out the fact that the hereditary principle, like all principles of legitimacy, has nothing of the transcendent, that it is empirical, limited, only partially rational and just, and therefore extremely fragile. Reason may easily demolish it, by showing that it is absurd and iniquitous. Consequently, during the first part of the period of legitimacy—the aristocratic and monarchic period, which lasted several centuries—the West must have recognized that it was establishing world order on such insecure foundations.

Is it surprising, therefore, that it did not dare to admit it? That it attempted to conceal the empiric nature of the first principle of legitimacy it had created by making it into an absolute and surrounding it with a sanctity that approached divinity? It was due to this that a great many generations in Europe obeyed the nobles, kings, and emperors with almost the same reverence that made them bow down to the pope and to God, without suspecting or wishing to admit that the principle of heredity was a fragile hypothesis, a problematical chance for stability and justice: it might or might not be realized; there was no absolute certainty.

Obviously, in order that this almost mystical state of exaltation might be perpetuated, it was better to believe in the first principle of legitimacy that the West had blindly created, as being unique and absolute, than to examine it to discover its origin and nature. To discuss principles of legitimacy might at that time have seemed a dangerous philosophical pastime. But this attempt to conceal the empirical nature of the hereditary principle could not succeed in the long run because it was counter to the fundamental nature of legitimacy. Little by little the peoples of the West came to perceive that heredity was only an empirical and conventional principle, so an antagonistic principle was born, grew in strength, and finally, with the help of historical accidents, unleashed a terrible struggle. At first the shock, instead of revealing the empirical, precarious, and limited nature of all principles of legitimacy, had the opposite effect of obscuring it still further. Each side believed in its own principle as a divine absolute; and they massacred each other pitilessly without knowing what they were doing. In the fury of the conflict, it was impossible to understand that two principles of legitimacy, equally reasonable and just or unreasonable and unjust, could exist and why they could. Each party looked upon the other principle as an evil, a lie, the work of the devil, which had to be annihilated. But in the struggle the two principles almost everywhere became paralyzed; save for a few rare exceptions, neither one nor the other was any longer capable of ensuring order in the world and of guaranteeing men against the evil of fear; almost everywhere men ended up by no longer believing in either of them, and by losing any notion of the conditions that are necessary before a monarchy and a democracy can become legitimate. Once this notion was lost, the very existence of principles of legitimacy, their nature and their role, became unintelligible, and the intellectual comprehension of the problem of legitimacy as impossible as its practical solution. That is the situation today, after many wars and revolutions, which the entire West is in, with the exception of a few privileged nations—Switzerland, England, and the United States, to cite only the most eminent examples. An extremely dangerous situation which has everywhere led to the formation of revolutionary governments and to the second great panic in Western history: more terrible than the first because it possesses methods of extermination that the first did not have. Because of the endless wars it has unleashed, if it is not promptly rendered powerless, this second great panic threatens to destroy the treasures of Western civilization and the very existence of all mankind. But what other course of treatment can one hope for to cure this disease than to make an appeal to intelligence, since instinct is no longer sufficient? If not all mankind, at any rate its elite is now facing a decisive turning point: it has become too well informed, too sure of itself, too skeptical to believe in a principle of legitimacy as a religious absolute, without wanting to know why. It wants to reason everything out, even principles of legitimacy. Therefore it must not remain content to reason only to the point where every principle of legitimacy appears absurd and unjust; it must go beyond that to the very bottom of the problem; it must discover the nature and the task of principles of legitimacy, so that from them it may deduce rules for a rational ethics of authority that will transform the former mystical veneration of government into a widespread knowledge and sentiment of respective duties: those of the government toward its subjects and those of the subjects toward the government. There is no other solution. The problem of government today looms before the West like an enormous and precipitous mountain, full of crevasses, glaciers, and avalanches, barring the path to all mankind. This Mt. Everest of history must be ascended if some day we are to descend into the fertile plains of the future: a dangerous ascent, which must be undertaken without a guide, for man has not yet risked its perils. But at least the mountain is marked off into successive levels, which the mind can successfully traverse and which form a gigantic stairway leading without fear of error to the summit. The broadest of these levels to be crossed number seven. As a conclusion to my work I am going to try to make the ascent of the mountain, by means of these successive levels, to the very summit, from which mankind will finally be able to see into the future. I will thus have occasion to return to, summarize, and underline the most important ideas that were developed during the course of the book.

First Level

"Liberalism is childishness, revolution a force," said Bismarck. Bismarck, the greatest statesman of the West in the second half of the nineteenth century! And yet what did he know of the fundamental realities of his age? Nothing: the above aphorism proves it. He, too, like all the others, and more than the others, for he had more initiative, played with fire in order to attain a few immediate results, without realizing what he did. Liberalism, that alleged childishness, was, for the majority of Western governments, nothing less than the condition of their legitimacy, that is, their *raison d'être*. Revolution, that alleged force, was nothing but a gigantic hoax.

Revolution, revolution: the word is constantly on our lips. But it is not certain that we know the real meaning of it. What do we mean when we say that Christianity, that the Renaissance, that the industrial revolution in the nineteenth century were great "revolutions"? We mean that Christianity, the Renaissance, the industrial revolution fundamentally altered the ideas, feelings, customs, institutions, and artistic tastes of a part of mankind; that they gave the human mind a different orientation in religion, ethics, philosophy, science, politics, and practical affairs. To confine ourselves to Christianity, in place of the unrestrained polytheism of the Mediterranean peoples, it substituted Semitic monotheism; in place of the belief in the divine superiority of dynasties and aristocracies, it substituted the doctrine of the moral equality of all men, sons of God by the same claim. The orientation of thought having changed on these two points, a complete reorganization of institutions and manners became necessary.

But we also say that in 1848 nearly all Europe broke out in revolution. What do we mean by "revolution" in this case? The revolt of the governed against the government: the republic in Paris, the Parliament in Frankfurt, the Austrian emperor in flight, Italy, Hungary, Croatia at war with the crown of the Hapsburgs.

"Revolution" is thus a word with a twofold meaning. Sometimes we mean by revolution a new orientation of human thought, sometimes the total or partial destruction of a pre-existing legal system, the more or less complete subversion of the laws that establish the right to govern and the duty to obey, beginning with the principle of legitimacy that justifies the government.

Now it seems perfectly obvious that new orientations and destructions of legal systems are historical events which are vastly different in spite of the common term. New orientations, which mark the great stages in the history of mankind, always have a remote and obscure origin, have profound meanings, manifest and impose themselves gradually. Sometimes centuries elapse before they triumph. Violence, which shatters will and smothers intelligence, has only a secondary role in their progress; the leading role devolves upon suggestion, which persuades, seduces, and carries away thought, reason, and emotion. Destructions of legal systems are always in the form of superficial tempests, violent but short; a few months, a few weeks, sometimes even a few days are enough to overthrow the most ancient and firmly established legal systems. In six weeks, from July 14 to the end of August, the Old Regime in France disintegrated. Here violence plays the principal role: the "revolution" that overthrows a legal system is essentially an act of violence that is more or less dangerous and difficult.

The causes and effects are also vastly different. The causes of the great new orientations of mankind are so complex and obscure that they are only accessible to the mind in fragments. On the other hand, every destruction of a legal system has the same cause as every other, and this can appear in different shapes but is always easy to understand: the weakening and decay of the ruling powers. Like the causes, the consequences of a new orientation are innumerable and comprehensible only in fragments. Who would delude himself into thinking that he could enumerate all the effects of the Christianization of Europe? On the other hand, the revolutions that have destroyed legal systems have always had one never-failing effect: they have all given rise to an access of fear. That is an almost astronomically perfect law: as soon as the legal system of a society is destroyed, even if the destruction is justified by the vices and weaknesses of the system, panic sweeps over everyone. The first to be affected are the destroyers; the panic originates in them and from them spreads to all.

There is nothing in common, then, between these two phenomena except for the term: a case of homonymy, which is merely imperfection of language. And yet for a century and a half the West has tended more and more to

confound the two revolutions. The French Revolution
began to confuse them both in thought and in action.
When the States-General assembled on May 5, 1789, at
Versailles, what did they intend to do? Their plan was to
give a new orientation to the history of France. They did
not want to destroy the Old Regime from top to bottom
but to reform it. They did not want to overthrow the monarchy but to complete it by giving it a legislative assembly
created by a popular franchise. They did not want to proclaim a republic but to make an end of the sale of offices
and the exploitation of public trusts. They wanted to remove a decayed, unbalanced, hidebound government that
had become incapable of governing France and substitute
a younger, more adaptable, more intelligent, more just,
and more efficacious government. They were in the right;
what they demanded was reasonable. France was direly in
need of a great reform; in particular she could no longer
allow the entire legislative and executive power to remain
in the hands of a six-man council chosen by the king, completely out of touch with the nation and having no responsibility.

But an enormous and mysterious historical accident, the
meaning of which has to this day escaped the knowledge
of mankind, made this grandiose attempt to provide a new
orientation coincide with the revolutionary apocalypse set
in motion by the storming of the Bastille. It was the other
revolution, the overthrow of a legal system, that began less
than three months after the convocation of the States-
General. The great mistake of historians has been to attribute the complete collapse of the monarchic system,
which followed the successful uprising of July 14, to the
efforts made by France to reform the Old Regime, the
decisive event of which had been the convocation of the
States-General. Like the attempts at reformation, the collapse of the monarchy is an effect of the decay and crystallization of the Old Regime, the violent explosion of the
disease which had been lurking in the monarchy for two

centuries and for which the new orientation, according to the program revealed in the *cahiers*, had a mild remedy. But after the collapse the French Revolution became a twofold revolution. It was at the same time one of the boldest attempts ever made to impart a new orientation to government and society, and one of the most gigantic, rapid, and violent destructions of a legal system. The two revolutions intermingled, merged, fought each other, disfigured each other to the point of becoming unrecognizable and in the end the great panic, caused by the complete destruction of the legal system of the Old Regime, smothered the new orientation and made the projected liberation of mankind lead to the creation of a revolutionary state—the most terrible of all despotisms.

A maelstrom of disorders, of fears, of tyrannies, of wars that made torrents of blood flow all over Europe for a quarter of a century: that was the consequence of this encounter in France, in 1789, between the two phenomena which we classify under the name of revolution. It would be unjust to place the blame for this terrible coincidence on France. It was a tremendous accident of history that no one desired or foresaw. France was the victim that suffered most: all the calamities she has endured for a century and a quarter, including the catastrophe of 1940, have been the result of that coincidence. The common responsibility of France and Europe is another one; it is to have drawn from that tremendous disaster, not the lesson that should have been drawn, but two epic legends: the Jacobin legend, dear to the leftist parties, and the Napoleonic legend, which, first created by the leftist parties, was later confiscated to their advantage by the rightist parties. The two legends completely distorted the meaning of the tremendous event by confounding the two revolutions instead of distinguishing between them, as should have been done in order to keep the Western mind balanced and clear-sighted. From generation to generation ever-increasing flocks of historians, philosophers, poets, and novelists

have been at work, and they have succeeded in spreading
that confusion to every corner of the earth and to every
layer of society. What does it consist in? It consists in the
belief that it is sufficient to destroy a legal system for a
new orientation of government and society, more intelligent, freer, and more just, to be accomplished; for a
people to be regenerated and liberated from all the evils
that have tormented them. By refusing to give an exact
definition to the word "revolution," by constantly equivo-
cating about its dual meaning, people ended up by attributing to the destructions of legal systems the profound
and definitive ameliorations in the lot of man, which only
the new orientations are capable of accomplishing. It is
not very difficult to discover why this error gained so
many followers. The destruction of a legal system is swift:
a few weeks, sometimes a few days suffice, if circumstances
are favorable. A new orientation always requires a great
deal of time and efforts that are slow and painful. If the
overthrow of a legal system were sufficient to free humanity from the misery that never ceases to afflict it, the
most intricate problems of life would be very agreeably
simplified.

For a century now this illusion has seized upon the
Western mind and dominates it in every class, party, institution, and school. The French Academy, the great general staffs of Europe, the Vatican are as contaminated as
the Sorbonne, the General Confederation of Labor, and
the Second, Third, and nth Internationals. For twenty-five
years we have seen revolutions in favor of taverns, caba-
rets, and *bistrots;* and also revolutions in favor of salons
and Palace Hotels. And yet there was no difference between these two kinds of revolution: they both consisted
in the rupture of a pre-existing legal system. They had not
all completely destroyed it, the German and Italian revolutions in part. But the difference was one of quantity not
quality: if one of these revolutions was good or bad, all
the others had to be the same. Why did American million-

aires, French academicians, and high Vatican prelates become enthusiastic about certain revolutions execrated by
the workers and vice versa? Because each of them hoped
that the destruction of the legal system would mean the
immediate relief of certain evils of which, rightly or
wrongly, they complained. But the majority of the forty
immortals, Wall Street, and the Vatican were not any
more clear-sighted or better inspired than the communist
workers and peasants of Europe and America. For a quarter of a century, rich and poor, wise and ignorant, admired, financed, encouraged, prayed for, prepared, and
accomplished, under the name of revolution, greater or
lesser destructions of the existing legal system. They all
hoped that the world would be transformed in part or
completely by these "revolutions." Instead, they managed
to provoke the second great panic of history, the only
immediate, crushing, and inevitable effect of every destruction of a legal system being universal panic. But,
whereas the first great panic of Western history, the one
that Europe suffered from 1789 to 1815, was the result of
a tremendous accident that no one had either wanted or
foreseen, the second was created on purpose by the folly
of man, who thought he could remake the world with the
help of a magic wand that he had just discovered.

Such is the profound significance of the drama that the
world has witnessed for the last quarter of a century. In a
hundred and fifty years Western civilization has completely lost any notion of law. Today the great problem
before the world is to recover it. By what means? To what
extent?

The Second Level

The revolutionary thaumaturgy now in fashion popularized the idea that it is easy to change existing principles
of legitimacy and to invent new ones. But that is only one
of the numerous illusions of our age. Not only are principles of legitimacy not numerous but no age has ever had

the opportunity to choose between them. Every age has only one principle of legitimacy, which it finds already established or in the process of formation; and it can choose only between this principle and a government that is either revolutionary or quasi-legitimate, that is, a reign of fear or the permanent danger of an unforeseeable catastrophe. There is an apparent choice for those periods that are being torn by the struggle between the two principles, such as the nineteenth century, but in reality it is more the choice of the battlefield or trench to defend it than the choice of the principle itself.

The following question is now raised: which is the principle of legitimacy from which our age cannot escape? The reply is not difficult: the delegation of the power by the people. The hereditary principle, which legitimized the aristocracies and monarchies of the past, required a social organization, a distribution of wealth, a mental orientation that no longer exist and have not existed for a long time. But a principle of legitimacy cannot be a myth; it is efficacious only if it is an effective and efficient reality. In our study of legitimate democracy we saw that the conditions for the effective and efficacious reality of the principle of delegation by the people or the sovereignty of the nation, may be summed up in a diptych: right of opposition and freedom of suffrage. Right of opposition and freedom of suffrage are the two central pillars of Western order.

But here a first and terrible difficulty arises: how to co-ordinate the right of opposition and the freedom of suffrage with universal suffrage. We have seen that universal suffrage is the logical outcome of the sovereignty of the nation or of the people. Once the principle has been accepted that the government is legitimate only when it represents the will of the nation or the people, the nation or the people must be defined, and this definition cannot stop at half measures. Logic obliges us to identify the nation or the people with the sum of the men and women who have reached the age of reason. In other words, universal suffrage. But we have also seen that the abhorrence of the upper classes for universal suffrage is one of the keys to the history of the Western world for the last hundred and fifty years. The French Revolution was the first to be frightened by it. The revolution of '48 was obliged to grant universal suffrage to France but it did not have a long life. Attacked by the right, which feared its revolutionary tendencies, and by the left, which considered it too conservative, universal suffrage survived in chains, losing its freedom and deprived of its complementary organ —right of opposition. Legitimate democracy having become impossible, the republic fell and was replaced by the revolutionary government of Napoleon III. It was not until the Third Republic that universal suffrage recovered its freedom and joined forces with the right of opposition; in other words, it was not until then that the conditions for a legitimate democracy existed in France. Switzerland had already provided the first example in Europe of a legitimate democracy. Switzerland since 1848, France since 1870 are the two European countries who first applied the formula of democratic legitimacy in its entirety, even to universal suffrage. After 1900 the question of widening the franchise, up till then more or less restricted, began to make itself felt to some extent all over Europe; but it was after 1919, at the end of the First World War, that universal male or male and female suffrage became widespread in Europe. It is above all free and is accompanied by the right of opposition; the essential conditions for a legitimate democracy seem to have been everywhere realized. But the old abhorrence of the upper classes for universal suffrage revived and everywhere, in Italy, Germany, and Spain, resulted in the same upheaval that it had caused in France after 1848. All the revolutions that have taken place in Europe since 1919 have, like the Second Empire, resulted in the fettering of universal suffrage and the suppression of the right of opposition, that is, in the destruction of the democratic legitimacy. The result: revolutionary governments and the reign of fear everywhere.

The strangest thing about this is that universal suffrage, so hated by the upper classes in Europe, is perhaps the last conservative force still in existence. I have told how conservative universal suffrage showed itself in France in the three great elections of 1848 and 1849, which were the first free expressions of the sovereignty of the people in Europe. Universal suffrage has not changed in any respect in the twentieth century. During the ten years that I collaborated on the *Illustration*—they were the first ten years of the great experiment in free universal suffrage in Europe—I did my best to convince my readers that the masses are always passive and stagnant, that it is impossible to convert to an extreme idea millions of men and women whose education, temperament, profession, and orientation are different. Extreme ideas are always the property of small, selected, homogeneous minorities, according to the community of interests, passions, or enthusiasms. Where a free universal suffrage exists, it is extremely difficult for a revolutionary party to seize the power, or to keep it if by some chance it succeeds in getting possession of it.

The explanation of this paradox lies perhaps in the fact that the upper classes in Europe have been and are so opposed to universal suffrage, especially because of their repugnance for the idea of equality. The aristocratic tradition in Europe is still very strong; as the institutions have been destroyed, it survives in instinct, in sentiment, in the orientation of thought. Contact with the masses in a great political act such as the delegation of power is repugnant to the upper classes at the same time that it alarms them as a threat to their age-old political predominance. Nevertheless there is a simple and decisive justification for universal suffrage that should suffice to eliminate this opposition. The Belgian king, Albert, once formulated it in my presence, with vehement candor, in answer, I believe, to the murmuring of the salons, who were disconcerted by the fact that, when he had been restored to his kingdom at the end of the war, he had approved a law giving universal suffrage to the Belgian people. "People are saying that it is absurd to recognize the same right to vote in a university professor, a great banker, or an industrialist, and in a bricklayer, a blacksmith, or a peasant. They forget that the bricklayer, the blacksmith, and the peasant have no other means of acting upon the state than by their vote. They are nothing but a passive mob, talliable and liable to forced labor, if it is taken from them. The industrialist, the banker, and the professor possess many other more direct and efficacious means of acting upon the state."

However that may be, it is obvious that universal suffrage is one of the great problems with which mankind is struggling at this point in its history. The fault of universal suffrage is not in being revolutionary but in being passive, slow to stir, of an intelligence that diminishes with the increase in the mass. In order that the participation of the masses in the formation of government be a reality, a way must be found to arouse their interest, at least in certain great problems involving the direction and orientation of the state—which is neither easy nor exempt from danger. Moreover, the heterogeneous state of the masses, especially in Europe, almost necessitates the multiplication of parties, which might become a serious complication for the plan. But it is exactly while we are confronting these difficulties that we must recall that a civilization does not have the choice of a principle of legitimacy; that the latter is always imposed by a historical evolution that lies beyond the scope of each generation's efforts and that it must accept with all its advantages and disadvantages: *Hic Rhodus, hic salta.* In the great period of the monarchy and aristocracy, there were other difficulties to be met: the whims of heredity, the impossibility of allowing the coexistence of authority and criticism, especially true in the monarchies. Today it is the masses who are the chief difficulty, simply because a free universal suffrage is a necessary condition for a legitimate government.

The Third Level

Authority comes from above: that we are agreed upon. This is one of man's necessities, expressed by a historical constant—authority comes from above, in democracies as in monarchies. But in monarchies as in democracies legitimacy comes from below. The government only becomes legitimate and is freed from fear by the active or passive, but sincere, consent of the governed. We must never forget this inverse dual movement of authority and legitimacy. It explains why democracy cannot be legitimized without an internal spiritual unity, if all the people are not in agreement both on the principle of legitimacy and on the great moral and religious principles of life. If that unity does not exist, the right of opposition becomes the battle ground for a struggle to the death. Political parties, instead of tilting at each other in tournaments of chivalry, seek to destroy each other. The competition between majority and minority will no longer be possible; at the first opportunity one of the conflicting parties will possess itself of the power by violence and will annihilate its adversary. There will be revolutionary government.

A terrible problem for Europe. It appears in two shapes: Christianity and socialism. One part of Europe still believe in God and in Jesus, while one party no longer does. If government and opposition try to find weapons for their contests in the arsenal of theological disputes, the tournaments of democracy might some day become the scene of a throat-cutting contest between two fanatics. In the Protestant countries the Church has agreed to hold apart from the great debates of political parties and preserve a benevolent neutrality toward them, so long as they observe the cardinal principles of morality. In the Catholic countries, political neutrality on the part of the Church is more difficult. In her greatest period, the Church was a theocracy. If her aspirations in the field of politics have become more modest, she has never completely given up the hope of an eventual condominium with Caesar. She has no objection against representative government, democracy, or the doctrine of the sovereignty of the nation. But she has always based her attitude toward the respective governments on the respect that the latter showed both for her spiritual mission and her temporal interests. The Church has never hesitated to prefer a revolutionary government to a legitimate or quasi-legitimate government if the revolutionary government happened to be favorable to it and the legitimate or quasi-legitimate government indifferent or hostile.

What will the Catholic Church do in the chaos that has come over mankind? There is one of the greatest problems of our age. The Church is a very powerful organization serving certain moral principles that might help the world to come out of the chaos. But on one condition: that the Church agree to collaborate on an equal footing with other forces. There is an isolationist school in the Catholic Church, a school which believes that only the Church will be capable of saving the world because the chief cause of the present disaster is the revolt against the Catholic Church. All who desire to collaborate in the righting of the world should then put themselves under her guidance. This position is untenable: if part of mankind revolted against the Catholic Church, it was not because of a whim or through folly but for extremely serious reasons. The causes of the present chaos are more complex and profound than the revolt against Rome, and it is not impossible that the Church may have a share in the responsibility. However, the present crisis is beyond the strength of the Catholic Church to remedy, just as it is beyond the strength of all the other spiritual and temporal powers of the universe. If this isolationist policy should prevail, the most likely effect would be that the Church would only help to increase the confusion and would finally be engulfed herself.

The second problem is socialism. Socialism makes the same claim as the Catholic Church, without having the justification of historical titles comparable to those of the Church: the claim that it alone possesses the secret of how to save the world. But this claim, on the part of a doctrine that is hardly a century old, is so exaggerated that it is not dangerous. There is another and more serious complication. Marxist socialism has popularized a doctrine of government that makes the principle of democratic legitimacy inapplicable. According to this doctrine the world is governed by capitalism; government is only an instrument in the hands of the bourgeois—industrialists, bankers, merchants, landlords—to exploit and oppress the masses; the latter are the slaves of capital in the state as in the factory; concealed beneath the political freedom proclaimed to the world by the French Revolution lies the dictatorship of the *bourgeoisie*, which succeeded the domination of the kings and nobles. The French Revolution was only the annexation of the state by the *bourgeoisie*. The world will become free on the day the proletariat in its turn, after that of the Third, launches the revolution of the Fourth Estate and accomplishes the final liberation of mankind. The class war is to be the great struggle that will result in the new era. Jaurès wrote a history of the French Revolution in which the *bourgeoisie* was held up to the people as the first example of a revolutionary class; the proletariat should take a leaf from their book and surpass them. That view of the French Revolution is completely fictitious. The French Revolution was the collapse of the Old Regime from old age, and not the revolt of the Third Estate against the monarchy and aristocracy. A large part of the Third Estate, which Jaurès glorified as the first example of a revolutionary class, fought against the Revolution on the side of the nobility and clergy! The *bourgeoisie* only became dominant in a small part of Europe during the nineteenth century; except for France, England, Belgium, Holland, and the Scandinavian countries, Europe was governed by monarchies until 1918. Similarly, capitalism has never been a political force in Europe except in the imagination of the socialists. High finance and great industry only acquired a certain political influence during the course of the nineteenth century in the democratic countries, and, moreover, for the same reason and at the same time as the other classes and organizations: the workers, for instance, and their unions. In the monarchic countries—Italy, Spain, the Balkans, Austria-Hungary, Germany, Russia—high finance and great industry had no political influence before the First World War, and that was a deficiency, a weakness, an inferiority of the monarchic regimes in comparison with the democratic and parliamentary regimes. Historical materialism is the wrong key to the history of the nineteenth century; the socialists, who believed they could explain everything, failed completely to understand the real state of things, which they wanted to change. Whence came the great mistakes they made every time they exercised power by themselves or in collaboration with other parties, and the difficulty they experienced in holding on to the power after having acquired it. But the key, though it is the wrong one and does not open any doors, is easy to carry, not being heavy, and gives those who pocket it the illusion of knowing all about history without having even studied a single chapter.

This explains its success, even in extreme rightist and Catholic circles. There are a number of Don Quixotes on the extreme right who imagine that they are battling with giants when they tilt at the windmills of bourgeois plutocracy that Marxism has scattered from one end of Europe to the other. As a matter of fact the Marxists have confused the alleged political domination of capitalism, which is a myth, with the influence that wealthy classes have exerted on government in every age and in every regime. In every age and in every regime, at least up till now, the government has come from the wealthy classes and has been in immediate contact with them, whereas it has only been in remote touch with the middle classes and the masses of the people. The passions, prejudices, virtues, vices, and interests of the wealthy classes have exerted a preponderant influence on the policy of every regime—monarchy and republic, aristocracy and democracy. The wealthy classes in turn have always been very jealous of their influence on the government, and have sought to prevent the middle and lower classes from disputing it. That preoccupation on the part of the wealthy classes is manifest all through the history of the West since the French Revolution. It explains in part their hostility to universal suffrage. But the persistent influence of the wealthy classes on the government has nothing in common with the bourgeois domination alleged in the Communist Manifesto: it is universal and permanent; it antedates the bourgeois regime and will survive it. It will exist as long as there is any wealth in the world, and will come to an end only when man has succeeded in leveling wealth and poverty in an equalitarian society. The attempt is being made in the far east of Europe: whether success is possible is another matter.

A fallacy, therefore. But the fallacy, in spreading through the masses and crystallizing into the political program of a very powerful party, has created an extremely serious obstacle to the formation of legitimate democracies, that is, to the only solution to the problem of power that is possible today. If the people believe that capitalism is dominant and that the *bourgeoisie* are using the government in order to tyrannize and exploit them, they can only be hostile to the government, even in a democracy. The state becomes their enemy; the political rights that democracy affords them can only provide them with the means to dispossess the wealthy classes simultaneously with property and the government, to destroy the bourgeois state instead of collaborating with it. An ultrarevolutionary program cannot be put into practice by a legitimate democracy, which demands that the opposition be a collaboration. I am raising problems that cannot be solved by the rivalry of majorities and minorities: they bring into conflict and overexcite the bourgeois arrogance and the insolence of the masses in revolt, all the fears of the rich and all the jealousies, grudges, and fears of the poor. The dialectical tournaments of democracy cannot survive under the impact of these passions: struggles begin which multiply and are aggravated until they lead to revolutionary government, that is, to the regime of fear.

The socialist party has always had a right wing, which has tried to make the masses collaborate in democratic government, eradicating as far as possible the revolutionary spirit of the program. But the program remains, and it is in contradiction with the aims of legitimate democracy. The latter tries to administer the collective interests of society together and harmoniously; socialism wishes to destroy the existing society and replace it with a more just and happier society. Only a prophet could say whether and to what extent this plan could be achieved; a historian must in these chaotic times confine himself to recall a few memories. For two centuries, Western civilization has been trying to create a society without dynasties or aristocracies, by means of the principle of democratic legitimacy. Kings and nobles have almost all disappeared, but the entire world has fallen into such a state of chaos that no one can foresee whether the long-drawn-out struggle will succeed, in spite of the enormous sacrifices it has cost. Socialism is still not satisfied, and wants to create a society that will not only be without kings and nobles but also without riches and without classes. That is doubling the difficulty at the very moment when no one knows whether the first difficulty has been overcome; it is attempting the French

Revolution to the second power. If they are regarded from this standpoint, the appalling obstacles that the Russian Revolution is up against and that provide ample material for myths become understandable. And they should be a lesson: the second great experiment after the French Revolution.

The Fourth Level

Authority comes from above: we agree on that. But if it comes from above why does it stop halfway between Heaven and earth? Why not have it proceed from God Himself? Is not the humanization of government the great weakness of the Western world? Did it not reveal the empirical and conventional nature of principles of legitimacy, and consequently their fragility, to all the world, even the crudest masses?

That idea, in various shapes, has obsessed Europe ever since the French Revolution. According to this point of view, incredulity is the cause of the immense chaos in which mankind is on the verge of losing itself. But it is far from certain that pious ages have been better governed than skeptical ones. They have been perhaps more tractable, which is not always a virtue. God is able to help man to stop short in his criticism of principles of legitimacy, at the point beyond which no principle appears either just or rational, but He cannot allay the discontent of men who feel themselves badly governed; rather does He aggravate it. It is far more painful for men to be maltreated by a government claiming divine origin than by a government that claims to be their fellow creature. If universal suffrage selects an incapable or dishonest deputy, it is unfortunate, but after all the error committed by a majority is easy to explain and repair. It is more difficult to explain why the grace of God sanctifies for his entire life a wicked, debauched, cruel, selfish, stupid king, who harasses the men to whom he should be a father. The regimes that have abused theological justifications have brought about revolts that, going beyond the government, have struck at God Himself. This has taken place in Europe at the end of the eighteenth century, and in Asia at the beginning of the twentieth. The skepticism of the West, after the eighteenth century, is merely the pursuit into the very realms of Heaven after the governments of the earth that sought their legitimation in the stratosphere of religion.

That religion can be of help to government, no one will deny. But faith must pre-exist and provide its own *raison d'être*. People believe in God because they want to, not because they want to have a good police force as inexpensively as possible. It is ridiculous to say to a skeptical age that it must believe in God if it wishes to have good government. That is the weakness of the position of M. Izoulet and of a number of other Catholic writers. For two centuries a growing coolness toward religion has swept over nearly all mankind; particularly in the West, even those who still practice some religion, are becoming less and less disposed to let themselves be guided by the Church in their political life. The Pope himself experiences this every day. Good or bad, here is the situation: man is now called upon to govern himself both in act and in principle, in complete autonomy from religion. So much the worse for him if the difficulties of the task are increasing; so much the better if religion can help him out.

The Fifth Level

Legitimacies grow old for two reasons: either because they abuse the prestige they possess and become incapable of governing, or because men's ideas undergo a new orientation and they can no longer suffer the absurdity and injustice that every principle of legitimacy contains within it. Then they want to eliminate the dominant principle of legitimacy and substitute a principle that will be more just and rational where man discovered the other to be weak, even if it be less so elsewhere. The two causes may

act separately or together, the two agings accompany each
other or occur separately. This results in vastly different
historical cases.

The French and Russian revolutions are the two great
examples of the agings occurring simultaneously and of
the frightful devastation that they can cause in man's
history. The two revolutions were preceded and in part
caused by a new orientation in thought, by the desire for
a great change. In France this desire was first limited to
representative government, and, after the downfall of the
monarchy, grew to the creation of a society without nobles
or kings. The Russian Revolution began with an even
vaster plan of reconstruction. It wanted to add economic
equality to the juridical and political equality of its French
counterpart, complete the sovereignty of the people by
means of the seizure and collectivization of all the wealth
in the world, create a new order, not only without nobles
and kings but without rich and poor.

But the Russian people were as little prepared for such
a change in orientation as the French people were in 1789
to construct a new state founded on the sovereignty of the
nation. In France as in Russia the new orientation was
the desire of an advance guard of pathfinders and vision-
aries. In France as in Russia it succeeded in seizing the
power only because the pre-existing legal system, consumed by age, discredited by its impotence, weakened by
the general discontent, had collapsed: in France during
July and August, 1789, after the storming of the Bastille;
in Russia between April and October 1917, after the abdication of Nicholas II, caused by reversals and universal
disorder. Then, in France as in Russia, the two panics
superimposed upon each other and intermingled: the
panic caused by the destruction of the legal system and the
panic caused by the new orientation, for which the people
were not yet prepared. The Russian Revolution is neither
the unprecedented marvel that sends its admirers into
transports of delight nor the unprecedented monstrosity

that terrifies its adversaries; it is a new performance, in a slower tempo, on a larger stage, and in modern dress, of the drama of the French Revolution. Like the French Revolution, it resulted in the sanguinary despotism of a revolutionary government; like the French Revolution, it has made and will make its people suffer; like the French Revolution, it set the horizon ablaze with the glow of a fire that terrified and will for centuries terrify the world. Impelled forward, in the midst of these hallucinatory fears, by the desire for a new orientation, which, though confused, has deep roots, mankind may some day benefit from it, as it has from the French Revolution. But not until the first terror has been dissipated.

There is nothing to expect from the other revolutions that shook Europe after the Russian Revolution. They are the consequence of the decay of the monarchic legitimacy: either through the sudden collapse or the irreparable weakening of the monarchies that ruled the greater part of Europe until 1917 and 1918, at the end of the First World War. They are not actuated or supported by any desire for a new orientation; they are no more than desperate attempts to prevent the advent of the representative state and of democratic legitimacy, and will result only in interminable wars.

There remains only history's masterpiece: a new orientation that rejuvenates a decaying legitimacy, without a rupture of the legal system—"revolution" without "revolution." These are extremely rare, and yet during the last three centuries of Western history in Europe there have been two.

England in 1688 succeeded in changing the dynasty and its orientation without destroying the principle of aristomonarchic legitimacy, without provoking the struggle between the two invisible Genii of the City, as one century later France was to do. I shall confine myself to quoting a few pages from Benjamin Constant's book, *De l'esprit de conquête et de l'usurpation*. In spite of some vagueness of expression, it would be impossible to find a better description of the antirevolutionary character of the English revolution of 1688—a new orientation accomplished without a rupture of the legal system.

The example afforded by William III at first glance seems a very strong objection against all the statements that have just been made. Should not William III be considered as the usurper of the throne of England from the Stuarts? Yet his reign was glorious and tranquil, and it is from that reign that England's prosperity and freedom date. Is that not a proof that usurpation is not always impossible in modern times and that its effects are not always disastrous?

But the name of usurper is not at all suited to William III. He was called, by a nation which wanted to live in freedom and peace, to the exercise of an authority in which he had elsewhere made his apprenticeship, and, already invested with power in another country, he did not come into possession of the throne through the usual methods of usurpation, guile or violence.

In order to understand what there was of unique and advantageous about his position, compare him with Cromwell. The latter was really a usurper. He did not have the support, the aura and splendor of an already occupied throne. Also, in spite of his personal superiority, he could only obtain questionable and ephemeral victories. His reign had all the characteristics of usurpation: it had the short duration, and death came just in time to save it from an impending and inevitable downfall.

The intervention of William III in the revolution of 1688, far from being a usurpation, probably saved England from a new usurper and at the same time delivered her from a dynasty against which too many national interests had declared themselves.

When threatening circumstances interfere with the regular transmission of power and when this interference is of fairly long duration, in order that all interests may become alienated, it is not a question of investigating whether the prolongation of that authority would have been a good thing, it is certain that its re-establishment would be an evil.

A people in that situation are exposed to diverse courses, two of which are good and two of which are bad.

First the power may revert to the former owner, which brings about a violent reaction, vengeance, and upheaval; and the counterrevolution that takes place is merely a new revolution. That is what happened in England under the two sons of Charles I, and the injustices that filled those two reigns are a memorable lesson which other nations might well take to heart.

Or else some individual without legitimate claim may seize the power, and all the hardships of a usurpation weigh upon the people. That is what also happened in England, under Cromwell, and what is being renewed in our age, even more terribly, in France.

Or, again, the nation may succeed in giving itself a republican form of government, that is wise enough to ensure its tranquillity as well as its freedom. Let no one say that this is impossible, as the Swiss, the Dutch, and the Americans have accomplished it.

Or, finally, this nation may call to the throne a man already famous elsewhere, who receives the scepter with appropriate restrictions. That is what the English did in 1688. It is what the Swedes have done in our time. Both nations met with good fortune. In this case, the recipient of the authority has another interest than that of aggrandizing and increasing his power. He is interested in bringing about the triumph of the principles that serve as guaranty to that power, and these principles are those of liberty.

A revolution of that type has nothing in common with usurpation. The Prince who is freely elected by the nation is strong both in his former position and in his new title. He pleases the imagination by the memories that charm it, and satisfies reason by the national suffrage that supports him. He is far from being reduced to using recently created instruments. He can command with confidence all the forces of the nation because he does not deprive it of a single part of its political heritage. Earlier institutions are not opposed to him; he associates himself with them and they agree to support him.

Let us add that the English had the good fortune to find in William III exactly what a people need in such a circumstance: a man not only familiar with governing but accustomed to freedom as the head of a republic; his character had been formed in the midst of tempests, and experience had taught him not to be frightened by the agitation that is inseparable from a liberal constitution.

Considered from this standpoint, the case of William III, far from being unfavorable to me, tends rather, I believe, to support me. His accession, not being a usurpation, certainly does not prove that usurpation is possible today. The happiness and liberty that England enjoyed under his reign in no way implies that a usurpation can ever be beneficial. Finally, the duration and tranquillity of this reign proves nothing in favor of the duration and tranquillity of usurpation.[1]

Switzerland is the second example. Every morning I pass by the foot of the monument that Geneva erected to General Dufour, and I often pass by his tomb in the cemetery of Plainpalais. And I always reflect on the deep and so little-known significance of the scene in history of which he was the brilliant protagonist. By defeating the *Sonderbund*, General Dufour made it possible for his country to achieve a new and decisive orientation without destroying the legal system, a great revolution without revolution. Between 1840 and 1848, Switzerland made a determined effort to extract from the uncertain and vacillating regime of 1815 a coherent democracy, based on the principle of popular sovereignty and inspired by the principles of the French Revolution and by the example of the United States. But this effort met with a lively opposition, that for a while tried to prevent the victory of the new orientation by force of arms. If the *Sonderbund* had been stronger, the government established in 1815 would have been overthrown, the "great panic" would have begun, and no one knows what would have happened to Switzerland. The defeat of the *Sonderbund* permitted the system. That is one of the reasons why Switzerland, the new orientation to triumph without the overthrow of

[1] Benjamin de Constant-Rebecque, *Ibid.*, pp. 101-105.

applying the principles of the French Revolution, succeeded in creating the legitimate state *par excellence,* a state in which the citizens are not afraid of the government and the government is not afraid of the citizens.

These two great revolutions explain why the history of England and that of Switzerland were so fortunate during the nineteenth century. France's great misfortune was that she did not succeed in passing from the aristo-monarchic legitimacy to the democratic legitimacy without one of the most terrible destructions of the legal system in history. The consequences of that mishap were tremendous, not only for France but for all Europe; of these, the creation of the first revolutionary government in Western history was the most serious. But the former principle of legitimacy could then give way to the new principle: France was able, at the cost of terrible sacrifices, to reconstitute a new legitimacy. The most dangerous case of all is when a people, rightly or wrongly dissatisfied with the legitimate power that governs them, overthrows it without having another principle to put in its place. They are then forced to submit to revolutionary government, with the danger of having to remain under it for a long time without hope, unless they retrace their steps and reconstruct what they have destroyed: something that is always difficult to do.

The Sixth Level

The major problem still remains to be solved: how can the world's order depend on principles that are so fragile? What is the significance, in the economy of the universe, of this fragility of every social structure that man creates, even the most imposing? What duties does this fragility impose upon the ruling elite of mankind?

We can no longer evade these questions, now that we have discovered the strange nature of principles of legitimacy. To answer them, I shall begin by recalling a passage from *The Reconstruction of Europe.*

If all human beings were to react similarly to a given set of circumstances, so that their actions could be foreseen, human society would resemble nothing so much as a beehive or an anthill. Intelligence and will power would have no functions to perform. The life of the individual and the history of the group, would, like that of the bees and ants, be reduced to a predetermined and invariable co-ordination of instinctive and unchanging actions.

But, in a universe which is governed by the law of causality, the human mind is alone distinguished by its freedom, a word used somewhat equivocally by certain philosophical schools. Every piece of iron exposed to heat always reacts in the same way. It expands, turns red, then white, softens, and finally liquefies. The forecast is unmistakable, and all human labor is based on the security afforded by countless similar forecasts. The reactions of the human mind to physical or mental forces acting upon it, are on the contrary variable and far more unpredictable. One man will react quite differently from another to the same circumstances; the same man will not necessarily react tomorrow as he reacts today. Collective reactions seem even more capricious and difficult to foresee than individual reactions. Every human mind is the condensation of a mysterious force which explodes under the shock of life with intensity and in different and unforeseen directions, at will or as it can. That is why no science of the mind and of history analogous to the science of matter and nature has been formulated; one is even forced to consider whether the word "science" can be applied in the same sense to the physical and intellectual life of men, to the chemistry and history of societies.

This sovereign independence through which the mind acts and manifests itself, is the essence of human nature. But it is also responsible for the agony and the hardship in man's existence. Obviously, in order to live together, men must be able to foresee, at least to a certain extent, and under not too exceptional circumstances, what their actions or reactions will be. Take, for instance, the family unit. Would it be endurable if the husband and wife, parents and children, never knew, among the daily vicissitudes of life, whether they could count on mutual respect, obedience, and love, or whether they should live in fear of revolt, indifference, and hate—an equally possible alternative? The same may be said for all human societies, even the greatest ones, like the state. If the central nucleus of the human mind enjoys unlimited freedom and is capable of ignoring fixed laws, social life becomes permissible only if each one of us can more or less foresee the conduct of the majority of our fellow creatures under every known circumstance.

Society, then, is founded upon a contradiction between human liberty and the social necessity for reactions that can be foreseen.[2]

This signifies that beehives and anthills are perfect models of society, because each member always and at the right moment performs the necessary actions, to the exclusion of all freedom and without any alternative. Human societies, on the contrary, are imperfect and approximate, because there is never any certainty that the members will perform their duties. And yet man is the social being *par excellence;* he exists only in groups, and is never seen, as is the case with most animals, in a solitary state. What is the explanation for the fact that he is always more or less in conflict with society, which he needs? What is his mysterious freedom, which makes him an unsociable creature in the very midst of the society without which he is unable to exist? For this is the crux of the alarming contradiction.

In order to reply to that question, it is first of all necessary to remark that every living creature must die and yet does not want to, struggles against death but, in the end, must succumb to it. In the vegetable kingdom this struggle is a passive one. Plants, being gifted neither with motion nor with consciousness, wait passively, without visible reaction, until their vitality is exhausted by time or until they are destroyed by an accident of nature. The struggle becomes active when movement and consciousness are born together. Every creature that is able to move makes use of the faculty to protect his existence; he utilizes space

[2] Guglielmo Ferrero, *The Reconstruction of Europe* (New York: G. P. Putnam's Sons, 1941), pp. 31-32.

as a battlefield to fight against death, that is, against time, time being the supreme and ultimate destroyer of all living things and their works. In man the cosmic drama of life and death, of space and time, attains its most complex and inconsistent form. No living being has a clear and exact notion of death in general and of his own inevitable death, as man. The only certainty that men have is that they must die. And yet they all live, until the arrival of death, as though they were immortal. Although they do not know exactly why they exist, although they often complain of life as a burden to bear, they fight against death until the very last moment; they utilize space as a battlefield in the fight against time, with an unparalleled wealth of expedients, of stratagems, of tactics, inventions, and instruments of every kind. The greater part of human labor is consumed in the struggle against time and death. But this struggle is not the task of society; each man engages in it on his own account. Society can help the individual in his struggle, by furnishing him with the means, and especially by acting as the repository of the record of experiments made by past generations. But it is each individual who must protect, not life in general, but his own individual life; and each individual protects it as he can, well or badly, with the means he possesses, according to a clear or confused plan, which he himself conceived, and as though his life were the only one to be protected, without relation to other lives. The fundamental essence of every human personality lies in the tactics and strategy that it employs in the struggle against death. Man is swept by very different passions: sexual love, parental love, friendship, hatred, malice, vengeance, cupidity, ambition for glory and power. But it is not hard to ascertain that all those passions are a rich outward flowering, which adorns and partly conceals from superficial observation a single stem: the passion to live, or the fear of death, which is only the reverse of the passion to live. Wealth and power, for instance, why are they so coveted? They can satisfy many other passions; but what are all those satisfactions—sensual pleasures, aesthetic tastes, vanity, pride, independence—in comparison with the means they can furnish man in his struggle against death and time? These means are the continual service that wealth and power render or seem to render to their possessors; all the other services are far more precarious, fleeting, bound up with precarious conditions.

The fundamental necessities in man's struggle against death seem to provide the explanation for the incurable imperfection of all human societies. It has been attributed to the vagaries of individualism or to the blindness of egoism. This would leave unexplained how and why individualism and egoism, if they are only superficial faults, could permanently jeopardize the social order, of which man is, nevertheless, so in need. Reason and experience should not have much difficulty in curing them, even to the point of extirpating them. But the individualism and egoism that make man an unsociable being in spite of his need for society, are not superficial faults; they have their roots in the very essence of human nature: in the need of each individual to defend his life against death and time, to the best of his ability and knowledge. This instinct of self-preservation has a common element shared by all men, at the same time that it has something particular and unique in every individual: that is why men can and desire to live in society, but it is also why they get along together only up to a certain point, constantly distrust each other, and react to the same circumstance in different ways that are difficult to foresee. The determination of each man to defend his own life as though it were a unique absolute, without relation to or bond with other lives is the "mysterious force which explodes under the shock of life with intensity and in different and unforeseeable directions, at will or as it can."

The consequence is that men, assembled in society, do not know how to rule or to obey except very imperfectly.

What would be the perfect government? A man or men so wise, just, and venerable, that they would know everything that men should do in order to live the social life, and whose precepts would be accepted and followed unresistingly and eagerly by all mankind. But, even if such men existed, would they be able to make themselves spontaneously and completely obeyed by millions of human beings, each of whom is isolated from the others in an anxious struggle to defend his life against real or imaginary dangers and by methods, whether efficacious or not, that are different from the dangers and methods of the others? All of whom, from the standpoint of that struggle, see life in their own way and desire a hundred different solutions to the same problems of life? Even the greatest of legislators, Moses, who spoke for the Eternal, was able to hold his people together and preserve a certain amount of order only with the assistance of a code of commandments and threats and the interposition of instruments of coercion. Commandments, threats, coercions; those are the essentials of every government that mankind has created and obeyed. Force alone is capable of imposing a few common laws on the vast crowd of individual wills, each dominated by its own personal passion to live as though it were unique. But force is the action of fear; and fear, we have seen, is contagious. It is impossible to inspire fear in men without ending up by fearing them: from this moral law springs the most fearful torment of life—the reciprocal fear between government and its subjects. Up till now man has discovered only two remedies to combat that scourge: first, the mystical philosophies and religions, then, in the last few centuries, the principles of legitimacy. Created by human beings, these principles cannot escape the imperfections inherent in the structure of the human mind, out of whose depths they sprang. But all the principles employed by man to distinguish between good and evil, beauty and ugliness, true and false, useful and harmful, to judge the world and himself, and to find his bearings in life, are not relative, as the skeptics maintain: they are incomplete, and they are incomplete because they are limited, like the human mind that created them. Each principle is of value only in knowing, judging, and finding one's bearings in one section of reality: it has no value in any other section. If the section changes, other principles are needed. I believe I have demonstrated this primordial truth at length in another book, and to it I refer the reader who wishes to go into the matter more thoroughly.[3] The principles of legitimacy are not exempt from this rule; they are limited and incomplete and are of use only in certain situations in history, determined by the orientation of thought, which is subject to change. If man succeeded in finding the principle of legitimacy that was absolutely rational and just, the problem of government would be solved for once and for all, Plato's republic would be created for all men and forever, revolutions would be over for good. There would no longer be the need for any reforms; the book of history could close, and mankind could go off into the country and play the flute in company with the shepherds of Theocritus. The social order is a structure perpetually to be reconstructed, because the principles of legitimacy that support it are all incomplete and limited, never impose themselves completely and finally. Man accepts them only after he has become accustomed to them, and then only for the time being; since he accepts them through habit, he gets tired of them and forsakes them. Being incomplete and limited, they wear out, which explains why they are born and die, have a childhood and an old age.

The Seventh Level

But then, since it has lived for a long time without knowing them, why could not mankind fall back into the ignorance and misery of old? We can no longer have any

---

[3] Guglielmo Ferrero, *Between the Old World and the New* (New York: G. P. Putnam's Sons, 1914).

illusions on the nature of the principles of legitimacy:
they are human, that is, empirical, limited, conventional,
extremely unstable. Any philosophical hack can demonstrate their absurdity; any dictator, at the head of a gang
of cutthroats, can supress them. Nevertheless, they are the
condition of the greatest good that mankind, as a collective being, can possess—government without fear. They are
fragile, but everything depends upon these fragile things.
How will Western civilization be able to save them? By
learning to respect them as sacred, even though they are
the fragile creations of its own contradictory mind, and
full of fears. They are the new spiritual plan to which the
elite of mankind must submit; if it is unable to, then I
do not see what use it can be any longer, or how it will
be able to direct the world. But from where can we draw
the inspiration to realize what the respect should be for
a human creation, independent in large measure from its
inevitable faults? From the respect that every man owes
to his parents. "Honor thy father and thy mother," is the
Commandment of God. The duty is not conditioned: the
father and mother may be full of faults; they may even
commit faults; it is not up to the sons to judge them, still
less to cite the faults as justification for abandonment, in-
gratitude, or revolt. When the father and mother have
accomplished their duties toward their children, the latter
owe them gratitude and respect for the rest of their days.
A similar imperative obliges us to respect the principle of
legitimacy which the last two centuries have so painfully
created, which alone today can inspire universal consent,
and which is one of the greatest acts of self-confidence on
the part of mankind because it places the government of
mankind in man's own hands. That principle is today the
universal guaranty against the most dreadful of all scourges
—the reign of fear; consequently it is the common property
of all, and might almost be called the precious safety valve
of the true social contract. Loyalty to the principle is a
sacred promise made by each to all and by all to each:

all are equally bound to respect and uphold it, no one has the right to judge it from a personal standpoint, to think himself free to accept or refuse it. It is easy to see its faults and lacunae; any young dilettante in history who has leafed through the revolutionary literature of the right or left, can easily do this. It is harder, but far more useful, to understand the frightful dangers and disadvantages resulting from a violation of the principle, even when this can be justified by the latter's faults.

Mankind can be saved only if it realizes that legitimate governments are all that can liberate it from the second great panic that engulfed it, and that, in this critical moment of history, legitimate governments can only be created by applying loyally, sincerely, sensibly, and fearlessly the formula of democratic legitimacy, as formulated by the last two centuries. The task is a hard one, but without it there is no hope of salvation. What is necessary so that the elite of mankind may succeed in accomplishing it? Two things, complementary to each other, are needed: that those who will have the fearful task of ruling according to the formula know that they must make untiring efforts to minimize as far as possible the faults and disadvantages of the formula, and that, in view of these efforts, all classes realize that they have the duty to tolerate the inevitable faults and disadvantages of the government to the extreme limits of human patience before destroying the system and, in pursuit of the myth of a nonexistent perfection, delivering themselves into the hands of a revolutionary government. Above all both government and subjects must realize that, principles of legitimacy being human, limited, and conventional, they must be applied in loyalty and good faith for what they are, and not with deception in the intent to use them as instruments of domination and obtain results contrary to their nature. As I said thirty years ago in *Between the Old World and the New*, when the world still seemed in order, honesty should become the çardinal virtue of modern civilization, in proportion as it breaks loose from religious absolutes to be guided in every circumstance and in every sphere by human and limited principles. Honesty should become the supreme virtue, particularly in the relations between the government and its citizens, as the democratic formula becomes the accepted guaranty of the government's legitimacy. For the last century discussion has been going on as to whether the principles of the French Revolution are immortal or decrepit, good or bad. They are excellent, and our age will owe them its salvation if they are applied, as they have been in Switzerland, with honesty and in accordance with their true nature: as moral principles that restrain the government and prevent abuses while at the same time requiring from the subjects an obedience that is not so much forced as consentient, but because of that stricter and more imperative. The "immortal" principles, the Declaration of the Rights of Man, become a scourge if the government makes use of them as a pretext to increase the burdens and taxes of the subjects, or if the latter take advantage of them to substitute the right to disobey for the duty to obey. In many countries, in France, in Italy, in Germany, during the nineteenth and twentieth centuries, the principles of the French Revolution have undergone that heinous falsification, for reasons and under circumstances that varied. It is one of the causes of the great catastrophe that is now upon us, but the principles themselves are innocent. It is the fault of those who applied them badly, with evil intentions, and more often than not, with their hearts full of hatred and fear.

It is a new erection of the mind and of the heart that is needed; an immense work, in which statesmen, writers, historians, artists, and philosophers should concur. Philosophers, as well. For Western philosophy no longer seems to be attuned to that supreme need of mankind. Man is capable of surrounding himself with only a precarious, unstable order, which he can maintain only by constantly reconstructing it, which is continually being threatened by the explosion of real and imaginary terrors inherent in its nature. Order is the exhausting Sisyphean labor of mankind, against which mankind is always in a potential state of conflict. Over a long period of his existence, God powerfully helped man to resign himself to his tragic fate, partly by frightening him, partly by concealing the frailty of his achievement from him, partly by consoling him with other hopes. The progressive secularization of thought and of life placed a new and terrible problem before man: where was man to find new strength for his exhausting Sisyphean labor, which he had formerly found in the fear or the love of God? There seems to be only one solution to the problem: that the elite of mankind acquire a consciousness of the limitation of the human mind, at once simple and profound enough, humble and sublime enough, so that Western civilization will resign itself to its inevitable disadvantages; so that it will not try to escape into the myths that pride, fickleness, and non-submission to his fate multiply around man; and so that it will deduce from it the code of personal and collective duties of man, especially the categorical imperative of the honesty of each individual toward others and toward himself. But, before he can attain the almost superhuman humility of this consciousness, man must realize that he is the prisoner of an infinite reality, beyond and superior to him, which encloses and surrounds him on every side. If he imagines that reality is only in his mind, and that the latter is the dominating force of the universe, he will never consent to be bound by conventional and fragile principles as though they were superior and inviolable laws; he will not accept order except as a perfect and divine work; and, being unable to create it perfectly, he will be overcome by the frenzy to destroy and remake it, until complete despair overwhelms him. That is what happened to Hindu thought.

Ever since Descartes, Western philosophy has become more and more detached from the solid realism of Greek philosophy, from the Bible, from Thomism, and from the good sense of mankind in general; and it has set itself to deny in part, in one way or another, the reality of the world. It has never attained the complete negation of Hindu philosophy; but it is on a declivity that will conduct it to the point which Hindu philosophy has attained through despair, especially if the horrors of the fear of government become ever more numerous and aggravated and at last permanently established in the heart of the West. It is impossible to see how a philosophy that is not sure of the world's reality could, in the midst of a civilization devastated by violence and fear, avoid turning in despair to the final consolation and destruction of Nirvana. A civilization that desires to liberate man from all his fears must begin with the recognition of time and space as the two supreme realities, because space is the battlefield on which man struggles against time, which is the destroyer not only of life but of all man's works, including principles of legitimacy. It is impossible for a civilization to preserve and respect the principle of legitimacy that ensures it against the most terrible of fears, if it does not realize how powerfully time works to destroy it, and that its fight against time in defense of the principle is the most serious and important of the realities.

INDEX

Abel, 33-37
Absolute monarchy(-ies), 41, 54, 56, 64, 67, 68, 154, 155, 158, 220, 245. *See also* Monarchy, Legitimate monarchy
Abuses of power, 66
Abyssinia, 242
Adams, John, 65
Aduwa, Battle of, 241, 242, 243, 244
Africa, 156, 221, 224, 243
Agriculture, 51, 55, 57, 157, 198, 238, 240,, 246
Ahriman, 211
Ajaccio, 107, 216
Alba, Duke of, 204
Albert I, 293-294
Alexander I, 109, 226, 275
Alexander the Great, 148
America, 55, 64-66, 156, 245, 258, 261, 306. *See also* United States
American Revolution, 64-65, 281
Ami du Peuple, 95
Amiens, Treaty of, 108, 206, 223
Amis des Lois, 9
Anarchy, 32, 87, 92, 95, 96, 189, 191, 203, 217, 232, 233, 274
Annunzio, d', 266
Aristocracies, *see* Aristocratic republics
Aristocracy, 56, 57, 63, 98, 116, 167, 171, 172, 183, 297; Roman, 142, 220-224, 226, 227. *See also* Nobility
Aristocratic republic (s), 21-23, 25, 26, 45, 50, 52, 62, 64, 107, 138, 141, 163, 170, 179, 186, 219, 248, 278, 285, 291, 294, 299. *See also* Democracy, Monarchy, Republic,

Aristo-monarchic principle of legitimacy
Aristo-monarchic principle of legitimacy, 21-22, 24, 49-50, 51, 54, 56, 58, 60, 62, 65, 68-69, 70, 72, 76, 80, 83, 84, 85, 87, 94, 97, 99, 101, 103, 107, 110, 111, 112, 115, 116, 118, 121, 124, 128, 135, 138, 142, 160, 162, 163, 164, 165, 166, 186, 198, 210, 211, 216, 218, 281-283, 304, 308. *See also* Hereditary principle of legitimacy, Legitimate monarchy, Principles of legitimacy
Aristophanes, 70
Aristotle, 57
Armaments, 238, 243
Artois, comte d', 86
Asia, 156, 166, 172, 220, 221, 229, 302. *See also* Orient
Assassination (s), 147, 148, 201, 202; of Julius Caesar, 3-4, 5, 225, 226; of King Humbert, 245, 252; of Matteoti, 6, 11
Assemblies, elective, 45, 59, 91, 92, 190; legislative, in France, 8, 193, 195-196, 216, 287. *See also* Parliaments, Diets, Estates, *Staende*
Assembly of Notables, 68
Assignats, 96
Augustus, 226-228, 229
Aulard, 91
Aurelian, 221-222
Aurelius, Marcus, 204
Austerlitz, Battle of, 108, 109, 208
Austria, 23, 44, 108, 123-124, 125, 127, 136, 146, 166, 172, 208, 247, 269, 275, 298
Authority, 40, 58, 61, 83, 97, 113, 115, 120, 121, 154, 155, 158, 160,

161, 169, 171, 182, 192, 229, 231, 232, 233, 248, 284, 295, 301, 305, 306. *See also* Government

Balkan countries, 125, 264, 298
Barricades, battle of the, 112, 118
Bastille, storming of, 82, 83, 84, 85, 93, 94, 95, 98, 134, 160, 189, 192, 211, 287, 303
Belgium, viii, 23, 136, 173, 275, 298
Berlin, 109, 128, 268
Berne, 111
Berry, duc de, 215
Between the Old World and the New, 18, 314, 316
Bible, the, 33-37, 39, 53, 154, 319. *See also* Sacred Scriptures, Gospel, the
Bien Informé, 9
Bismarck, 242, 284
Bolognini, Duchess Letta, 127
Bonaparte, Joseph, 106
Bonaparte, Louis, 106
Bonaparte, Lucien, 44-45, 223
Bonaparte, Napoleon: Consulate of, 7-12, 44-48, 193-199, 201, 205-206; fear of, 7-12, 43-48, 193-195, 196-199, 201, 275; invasion of Italy, 43-44, 248; and Julius Caesar, 222-223; and revolutionary govt., 196-199, 205-206. *See also* Napoleon
Bordeaux: Archbishop of, 88; duc de, 215
Bossuet, 154
Bourbon dynasty, 121, 163, 216, 217, 231, 233, 234
Bourgeois (-ie), 3, 5, 63, 91, 121, 171, 172, 210, 249, 259, 260, 297-300. *See also* Middle classes
Brin, engineer, 127
Bruhl, Levy, 31
Brumaire 18, 7, 9, 43-45, 104, 193-194, 210, 216, 224, 276
Budapest, 128
Buddha, 25
Buddhism, 279-280
Bulgars, 132

Cadoudal, conspiracy of, 202

Caesar, Julius, 10, 142; assassination of, 3-4, 5, 225; dictatorship of, 3-4, 219, 222-226
Cahiers, the, 76-77, 79, 94, 133, 288
Cain, 33-37
Calonne, 68
Calvin, 55, 57
Campania, the, 13
Campo-Formio, Treaty of, 43-44, 209, 223
Capetians, 132
Capitalism, 297-300
Caracalla, 204
Carolingians, 132
Catholic Church, 22, 180, 295-297. *See also* Church, the, Clergy, the
Catholics: in France, 11, 46, 103, 181; in Italy, 244, 247, 256, 265
Cavaignac, General, 121
Cavalotti, Felice, 257
Cavour, 151, 264
Censorship, vii, 197-198
Ceremonial, in Old Regime, 54
Charles I, 306
Charles II, 306
Charles X, 112, 113, 213-215
Charter, English, 56
Charter, of Louis XVIII, 110-113, 125, 215, 231-232
Chef du Cabinet, 9
China, 278
Chinese Revolution, 166
Christianity, 29, 39, 52-53, 142-143, 148-149, 151, 154, 221, 223, 278, 280, 285, 295
Church, the, 51, 52, 53, 57, 68, 86, 90, 92, 93, 94, 102, 149, 189, 212, 246, 258, 302. *See also* Catholic Church
Cinq Cents, the, 44
Cisalpine Republic, 197
Citizens: active, 90; passive, 90-91
Citoyen Français, 9
Civil Code, of France, 199
Civil wars, 147, 148, 271; in Rome, 221-226, 227
Civilization, 42, 50, 94, 294; defined, 28-30, 38-39, 48, 319
Cleopatra, 151
Clergy, in France, 10, 57, 67, 69, 71,

73, 74, 76, 78, 79, 93, 94, 95, 97, 116, 157, 171, 189, 190, 298. *See also* Church, the, Upper classes
Cochin, Auguste, 69, 70, 98, 100, 159
Coercion, in government, 34-36, 46, 107, 175, 248, 313. *See also* Force, Violence
Comitia, 219, 225, 227, 278
Commerce, 52, 54, 57, 65, 88, 89, 156, 198, 246
Committee of Investigation, 96
Commodus, 204
Commons, House of, 56, 98, 157
Communist Manifesto, 299
Confederation of the Rhine, 108
Confiscations, 98
Congress of Vienna, reconstruction at, ix, 265, 275
Conscription, universal, 44, 53, 164
Conservatives, in Italy, 237-241, 247, 253, 256, 259, 262, 263, 265, 269. *See also* Liberals, Radicals, Republicans, Socialists, Syndicalists
Consiglio Maggiore, 23, 71, 136
Conspiracy (-ies), 4-5, 97, 147, 195, 202
Constant, Benjamin, 11, 47, 202-205, 304-307
Constantine, 148
Constituent Assembly, 199
Constituent power, 74, 77, 78, 79, 92
Constituted power, 74, 77
Constitution(s): American, 45; English, 45, 91, 236; of French monarchy, 91; Italian, 236-239; of National Assembly, 87-92, 95, 97; of 1791, 189; of Year III, 191; of Year VIII, 7-8, 10, 45-46, 104-105, 106, 107, 114-115, 189, 192-196, 210
Constitutional law, English, 236
Constitutional monarchy, 80, 218. *See also* Monarchy, Legitimate monarchy
Constitutional power, 79
Contrat Social, 58-64, 65, 66, 73, 74, 100, 167-168, 183
Convention, the, 99, 184, 190-191, 196

Copernicus, 55
Corriere della Serra, 266
Council of State, in French Constitution of the Year VIII, 8
Council of Two Hundred, in Geneva, 57, 167-168
Councils, 8, 22, 54. *See also* Parliaments, Assemblies, Diets, Estate, *Staende*
Coup d'état, 12, 98, 191; Mussolini's, 4, 5, 218; Napoleon's, 9, 10, 43-45. *See also* Brumaire 18
Court of Cassation, 8
Court(s), the, 51, 55, 67, 68, 79, 84, 86, 92, 93, 94, 95, 96, 97, 113, 115, 125, 152, 244. *See also* Crown, the
Criminal law, reformed, 90
Crise de la conscience européenne, 1680-1715, la, 58
Crispi, 238-239, 241, 242-243
Croatia, 285
Cromwell, 305, 306
Crown, the 56, 83, 89, 98, 162, 236, 272, 273. *See also* Court(s), the

Darwinism, 180
Death, man's fight against, 310-313
Décade philosophique, 9
Declaration of Independence, 65-66
Declaration of the Rights of Man, 87-89, 90, 93, 95, 183, 317
Delations, 98
Delegation of power, 168-170, 173, 182, 291, 293
Democracy(-ies), 6, 20, 22, 24, 25, 26, 50, 63, 107, 116, 123, 127, 132, 138, 140, 144, 166, 188, 189, 192, 219, 220, 283, 295, 296, 299, 307. *See also* Aristocratic republic, Monarchy, Republic, Legitimate democracy, democratic principle of legitimacy
Democratic principle of legitimacy, 21, 49, 50, 59, 70, 94, 97, 98, 99, 101, 103, 104, 106, 107, 110, 111, 113, 115-116, 117, 118, 120, 123, 124, 128, 129, 135, 138, 139, 145, 155, 160, 161, 162, 164, 166, 172, 184, 188, 191, 193, 196, 198, 205,

208, 210, 211, 216, 218, 271, 273, 282-283, 292, 293, 297, 300, 304, 308, 316, 317. *See also* Elective principle of legitimacy, Legitimate democracy, Principles of legitimacy

Deportations, 98

Depretis, 237-238, 240, 251

Descartes, 318

Despotism, 41, 45, 47, 202-205. *See also* Usurpation

Deuteronomy, 150

Dictator(s), 4-7, 11, 27, 42, 48, 219, 222, 256, 315; Julius Caesar as, 3-4, 222-226. *See also* Bonaparte, Napoleon

Diets, 22, 54, 56, 155. *See also* Parliaments, Assemblies, Estates, Councils, *Staende*

Diplomatic Committee, 96

Directory, the, 7, 11, 43-44, 102-104, 191-192, 194, 196, 199

Divine right, 23, 110

Doge, of Venice, 22, 23, 219

Dreibund, 268, 275

Dreyfus affair, 242

Dual Entente, 268

Ducos Roger, 194

Dufour, General, 307

Ecclesiastical principalities, 163

Ecclesiastics, 154

Economic interests, 51, 144

Edward VIII, 152

Efficacy, in government, 132, 134, 135, 136-137, 143-144, 152

Egypt, 142, 151, 224; Bonaparte's expedition to, 44, 223

Eighteenth century, viii, 15, 21, 45, 51, 53, 54, 55, 57, 58, 71, 72, 85, 88, 98, 110, 152, 158, 159, 160, 163, 170, 171, 211, 218, 266, 302

Elections, 21, 22, 23, 59, 75, 125, 168-170, 176; in France, 91, 92, 95-96, 106-107, 111, 114, 117, 118-119, 120-122, 123, 158, 189, 190, 191, 193, 195, 216, 231, 233, 293; in Italy, 237, 241, 247-248, 254-256, 261, 262, 266, 267, 271

Elective principle of legitimacy, 21,

49, 50, 56, 64, 69, 92, 95, 105, 135, 138, 168. *See also* Democratic principle of legitimacy, Elections, Principles of legitimacy

Electoral colleges, 22

Émigrés, 10, 95. *See also* Nobility, in France

Empiricism, 57

Encyopedists, the, 69, 88

Enghien, duc d', abduction and trial of, 202

England, viii, 23, 45, 56, 64, 65, 71, 75, 80, 88, 97, 108, 113, 128, 129, 130, 136, 155, 156, 157, 161, 164, 173, 178, 187, 206, 215, 241, 242, 268, 269, 275, 276, 283, 298, 304-308

Enquête sur la monarchie, 131-132

Equality, 16, 88, 120, 121, 165, 186, 220, 259, 285, 293, 303

Estates, 22, 54, 56, 68. *See also* Parliaments, Assemblies, Diets, Councils, *Staende*

Executive power, 8, 20, 21, 59, 60, 71, 80, 89, 90, 92, 96, 110-112, 113, 114, 125, 157, 219, 287. *See also* Legislative power

Exemptions, 90

Falernian wine, of Horace, 13-14

Fascist revolution, 4, 48, 129, 218, 274-275, 289

Fear: of Bonaparte, 45-48, 106-110, 197-198, 201, 207-208; between govt. and subjects, 27, 30-37, 38-43, 48, 99-100, 112, 116, 123, 140, 147-148, 179, 190, 192, 203, 206, 220, 221, 234, 273, 278-281, 283, 286, 291, 295, 313, 315, 319

February Revolution, 118, 119, 120

Federal Council, Swiss, 20

Ferrero, Leo, 53, 128

Feudal Committee, 96

Fifteenth century, 51, 54

Financial Committee, 96

First Consul, the, *see* Bonaparte

First Empire, of France, 47, 106, 122, 123, 188, 199, 202, 216, 231. *See also* Napoleon

First World War, viii, 4, 6, 18, 49,

128, 152, 162, 165, 184, 186, 267-270, 272-273, 274, 275, 276, 292, 298, 304

Florence, 218; archbishop of, 15; prefect of, 6

Force, in government, 40-41, 48, 61, 187, 234, 278, 313. *See also* Coercion, Violence

Fouché, 201

Fourteenth century, 223

France, vii, viii, 14, 16, 23, 56, 57, 58, 60, 64, 125, 127, 128, 129, 136, 139, 145, 146, 163, 166, 171, 173, 180, 211, 219, 223, 224, 238, 241, 242, 258, 260, 261, 263, 265, 268, 269, 273, 275, 276, 293, 298, 306, 317; Bonaparte and, 7-12, 43-47, 106-110, 194-202, 206; under Old Regime, 67-72, 156, 158-160, 163; and Louis Philippe, 113-118, 161, 213-217, 230-235, 252; and Restoration, 110-113, 134; and Revolution, 73-105, 133-134, 159-160, 182-184, 188-193, 211, 286-288, 303, 304, 308; and Second Republic, 118-122, 292; and Second Empire, 122-124; and Third Republic, 124, 292. *See also* French Revolution, Napoleon, Restoration, July Monarchy, etc.

Francesco, Don, 13-14

Franchise, qualified, 117. *See also* Suffrage

Francis II, 109

Francis Joseph, 165

Frankfurt Parliament, 285

Franklin, Benjamin, 65

Franks, 221-222

Frederick II, 146, 153

Freedom(s), 16, 50, 87-88, 95, 98, 103, 107, 111, 115, 125, 173, 175, 180, 191, 193, 205, 217, 236, 237, 244, 250, 259. *See also* Liberty (-ies)

French Academy, 198, 289, 290

French Revolution, vii, ix, 6, 41, 43, 49, 53, 69, 70, 71, 72, 81, 110, 111, 114-115, 129, 133-134, 141, 150, 152, 158, 159-160, 164, 171, 172, 175, 182, 183-184, 197, 203, 204, 211, 212, 220, 224, 230, 235, 240, 245, 265, 276, 281, 288, 292, 297-298, 299, 300-301, 303-304, 307, 308, 317; Bonaparte and, 7-11, 45-48, 106-110, 193-194, 196-202, 205, 206-211; Constitution of the Year VIII, 7-11, 45-46, 104-106, 189, 192-196, 211; Convention, 99-100, 190-191; Directory, 43-44, 102-104, 191-192, 104; Legislative Assembly, 99, 189-190; National Assembly, 79, 80, 86, 87-99, 103, 104; Revolt of the people, 82-86, 88, 89, 92-93, 95, 96, 97, 286; States-General, 45, 67-68, 73-79, 80, 83, 85, 94, 287

Galileo, 55

Gamble, The, vii

Gazette de France, 9

General Confederation of Labor, 289

General Council, of Geneva, 57, 60, 63, 64, 73, 167-168

General will of the people, 58-64, 73, 74, 75, 77, 78, 80, 87, 100, 102, 103, 173-177, 178, 182, 190, 205. *See also* Rousseau

Genesis, 33, 36, 280

Geneva, Republic of, 73, 111; government, 57; and Rousseau, 60-64, 167-168

Geneva, University of, 7

Geneva Disarmament Conference of 1932, 31

Genii of the City, 39, 51, 68, 70, 77, 94, 98, 107, 110, 112, 116, 118, 123, 124, 127, 137, 145, 160, 210, 217, 220, 245, 246, 247, 304; defined, 17-18, 26-27. *See also* Genius of the Old Regime. Genius of the Revolution, Principles of legitimacy

Genius of the Old Regime, 50, 51, 70, 72, 76, 77, 78, 79, 97, 98, 101, 122, 128, 215. *See also* Old Regime, Genii of the City

Genius of the Revolution, 50, 51, 72, 76, 77, 78, 97, 101, 103, 122.

See also French Revolution, Revolution of '48, Genii of the City
George VI, 152
Gerard, General, 213
German Empire, 16
German Revolution, in 1933, 129, 289, 292
Germany, 64, 108, 109, 124, 125, 127, 128, 129, 139, 161-162, 163, 166, 172, 241, 242, 265, 267, 268, 275, 292, 298, 317
Ghibelline, 249
Giolitti, 126-127, 240-241, 251, 253-267, 269-276
Giornale d'Italia, 263
Golden Book of Venice, 23, 136
Gospel, the, 220. *See also* Bible, the, Sacred Scriptures
Government, 277-319. *See also* Legitimate, Illegitimate, Prelegitimate, Quasi-legitimate, Revolutionary, Totalitarian govt., Legitimacy in govt., Illegitimacy in govt., Legitimate democracy, Legitimate monarchy, Principles of legitimacy
Gracchi, the, 220
Great Britain, *see* England
Greatness and Decline of Rome, The, 18
Great panic, the, 17, 85-87, 93, 94, 96, 97, 98, 100, 104, 106, 189, 211, 283, 288, 290, 303, 307, 316. *See also* Fear
Greece, 221, 224
Greek science, 29
Group interests, 71, 72, 90
Guelf, 249
Guizot, 114, 117-118, 127, 217, 251, 253, 254, 255

Hapsburg dynasty, 43, 121, 128, 156, 163, 285
Hauterive, E. d', 9
Hazard, Paul, 58
Henry V, *see* Bordeaux, duc de
Hercules, 43
Hereditary principle of legitimacy, 21-23, 24, 26, 49, 54, 55, 57, 60, 62, 63, 64, 65, 71, 92, 135, 136,

138, 139, 146-153, 155, 161, 162, 168, 170, 199, 231, 233, 281-283, 291, 294. *See also* Aristo-monarchic principle of legitimacy, Principles of legitimacy
Hindu philosophy, 279-280, 318-319
Hohenzollern dynasty, 121, 128, 163
Holland, viii, 23, 136, 156, 173, 204, 298, 306
Holy Roman Empire, 22, 108, 156
Horace, 13-14
Hortense, Queen, 121
House of Representatives, 45
Humbert, King, 126-127, 239-240, 241, 243, 246-249, 252, 253, 257, 261, 272; assassination of, 244-245; character, 250-251
Hume, 88
Hungary, 285, 298

Idées napoléoniennes, Les, 121
Ideological war, 98
Ides of March, 10
Illegitimacy, in government, 41, 106, 123, 132, 208, 209. *See also* Illegitimate govt.
Illegitimate government(s), 130, 187, 188, 197, 198, 206, 217, 278. *See also* Revolutionary govt., Totalitarian govt., Illegitimacy in govt.
Illuminism, 69
Illustration, 293
"Imperator," 228-229
Imperium proconsulare, 227
Industry, 28, 29, 51, 52, 55, 57, 88, 156, 157, 164, 198, 246, 259, 298
Infallibility, 26, 155-157, 160-162, 166, 172, 184
Isaiah, 146
Islam 39. *See also* Mohammedanism
Italy, 7, 13, 14, 15, 18, 108, 124, 125-127, 151, 156, 172, 217-218, 224, 285, 292, 298, 317; fascism in, 4-7, 12, 129, 218; Napoleon's invasion of, 41, 43-44, 46, 248-249; pre-fascist govt., 236-276
Izoulet, 169, 302

Jacobin clubs, 95
Jacobins, 100, 206, 214, 288

James II, 306
Jaurès, 297
Jefferson, Thomas, 65
Jena, Battle of, 108, 208
Jeremiah, 146
Jesus Christ, 148, 180
Journal des Débats et Décrets, 9
Journal des Défenseurs de la Patrie, 9
Journal des Hommes Libres, 9
Journal de Paris, 9
Journal du Soir, 9
Judaism, 29, 39
Judiciary, 20, 80, 89, 90, 190
Julian-Claudian family, 229
July Monarchy, 113-118, 123, 216-217, 231-235, 250. *See also* Louis Philippe
June Days, 119-120, 121, 184
Jury, introduced in France, 90
Justice, 4, 17, 29, 54, 58, 66, 87, 88, 89, 168, 179, 201, 237, 282

Kelsen, Hans, 132
König der Franzosen, 230-234

Lafayette, 213-215
Lafitte, 214-215
Langue hébraïque Restituée, La, 33-37
Law(s), 6, 57, 62, 71, 83, 84, 88, 89, 90, 95, 96, 98, 160, 228-229, 236, 277, 278, 285
League of Augsburg, 158
League of Nations, failure of, ix
Legions, of Rome, 220, 222, 223, 225-227, 229
Legislation, initiation of, 8
Legislative Assembly, 99, 189-190, 196, 199
Legislative power, 8, 20, 21, 57, 59, 60, 71, 73-74, 76, 77, 79, 80, 83, 89, 90, 92, 110-112, 113, 115, 125, 157, 219, 287. *See also* Executive power
Legislature, in French Constitution of the Year VIII, 7-11, 45
Legitimacy, of government, 55, 61, 62, 66, 73, 78, 80, 94, 124, 145, 214, 229, 278, 280-281, 284

Legitimate Democracy, 167-186, 190, 291, 292, 299, 300
Legitimate government(s), ix, 41, 53, 63, 74, 75, 130, 192, 194, 195, 200, 205, 209, 217, 218, 246, 260, 272, 273, 276, 295, 296, 316; defined, 41-42, 131-144, 187, 207. *See also* Legitimate monarchy, Legitimate democracy, Legitimacy in govt., Principles of Legitimacy
Legitimate monarchy, 145-166, 217
Legitimists, 119. *See also* Orleanists, Royalists, Monarchists
Leman, Lake, 57, 62
L'esprit de conquête et de l'usurpation, De, 202-204, 304-307
Lettres écrites de la montagne, 60
"Lex Regia," 229
Liberalism, 181, 223, 257, 260, 284
Liberals, in Italy, 237-241, 244, 247, 253, 254, 256, 259, 262, 265, 269. *See also* Conservatives, Radicals, Republicans, Socialists, Syndicalists
Liberian Republic, 15
"Liberticidal" Bills, 244
Liberty(-ies), 6, 56, 65, 87, 88, 89, 90, 158, 180, 181, 193, 194, 245, 253, 254, 258, 276, 306. *See also* Freedom(s)
Livy, 142
Locke, 88
Lombardy, 243
Lombroso, Gina, 51
London, 109, 195
London Treaty, 269
Lords, House of, 56, 157
Louis XIII, 152, 155
Louis XIV, 15, 146, 152, 153, 155, 156
Louis XV, 15, 152, 215, 217
Louis XVI, 71, 73, 76, 77, 79, 80, 83, 85, 86, 88, 89, 90, 92, 93, 99, 133-134, 163, 215
Louis XVIII, 110-113, 124, 125, 126, 127, 134, 161, 166, 215, 217, 226, 275
Louis Napoleon, 120. *See also* Napoleon III
Louis Philippe, 113-118, 123, 124,

125, 127, 128, 161, 162, 166, 215, 229, 230-235, 250, 251, 252, 261, 262, 271

Lower classes, 57, 220, 243, 248, 257

Lunéville, Treaty of, 108

Luxembourg Palace, 7, 8, 45

Luxury, under the Old Regime, 52, 141-142, 149-150, 185-186, 248

Luzzatti, 262, 263

Lybia, 266

Lyons, 202

Maistre, Joseph de, 91

Majority rule, 20-21, 22, 23-24, 25, 26, 58, 75, 103, 115, 126, 133, 135, 140, 144, 173-178, 179, 181, 185, 190, 191, 193, 239, 241, 246, 254-256, 257, 270, 271, 295, 300. See also Minority rights

Marat, 95, 100

Marie Louise, 107

Marius, 221, 222, 223

Marxism, 240, 260, 297-298. See also Socialism

Masséna, 44

Masses, the, 40, 51, 55, 83, 86, 95, 97, 116, 118, 140, 145, 149, 150, 159, 163, 165, 166, 170, 172, 178, 182, 184, 185, 189, 195, 210, 259, 263, 267, 293, 294, 295, 297, 299, 300

Matteoti, assassination of, 6, 11

Maurras, Charles, 131-132

Maya, veil of, 279

Mazarin, 271

Mediterranean World, 29, 39

Mémoires, of Metternich, 231-234; of Talleyrand, 19, 135, 277

Memoirs, of Giolitti, 126

Mentalité primitive, La, 31

Metternich, 199, 230-235, 250, 252, 262, 271

Middle Ages, the, viii, 51, 52, 55, 76, 146, 149, 150, 155

Middle classes, 54, 69, 83, 94, 164, 172, 189, 220, 240, 243, 248, 256, 257, 273, 275, 298. See also Bourgeois(-ie)

Milan, 243, 270

Military Committee, 96

Minority rights, 21, 54, 75, 140, 173-178, 179, 180, 181, 182, 185, 190, 191, 193, 237, 246, 247, 263, 295, 300. See also Majority rule

Mirabeau, 78-79, 80, 90, 183

Mocenigo, Alvisio, 23, 136

Modena, 218

Mohammedanism, 29. See also Islam

Moloch, 191, 220

Mommsen, 229

Monarchists, 119, 122, 139. See also Royalists, Legitimists, Orleanists

Monarchy(-ies), viii, 14, 21, 22, 25, 26, 50, 52, 53, 54, 62, 63, 68, 99, 102, 107, 112, 116, 120, 121, 122, 124, 125, 127, 138, 141, 142, 144, 169, 170, 171, 172, 173, 174, 175, 178, 179, 183, 185, 186, 188, 192, 210, 215, 216, 217, 218, 219, 229, 230, 231, 233, 243, 244, 248, 258, 278, 283, 287, 291, 294, 295, 297, 298, 299, 300, 303. See also Aristocratic republic, Democracy, Republic, Legitimate monarchy, Aristo-monarchic principle of legitimacy

Moniteur Universel, 9

Montesquieu, 88, 110, 111, 112

Monza, 244-245

Moreau, General, 202

Morocco, 265

Mortemart, duc de, 213, 214, 215

Moscow, 128

Moses, 100, 150, 313

Mussolini, 5-7, 11, 274-275

Mysticism, 279-280

Nachgelassene Papiere, 230-234

Naples, 218

Napoleon, ix, 103, 114, 116, 120, 121, 122, 123, 124, 184, 202, 231, 232, 234, 235, 288; Consulate of, 106, 107, 199; empire of, 106, 108, 110, 188, 216, 217; fear of, 106-110, 207-208; foreign policy, 108-110, 208-209; and Julius Caesar, 219, 223; and propaganda, 199-200; and revolutionary govt., 207-211. See also Bonaparte, Napoleon

Napoleon III, 122-124, 184, 292.
   See also Louis Napoleon
"Napoléon et la presse," 9
National Assembly, 79-80, 86-99,
   104
National Council, Swiss, 20
National plebiscite, in France, 106,
   107, 216
National will, 73, 77, 78, 94, 106.
   See also General will of the peo-
   ple
Nationalism, in France, 116
Nationalists, in Italy, 259, 260, 264,
   268, 269
Necker, 88
Nero, 229
New York, vii, 6, 11
Nicholas II, abdication of, 303
Nineteenth century, 26, 27, 33, 41,
   43, 47, 51, 52, 64, 84, 111, 113,
   115, 122, 128, 129, 130, 132, 159,
   160, 161, 162, 163, 164, 165, 167,
   168, 176, 183, 199, 218, 219, 223,
   233, 235, 242, 249, 251, 260, 261,
   284, 285, 291, 298, 308, 317
Nirvana, 319
Nobility, 51, 53, 54, 56, 210, 258; in
   France, 10, 57, 67, 68, 69, 71, 73,
   74, 76, 78, 79, 86, 93, 94, 95, 97,
   157, 190, 298. *See also* Aristocracy,
   Upper classes
Normans, 132

Old Regime, 41, 45, 71, 80, 115,
   121, 125, 141, 165, 186, 248-249,
   260; and the Revolution, 49-66,
   76, 94, 98, 103-104, 105, 107, 108,
   128, 160, 171, 189, 199, 206, 214,
   216, 220, 230, 245, 246, 286-288,
   297. *See also* Genius of the Old
   Regime
Old World, the, vii, viii. *See also*
   Old Regime
Oligarchy, 44, 60, 64, 105, 117, 223,
   224
Olivet, Fabre d', 33-37
Olympia, Mother of Alexander, 148
Opposition, Right of, 21, 26, 47, 54,
   56, 64, 75, 87, 103, 111, 114, 115,
   117, 123, 125, 140, 153, 155, 160,
   161, 162, 166, 174-178, 180, 181,
   184, 191, 193, 194, 195, 196, 197,
   216, 238, 239, 241, 253-254, 257,
   262, 263, 266, 267, 291-293, 295.
   See also Minority rights
Order, 16, 17, 50, 54, 58, 84, 89,
   168, 190, 211, 232, 234, 281, 291,
   317-318
Organization, 16, 242
Orient, the, 156, 160. *See also* Asia
Orlando, 274
Orleanists, 119. *See also* Royalists,
   Monarchists, Legitimists
Orléans, duc d', 214-215. *See also*
   Louis Philippe
Ormazd, 211
Ottoman Empire, 264, 265, 266

Palais Royal, 10
Palazzo Braschi, 264
Palazzo Riccardi, 6
Pan-Germanism, 259
Pantheism, 57
Papacy, the, 15, 156. *See also* Pope,
   the
Paris, vii, 9, 11, 83, 85, 89, 93, 109,
   112, 200, 213, 214, 216; Arch-
   bishop of, 95
Parliament (s), 22, 23, 25, 54, 56,
   125-126, 155, 176, 179; English, 45,
   56, 75, 80; French, 7-11, 44-45,
   90, 93, 111-116, 161, 213, 214, 215;
   Italian, 5-6, 127, 236, 237-241, 243-
   244, 247, 250, 253-256, 258, 259,
   262, 263, 266, 270, 271, 272, 273.
   See also Legislative assemblies,
   Diets, Estates, *Staende,* Roman
   senate, etc.
Parma, 218
Parthians, 225
Party(-ies), political, 23, 24, 41, 58,
   75, 80, 113, 162, 185, 200, 271,
   294, 295; in Italy, 236, 237-241,
   243-244, 247, 250, 251, 253-254,
   256-257, 261, 262, 266, 273
Pascal, 277
Paternal authority, 23, 35, 315
Peasants, 83, 240, 261, 265, 267, 290
Pelloux, General, 127, 244, 251, 254
Perier, Casimir, 213

Persians, 221-222
Philip II, of Spain, 204
Philip of Macedon, 148
Philippism, 125-127, 252, 253, 257, 260, 266, 269. See also Louis Philippe
Philosophy, 18, 48, 53, 57, 69, 88, 98, 100, 110, 159, 198, 249, 259, 260, 277-280, 285, 317-319
Physiocrats, the 88
Pichegru, General, 202
Piedmont, 108, 124, 218
Pisa, 236
Plato's republic, 314
Plurality, 75. See also Majority rule
Po Valley, 43
Police, the, 4, 11, 82, 83, 84, 87, 88, 89, 96, 97, 99, 134, 157, 160, 190, 201, 302
Polignac, prince de, 213
Politique tirée des propres paroles de l'écriture sainte, 154-155
Pontchartrain, 158
Pope, the, 22, 55, 106, 107, 247, 248, 282, 302. See also Papacy, the
Popular sovereignty, 20-21, 59-64, 91, 92, 100, 102, 103, 139, 173-174, 180, 181-185, 189, 307. See also Sovereignty of the people
Popular will, 115. See also General will of the people, National will
Potestas tribunicia, 227
Power, see Government
Preligitimate government, 148, 186, 189, 190, 191, 192, 193, 278; defined, 139-140, 187-188
Press, freedom of, 8-9, 47, 87, 103, 112, 161, 175, 193, 194, 195, 197, 204, 253, 256
Pressburg, Treaty of, 108
"Princeps," 228-229
Principles of legitimacy, 19, 52, 56, 62, 63, 72, 77, 100, 106, 127, 170, 172, 180, 217, 219, 220, 231, 233, 234, 235, 236, 285, 290-291, 294, 295, 301, 302, 308, 319; nature of, 20-27, 40-42, 48, 49-51, 102, 117, 134-141, 144, 169, 182, 197, 206, 277-284, 313-314, 315-316. See also Aristo-monarchic, Demo-cratic, Elective, Hereditary principle of legitimacy, Genii of the City, Legitimate govt., Legitimate monarchy, Legitimate democracy
Privileges, 90, 144
Progress, 42, 50, 164, 281; defined, 28-30, 38-39
Propaganda, 199-200, 206-207
Proscriptions, 98
Protectionism, in Italy, 238, 240
Protestant Church, 295-296
Protestantism, 156
Prussia, 23, 108, 109, 124, 125, 136, 162, 208
Ptolemy Auletes, 151
Public good, 131-133
Public harm, 131-132
Public Safety, 191
Public welfare, 132-133, 196
Publiciste de Paris, Le, 9, 95

Qualitative civilization(s), 52
Quantitative civilization(s), 164, 165, 179, 260, 261
Quantitative revolution, 52
Quasi-legitimate government, 278, 291, 296; defined, 217; in Italy, 217-218, 236-276; July Monarchy, 217, 230-236; Roman Empire, 218-229
Qu'est-ce que le Tiers-Etat?, 73-76
Quirinal Palace, 246, 257

Radicals, in Italy, 238, 243-244, 253, 254, 256, 257, 269, 273. See also Liberals, Republicans, Socialists, Syndicalists, Conservatives
Rambouillet, château de, 215
Rattazzi, Urbano, 126
Reactionism, in Italy, 243, 244, 254
Reconstruction of Europe, The, vii, 308-310
Referendum, 20
Reformation, the, 54-55
Religion, 18, 50, 51, 52-53, 142-143, 144, 149, 277, 278, 279, 285, 302; as progress, 38-39. See also Christianity, Catholic Church, Church, the, Protestant Church, Islam, Mohammedanism, Buddhism

Religious orders, in France, 71

Renaissance, the, 55, 285

Representative government, 6, 63-64, 75, 87, 92, 105, 113, 114, 116, 128, 189, 193, 195, 211, 218, 246, 296, 303, 304. See also Democracy, Legitimate democracy, Democratic principle of legitimacy

Republic(s), viii, ix, 50, 52, 54, 56, 65, 107, 111, 118, 120, 124, 128, 129, 138, 166, 170, 186, 210, 215, 217, 218, 219, 231, 233, 243, 287, 299, 306, 307. See also Monarchy, Democracy, Aristocratic republic

Republicans: in France, 46, 119, 122, 195; in Italy, 238, 244, 253, 254, 256, 269. See also Royalists, Monarchists, Conservatives, Liberals, Radicals, Socialists, Syndicalists

Restoration, of French monarchy, 110-112, 117, 123, 214. See also Louis XVIII, Charles X

Revolt against coercion of government, 34-36, 40-43, 45, 46-47, 197, 205, 207, 208, 258-259, 279, 281

Revolution(s), viii, 3-7, 12, 16, 41, 46, 112, 119-120, 121, 125, 128, 129, 132, 136, 146, 166, 172, 184, 211, 213, 214, 218, 224, 225, 242, 276, 284-288, 289, 292, 297, 304, 305-308. See also American, Chinese, Fascist, French, German, Russian, Spanish, Turkish revolution, revolution of '48, February Revolution, June Days, Revolt

Revolution of '48, 118-120, 128, 184, 219, 234, 235, 292

Revolutionary government(s), ix, 186, 217, 234, 273, 275, 276, 283, 288, 291, 292, 295, 296, 304, 308, 316; defined, 187-189, 196-198, 199-200, 205-206, 209-210; French Revolution, 189-212. See also Illegitimate govt., Totalitarian govt.

Revolutionary spirit, 26, 27, 62, 63, 64, 66, 137, 300

Revue des deux mondes, 9

"Rex," of Rome, 218-219, 226, 227-229

Richelieu, 133, 155, 156, 157, 186, 271

Risorgimento, 236

Robespierre, 102

Rocca di Cavour, 255, 262, 267, 270

Rochefoucauld, duc de la, 15

Romanov dynasty, 163

Rome, ancient, 13, 17, 142, 146, 204, 219-229, 257, 278; Empire, 146, 148, 218-229; Republic, 3, 218-227, 229, 278; Senate, 3-4, 5, 219, 220, 225, 227, 228, 278

Rome, modern, 6, 11, 48, 237, 255, 263, 264, 267, 268, 270; march on, 5, 275

"Rosina," 151

Rousseau, 41, 58-64, 66, 73, 74, 75, 77, 80, 88, 90, 100, 167-168, 175, 183

Royal Council, 71, 104, 157, 159, 287

Royalists, in France, 11, 46, 103, 195, 201. See also Monarchists, Legitimists, Orleanists

Rubicon, crossing of, 4, 79

Rudini, Marquis, 239, 243, 244, 251

Rudolph, Archduke, 151

Russia, 23, 108, 109, 128, 136, 160-161, 166, 172, 208, 268, 269, 298, 299, 303

Russian Revolution, vii, 128, 129, 146, 301, 303-304

Sacred Scriptures, 180. See also Bible, Gospel

Saint Augustine, Confessions of, 212

Saint Cloud, 45, 214

St. Gervais quarter, 60

St. Paul's Epistle to the Romans, 155

St. Petersburg, 109

St. Pierre quarter, 60, 62

Salandra, 253, 263, 267-270, 272, 274

Sardinian kingdom, 165, 218, 245, 246, 247

Sarmatians, 221-222

Savoy dynasty, 163, 218, 245-247

Scandinavian countries, viii, 23, 136, 173, 298

Scholarship, 55

Science, 28, 29, 38-39, 51, 55, 57, 69, 144, 260, 285

Secolo, the, 243-244, 257

Second century, 228

Second Empire, of France, 122-124, 184, 210, 292. *See also* Napoleon III

Second International, 289

Second Republic, 118-122, 172, 285, 292

Second World War, viii

Security, 58

Senate, in French Constitution of the Year VIII, 7-8, 45, 115, 194-196, 199; U. S., 45. *See also* Rome, ancient, Senate

Senatus populusque romanus, 219, 220, 225

Seventeenth century, 15, 51, 54, 55, 56, 157-158, 160, 266, 280

Sicily, 13, 242

Siéyès, 85, 92, 160, 183; author of Constitution of the Year VIII, 103-105, 106, 107, 114-115, 192-195; and the third estate, 73-80

Sixteenth century, 15, 55, 278

Small Council, of Geneva, 57, 167-168

Social contract, the, 41-42, 58-64, 181, 315

Socialism, 295, 297-300

Socialists: in France, 116, 119; in Italy, 242, 243, 244, 249, 253, 254, 256, 259, 260, 262, 267, 269. *See also* Syndicalists, Radicals, Republicans, Liberals, Conservatives

Sociétés de Pensée et la Democratie, Les, 70

Society of Friends of the Constitution, 95. *See also* Jacobins

Sonderbund, 307

Sonnino, 253, 263, 269

Sorbonne, the, 289

Sorel, Georges, 259

Sovereign Council, of Geneva, 57

Sovereignty of the people, 3, 7, 8, 24, 59-64, 87, 112, 117-120, 170, 171, 220, 248, 263, 291, 296, 303. *See also* Popular sovereignty

Spain, 108, 109, 125, 127, 128, 129, 172. 208, 224, 292, 298

Spanish Republic, 139

Spanish revolution, vii, 125, 129, 292

Special tribunals, 201

Stael, Mme. de, 11, 47

Staende, 54, 155

States Council, Swiss, 20

States-General, 45, 67, 68, 73, 74, 76-79, 80, 83, 85, 94, 133, 157, 287

Strikes, 253

Stuarts, the, 305

Succession, rule of, 147-152, 174. *See also* Hereditary principle of legitimacy

Suetonius, 228

Suffrage, 173, 175, 176, 192-193, 195, 196, 197, 261, 306; universal, 24, 117-120, 122, 123, 124, 128, 139, 170, 174, 182-185, 190, 230, 262-263, 266-267, 291-295, 299, 301; universal male, 20, 174. *See also* Elections

Sulla, 221, 222, 223

Sweden, 306

Switzerland, 15, 108, 124, 145, 163, 173, 178, 180, 211, 273, 275, 283, 292, 306, 307-308, 317; government, 20-21, 22, 187

Syndicalists, In Italy, 259, 269. *See also* Socialists, Radicals, Republicans, Liberalists, Conservatives

Tacitus, 228

Talleyrand, 19, 90, 107, 135, 138, 188, 209, 226, 232, 233, 265, 275, 277

Taxes, 15, 53, 56, 57, 67-68, 76, 83, 88, 89, 117, 155, 157, 182, 256

Ten Commandments, the, 4, 313

Tennis Court Oath, 79, 85

Terror, the, 98, 99, 102

Theocritus, 314

Theology, 55

Thermidor, 9, 191

Third century, 221-222

Third estate, in France, 57, 67, 69, 73, 74, 76-81, 84, 86, 94, 103, 104, 157, 183

Third International, 289

Third Republic, 15, 16, 124, 139, 172, 178, 180, 292

Thomism, 57, 319

Tiberius, 204, 228

Tibet, 25

Tithes, church, 90

Totalitarian government, 16, 41, 47, 188, 197, 198, 210, 211, 219. *See also* Revolutionary government, Illegitimate govt.

"Transformism," 237-238

Trent, Council of, 54-55

Tribunate, in French Constitution of the Year VIII, 7-11, 45

Tripoli, 264, 265, 267, 268

Tuileries, the, 110, 123

Turin, 86, 236, 270; senate of, 165

Turkey, 264

Turkish revolution, 166

Tuscany, grand-duchy of, 15

Twentieth century, 47, 51, 84, 132, 161, 210, 219, 224, 302, 317

Tyrtaeus, 266

Unanimity, 58, 63, 64, 74-75, 94, 173

United States, vii, ix, 65-66, 69, 110, 180, 186, 283, 307. *See also* America

Upper classes, 55, 57, 69, 83, 94, 95, 120, 172, 176, 182, 184, 189, 195, 210, 240, 244, 247, 257, 258, 265, 267, 292, 293. *See also* Nobility, Clergy

Usurpation, 202-204, 215, 216, 245, 305-307. *See also* Despotism

Usurper, 188, 203-204, 216, 276, 305

Vatican, the, 289, 290

Venetia, 243

Venice, Republic of, 22, 23, 44, 71, 136, 219

Venus, 142

Versailles, 60, 71, 76, 79, 85, 86, 87, 93, 94, 134, 183, 287

Vespasian, 229

Veuillot, 181

Vichy, 267

Victor Emmanuel II, 126, 151, 247

Victor Emmanuel III, 4, 127, 253-255, 257, 259, 263, 268, 270, 271, 272, 273, 274

Victorian age, 242

Vienna, 43, 109, 128, 165, 268

Violence, of government, 99, 140, 254, 286, 305. *See also* Coercion, Force

Voltaire, 88

Wagram, Battle of, 208

Wall Street, 290

Washington, D.C., 45, 111

Weapons, 31-33

Weimar Republic, 139

Wellington, 216

West, the, 28, 65, 149, 150, 155, 170, 183, 188, 189, 209, 211, 221, 277, 278, 280, 281, 282, 283, 284, 286, 299, 302, 319. *See also* Western civilization, Western world

Western civilization, viii, 21, 135, 136, 289, 300, 315, 318. *See also* West, Western world

Western world, 52, 62, 96, 129, 137, 144, 196, 210, 224, 276, 292, 301. *See also* West, Western civilization

William II, of Germany, 161

William III, of England, 305-307

Wittelsbach, 121, 128

Workers, 83, 240, 261, 265, 290

Zanardelli, 239-240, 241, 253

Zurich, 44, 111

WORLD AFFAIRS: National and International Viewpoints
An Arno Press Collection

Angell, Norman. **The Great Illusion, 1933.** 1933.

Benes, Eduard. **Memoirs:** From Munich to New War and New Victory. 1954.

[Carrington, Charles Edmund] (Edmonds, Charles, pseud.) **A Subaltern's War.** 1930. New preface by Charles Edmund Carrington.

Cassel, Gustav. **Money and Foreign Exchange After 1914.** 1922.

Chambers, Frank P. **The War Behind the War, 1914-1918.** 1939.

Dedijer, Vladimir. **Tito.** 1953.

Dickinson, Edwin DeWitt. **The Equality of States in International Law.** 1920.

Douhet, Giulio. **The Command of the Air.** 1942.

Edib, Halidé. **Memoirs.** 1926.

Ferrero, Guglielmo. **The Principles of Power.** 1942.

Grew, Joseph C. **Ten Years in Japan.** 1944.

Hayden, Joseph Ralston. **The Philippines.** 1942.

Hudson, Manley O. **The Permanent Court of International Justice, 1920-1942.** 1943.

Huntington, Ellsworth. **Mainsprings of Civilization.** 1945.

Jacks, G. V. and R. O. Whyte. **Vanishing Lands:** A World Survey of Soil Erosion. 1939.

Mason, Edward S. **Controlling World Trade.** 1946.

Menon, V. P. **The Story of the Integration of the Indian States.** 1956.

Moore, Wilbert E. **Economic Demography of Eastern and Southern Europe.** 1945.

[Ohlin, Bertil]. **The Course and Phases of the World Economic Depression.** 1931.

Oliveira, A. Ramos. **Politics, Economics and Men of Modern Spain, 1808-1946.** 1946.

O'Sullivan, Donal. **The Irish Free State and Its Senate.** 1940.

Peffer, Nathaniel. **The White Man's Dilemma.** 1927.

Philby, H. St. John. **Sa'udi Arabia.** 1955.

Rappard, William E. **International Relations as Viewed From Geneva.** 1925.

Rauschning, Hermann. **The Revolution of Nihilism.** 1939.

Reshetar, John S., Jr. **The Ukrainian Revolution, 1917-1920.** 1952.

Richmond, Admiral Sir Herbert. **Sea Power in the Modern World.** 1934.

Robbins, Lionel. **Economic Planning and International Order.** 1937. New preface by Lionel Robbins.

Russell, Bertrand. **Bolshevism:** Practice and Theory. 1920.

Russell, Frank M. **Theories of International Relations.** 1936.

Schwarz, Solomon M. **The Jews in the Soviet Union.** 1951.

Siegfried, André. **Canada:** An International Power. [1947].

Souvarine, Boris. **Stalin.** 1939.

Spaulding, Oliver Lyman, Jr., Hoffman Nickerson, and John Womack Wright. **Warfare.** 1925.

Storrs, Sir Ronald. **Memoirs.** 1937.

Strausz-Hupé, Robert. **Geopolitics:** The Struggle for Space and Power. 1942.

Swinton, Sir Ernest D. **Eyewitness.** 1933.

Timasheff, Nicholas S. **The Great Retreat.** 1946.

Welles, Sumner. **Naboth's Vineyard:** The Dominican Republic, 1844-1924. 1928. Two volumes in one.

Whittlesey, Derwent. **The Earth and the State.** 1939.

Wilcox, Clair. **A Charter for World Trade.** 1949.